# WITH THE 1/5th ESSEX IN THE EAST.

BY

LT.-COL. T. GIBBONS, D.S.O.
5th Bn. The Essex Regt.

The Naval & Military Press Ltd

Published by
**The Naval & Military Press Ltd**
Unit 10 Ridgewood Industrial Park,
Uckfield, East Sussex,
TN22 5QE England
Tel: +44 (0) 1825 749494
Fax: +44 (0) 1825 765701
www.naval-military-press.com
www.military-genealogy.com
www.militarymaproom.com

*In reprinting in facsimile from the original, any imperfections are inevitably reproduced and the quality may fall short of modern type and cartographic standards.*

TO MY COMRADES

ON BOTH SIDES OF THE VEIL

THIS BOOK IS

DEDICATED.

# PREFACE.

My primary object in making this, my first—and last—attempt at writing a book, is to recall to the minds of my old comrades of all ranks of the 1/5th Battalion The Essex Regiment some of the incidents of the campaigns in Gallipoli and Palestine so far as they concerned the Battalion, and of our sojourn in Egypt in 1916 and again in 1919.

I have endeavoured to make it as far as possible a record of the Battalion's service overseas, drawn from my official War Diary—a very dull document—Battalion routine orders—a duller document still—and my own memory—the dullness of which I can hardly contemplate without tears!

I kept no private diary on Service. Operation orders were always "very secret" and were destroyed, except a few important ones, which found their way into the appendix to the War Diary. And my letters home were strictly censored by a very fussy and officious censor—myself.

For the above reasons I cannot claim for my effort either the fullness or the accuracy to make it an official record of the Battalion, although I hope and believe it is free from inaccuracy. Still less is it an attempt to write a history of the campaigns in which we took part, or of the countries in which we fought and marched and rested. I have written down events as far as I can remember them, as they struck me at the time they happened; I have added some of my own reflections thereon; and I have included some notes on the wonderful ancient history of Palestine. With regard to the latter, although they may possibly bore the general reader, I hope they may add to the pleasure with which the old 5th Essex soldier will fight his battles and do his marches over again by his fireside; and perhaps to the pleasure of his children and his grandchildren as he tells them the story of his share in the great campaign in that historic land. To me it has been a matter of great regret that I did not know more of the history of the country in which we were privileged to fight—a history which for many centuries might almost be said to be the history of the world.

I have to acknowledge with gratitude the valuable assistance of Major W. E. Wilson, D.S.O., who was for over two years my second in command, for filling up the gaps caused by my temporary absences from the Battalion; to Captain J. F. Finn, M.C., my Adjutant for a similar period, for supplying me with some of his notes and a complete list of casualties from the archives of the 3rd Echelon, G.H.Q. Alexandria; to Rev. B. K. Bond, M.C., C.F., for some excellent photographs; to Captain L. D. Womersley for his effective paper-cover design; and to the Officer i/c. No. 2 Infantry Records, Warley, for furnishing me with much of the information contained in the Appendices.

For historical allusions I am indebted to Dr. J. Adam Smith's "Historical Geography of the Holy Land"; to Dean Stanley's "Sinai and Palestine"; to Colonel C. R. Conder's "Palestine"; to the various quarterly statements published by the Palestine Exploration Fund; to the excellent official guide to the Galleries of the British Museum; and to those valuable enemy publications the Palestine Guide books of Meistermann and Baedeker. I am also indebted to the Palestine Exploration Fund for kindly giving me permission to make use of their excellent maps of the country which form the basis for most of the maps published herewith.

I am only too conscious of the many shortcomings of this book, due to my inexperience as a writer, and to the fact that it has been written at odd moments snatched from a rather busy life. I apologise to the reader for the frequent occurrence of the first personal pronoun—a fault again due to the said inexperience and not to any desire to attach undue importance to my own small share in the events recorded.

I have probably omitted to mention many meritorious services and gallant acts on the part of all ranks of my comrades in arms. This again, I hope, will be attributed by the indulgent reader, not to any want of appreciation of services rendered, still less to any desire to discriminate unfairly between individuals, but to ignorance and a bad memory. Many such deeds went unnoticed, except by those who did not live to tell of them. But in the "day when the hearts of all men are revealed" they will assuredly be taken into account.

T. GIBBONS.

DUNMOW, ESSEX,
*May*, 1921.

# CONTENTS.


Pages

AUTHOR'S PREFACE .. .. .. .. .. .. vii.–viii.

CHAPTER I.—GALLIPOLI .. .. .. .. .. .. 1–29

Leaving Plymouth—historic waters—Gibraltar—Malta—Alexandria—Mudros—Good-bye to the "Grampian"—a race in the dark—Imbros—first view of the Peninsula—the landing at Suvla Bay—movements by night—spies—under fire—getting in wounded—the advance across the plain—steadiness of the Bn.—casualties—a patrol ambushed—holding the lane—taking over the "Razorback"—Jephson's Post—the destroyer—the battle of Aug. 21st—Sickness—Hill 60—move to Anzac—close trench warfare—primitive bombs—"Laindon Hill"—the rains—Gallipoli glue—sniping—wonderful sunsets—"The Soul of Anzac"—gallery trenches—patrolling and digging—the relief—a deluge—The blizzard—weather bound—piers washed away—off at last—reflections—casualties.

CHAPTER II.—THE LAND OF EGYPT .. .. .. 30–38

Rest at Mudros—reinforcements—Alexandria—Mex Camp—The Senussi campaign—El Hammam—Camel patrols—the armoured train—armoured cars—bathing—the aeroplanes—Van Ryneveld—wonderful ruins—sandstorms—Jennings Bramly Bey—Friendly Arabs—rout of the Senussi—journey through the Delta—Cairo—The Pyramids.

CHAPTER III.—THE WILDERNESS .. .. .. .. 39–53

The Turks and the Suez Canal—Arrival at Shallufa—"Manchester Post"—record heat—laborious digging—sand, sand, sand—chameleons—Railways and roads in the desert—route marching—"Salford" and "Oldham Posts"—Geneffe—Ballah and "Ballybunion"—The Land of Goshen—Battle of Romani—gallant Machine gunners—Turkish prisoners—back again—A "Gyppo" entertainment—Ferry Post—The Navy—Xmas pantomime—Ismailia—duck shooting—refitting—the march to the Promised Land—Kantara—The Wire road—Romani—the battlefield—daily marches—Bardawil—a Crusader's Church—El Arish.

CHAPTER IV.—THE OLD ROAD .. .. .. .. 54–60

The River of Egypt—a historic highway—back through the ages—The nomads—Abraham—Joseph—The Pharaohs—Amasis—Thotmes—The Syrians—Rameses—Seti—Ebb and flow of armies—Phœnician caravans—Solomon's emissaries—the daughter of Pharoah—Shishak's invasion—The messengers of Hoshea—Sargon—Assyrian and Egyptian armies—Sennacherib—Pharoah Necho—Jehoahaz the captive—Nebuchadnezzar—The remnant of Judah—Cambyses the Persian—Artaxerxes—Darius—Alexander the Great—Ptolemy—Cleopatra—The Holy Family—Titus—Zenobia—The Romans—Chosroes—The Moslems—Saladin—Louis of France—The Turks—Napoleon—Mahomet Ali—Ibrahim—The Turks again—The British.

CHAPTER V.—THE PROMISED LAND .. .. .. 61–66

Rafa, on the frontier—Khan Yunus—The Philistines—In Seirat—First View of Gaza—The plain of many battles—Ali Muntar—Samson—The scheme of attack—The Turkish positions—Task of the Essex Brigade.

CHAPTER VI.—THE FIRST BATTLE OF GAZA .. .. 66–71

Start of the Cavalry—a misty morning—movements of the Battalion—the battle opens—shell fire—orders for the attack—Green Hill and The Labyrinth—a "drill book" attack—fine behaviour of all ranks—absence of cover—the position taken—getting in the wounded—heavy casualties—The order to withdraw Why?—the advance repeated—reinforcement of the enemy—the dressing station shelled.

Pages

CHAPTER VII.—MARCH 26 AND 27, 1917 (Major Wilson's Narrative) .. .. .. .. .. .. .. 72–80

Description of the attack—regaining touch—Turkish demoralization—orders for withdrawal—Turkish counter-attack beaten off—the concentration—difficult night march—re-organization—Honours and awards—individual acts of heroism—laudatory orders—The Brigadier's appreciation.

CHAPTER VIII.—THE SECOND BATTLE OF GAZA .. 81–82

High hopes—Artillery—Tanks—Sheikh Abbas position taken—strengthened defences—Heavy fighting by the Division—failure of The Tanks—the battle for Outpost Hill—heavy casualties—the advance checked—attack abandoned—gallantry of the troops—the "Chief's" appreciation.

CHAPTER IX.—TRENCH WARFARE .. .. .. .. 83–93

Positions consolidated—"Dumbell Hill"—The Imperial Camel Corps—Sheikh Abbas—Night bombing by the Turks—a fight on "Essex Hill"—Letter from Sir Evelyn Wood—In reserve at "Regent's Park"—the Coastal Sector—Blazed Hill—Indian Visitors—propaganda—Gallant airmen—Raids on "Umbrella Hill"—heavy shelling—relief after 8 weeks in the line—training—advance of the line—wiring under fire—preparations for the next attempt—a patrol encounter—"Cuthbert" the terrier—our objectives for the attack—trench models—The tanks—an interrupted concert.

CHAPTER X.—THE THIRD BATTLE OF GAZA .. .. 94–102

The Bombardment—wire-cutting—The plan of attack—Fall of Beersheba—The night attack on "Rafa" Redoubt and "Zowaid" Trench—Taking of Umbrella Hill—Contradictory reports—breakdown of the Tanks—The positions taken with the bayonet—the loss of direction—some good leadership—Stubborn resistance of the Turks—retaliation—counter-attack beaten off—heavy casualties—a fine performance—individual acts of gallantry—Success of the main attack.

CHAPTER XI.—THE FALL OF GAZA AND THE ADVANCE THROUGH PHILISTIA (Major Wilson's narrative) .. 103–114

Heavily shelled—consolidation—relief—fall of Gaza—abandoned material—the pursuit—incidents of the march—outpost duty—the rains—Ramleh—Selmeh—Sarona—Action on the river Auja—The Turks make a stand—and occupy Mulebbis—a successful raid—marching in the mud—terrible bivouacs—the capture of Mulebbis—billets at last.

CHAPTER XII.—"GENERAL MUD" CHECKS THE ADVANCE 115–121

Ludd—Tomb of St. George—Ramleh—The Plain of Sharon—Jaffa—Capture of Mulebbis—delight of the Jewish Colony—Xmas festivities—Antipatris—Gilgal—A day's shooting—The Judean hills—Ruins.

CHAPTER XIII.—IN SHARON AND EPHRAIM .. .. 122–136

Capture of Mejdel Yaba—Kefr Ana (Ono)—Yehudieh (Jehud) Wilhelma—the Boche cows—In the hills—wild flowers—insects—Departure of troops to France—increased activity of the enemy—a spirited patrol action—fighting mosquitoes—The Crusaders—In the orange groves—patrolling the plain—good work—orders for France—cancellation—Brigade race meeting—Beit Nebala (Neballat)—Road making—In the Olive grove—Haditheh (Hadid)—The Maccabees—The Bureid Ridge—The Boche airman.

Pages

CHAPTER XIV.—THE BATTLE IN THE FOOTHILLS.. .. 139–147

The plan of operations—task of the Essex Brigade—equipment—the start at 1 a.m.—Apprehension of the enemy—The attack—Lewis gun among the rocks—capture of Kefr Kasim village and wood—a short check—on again—Taking of Sivri Tepe—a fine position—Turkish field kitchens—Breakfast all hot—casualties—pressing on—night outposts—our task completed—The "Brook Kanah"– a strenuous day's work—individual acts—hats off to the Lewis gunners.

CHAPTER XV.—ON TREK .. .. .. .. .. 148–157

Details for the march—start on Sept. 29—Kakon—streams of prisoners—The Dead river—extinct oak forest—Caesarea—Zimmarin—The Crocodile river—The port of Dor—Athlit—the last stronghold of the Cross—Haifa—Carmel—scorpions—The brook Kishon—The river Belus and the discovery of glass—Acre—Achzib—The ladder of Tyre—The pools of Solomon—Tyre—The river Leontes—Sarepta—Sidon—the Battalion drums—the landing place of Jonah.

CHAPTER XVI.—TURKEY THROWS UP THE SPONGE .. 158–164

News of the Armistice—the extent of the Turkish debacle—the fruits of victory—rumours from Europe—the march through Beyrout—joy of the inhabitants—our camp—The Lebanon—Turkish defences—sufferings of the Lebanese—The rains—the armistice with Germany—Prince Feisal—embarkation for Egypt.

CHAPTER XVII.—BACK TO EGYPT .. .. .. .. 165–172

Helmieh Camp—recreation—The march through Cairo—A merry Xmas—Educational training—sports—the Brigade Championship—the concert party—Nationalist riots—Demobilization stopped—in the provinces—the battle of Benha—order restored in the town—communication cut off—gratitude of the Greeks—Race meetings at Quesna—return to Cairo—Demobilization—The Citadel—return of the cadre to England—break up of the Bn.—appreciation.

APPENDIX I.—CASUALTIES .. .. .. .. .. 173–191

APPENDIX II.—HONOURS AND AWARDS .. .. .. 192–194

APPENDIX III.—LIST OF OFFICERS WHO SERVED WITH THE BATTALION .. .. .. .. .. .. 195–198

# LIST OF ILLUSTRATIONS.


| | Facing Page |
|---|---|
| Anzac Cove .. .. .. .. .. .. .. | 17 |
| The Front Line on Laindon Hill, Anzac .. .. | 18 |
| Sick and Wounded Arriving at the Hospital Ship .. | 25 |
| Walker's Ridge, Anzac .. .. .. .. .. | 29 |
| Coming to Market, El Hammam .. .. .. .. | 33 |
| The Battalion Arrives at Shallufa (Suez Canal) .. | 39 |
| A Halt in the Desert, Breakfast .. .. .. .. | 43 |
| The Wire Road .. .. .. .. .. .. | 50 |
| A Short Halt .. .. .. .. .. .. .. | 53 |
| Helping an Armoured Car Over the Wadi Ghuzzi, March 26, 1917 .. .. .. .. .. .. .. .. | 66 |
| Behind The Mansura Ridge, March 26, 1917 (The Brigade Moving up to the Attack) .. .. .. | 68 |
| The Battalion in Action in the Attack, March 26, 1917 | 70 |
| The Top of the Hill, Ali El Muntar .. .. .. | 78 |
| Behind the Sheikh Abbas Ridge, 2nd Battle of Gaza, April 19, 1917 .. .. .. .. .. .. .. | 81 |
| Battalion Headquarters at Sheikh Abbas .. .. | 84 |
| Turkish Prisoners .. .. .. .. .. .. | 86 |
| View of Gaza from the Enemy's Front Line .. .. | 105 |
| Memorial Cross on the Green Hill .. .. .. | 107 |
| Mejdel Yaba, Captured March 12, 1918 .. .. .. | 125 |
| Ras-el-Ain (Antipatris) .. .. .. .. .. | 129 |
| Enemy Gun-Limber in the Wadi Kanah .. .. .. | 145 |
| The Brook Kishon from the Slopes of Carmel .. | 150 |
| The Head of the Battalion in the Opera Square, Cairo, December 20, 1918 .. .. .. .. .. .. | 165 |
| The Football Team, Egypt, 1919 .. .. .. .. | 169 |
| The Hockey Team, Egypt, 1919 .. .. .. .. | 171 |


# LIST OF MAPS.


| | Facing Page |
|---|---|
| Sketch Map of Suvla and Anzac .. .. .. .. | 1 |
| The Route from the Suez Canal to Gaza .. .. | 54 |
| Gaza and the Surrounding Country .. .. .. | 66 |
| The Coastal Plain—Jaffa District .. .. .. | 115 |
| The Battle in the Foothills, Sept. 19, 1918 .. .. | 139 |
| The Palestine Theatre of War .. .. .. .. | 158 |

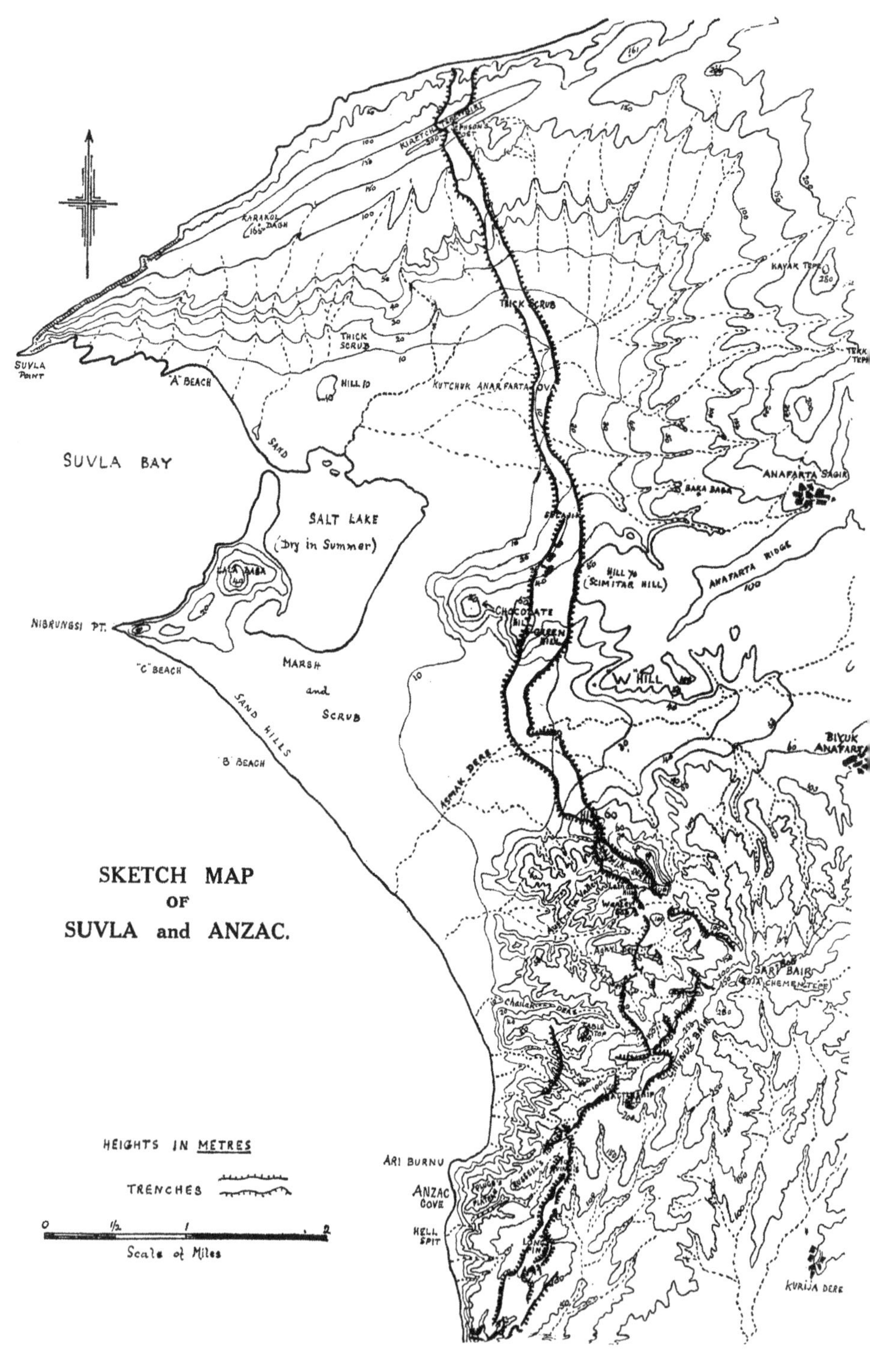
SKETCH MAP
OF
SUVLA and ANZAC.
HEIGHTS IN METRES
TRENCHES
0
1/2
1
2
Scale of Miles
SUVLA POINT
"A" BEACH
SUVLA BAY
SAND
SALT LAKE
(Dry in Summer)
LALA BABA
NIBRUNGSI PT.
"C" BEACH
SAND HILLS
"B" BEACH
MARSH
and
SCRUB
HILL 10
THICK SCRUB
THICK SCRUB
KARAKOL DAGH
KUTCHUK ANAFARTA OVA
KAYAK TEPE
ANAFARTA SAGIR
BAKA BABA
ANAFARTA RIDGE
HILL 70
(SCIMITAR HILL)
CHOCOLATE HILL
GREEN HILL
W HILL
BIYUK ANAFARTA
ASMAK DERE
Chailak Dere
SARI BAIR
ARI BURNU
ANZAC COVE
HELL SPIT
KURIJA DERE

# With the 1/5th Essex in the East.

## CHAPTER I.

## GALLIPOLI.

N July 21st, 1915, the 1/5 Battalion Essex Regiment had completed nearly a year's war service in England. Much dissatisfaction had been felt, and expressed, that the Battalion had not been called upon earlier for foreign service. We somehow felt that we were as good and as keen as the units which for some time past had been sent to swell the Army in France. The official reason, which was no doubt the true one, was that trained troops were required for home defence and that this was the particular job of the Territorial Force. Hence it was that many Divisions of the new Army—the "First Hundred Thousand," whose exploits have been immortalized by the pen of Ian Hay—had already been sent abroad and were shewing the stuff they were made of.

The Territorial Force was, of course, represented in France at a very early date. Selected Battalions were sent out, including three from our own East Anglian Division, and had shewn themselves to be worthy representatives of their County Regiments. The Essex Yeomanry had already proved itself one of the finest Cavalry Regiments in France, and had got well ahead with a record which was second to none. Early in the year a complete Territorial Division—the North Midland—had taken the field and it was followed by others during the spring. The North Midland Division had been training in Essex and their departure made still harder to bear the thought that the East Anglian was still in England. It was some consolation to be told that the strategic importance of East Anglia was such as to necessitate a strong defence force and elaborate works, and that the East Anglian Division must necessarily perform these duties until sufficient second-line Territorials could be trained to take their places. It is unnecessary here to go into the question of the advantages conferred on the New Army over the Territorial Force in the matter of recruiting, the services of Regular officers and non-commissioned officers, etc. We were given the rôle of defending East Anglia, and it was up to us to do it, and to possess our souls in patience while our comrades of the Territorial Force from other parts of the Kingdom and of the New Army were being given places of honour on the Continent. Could we have seen into the future we might have been satisfied that our chance would come soon enough to enable us yet to play an important part in the most tremendous task ever imposed on a nation. But at that time short odds were being taken that the war would be over by Christmas, and the "pessimist" who gave it another year demanded—and often obtained—long prices.

However, in the summer of 1915 indications were not wanting that something was going to be done at last with the East Anglian Division; and when eventually we were fitted out with khaki drill and helmets excitement ran high. At that time it was widely held (by people who didn't know—and who did?) that the war was going to be won in the East, and we began to feel that after all our part was not going to be an unimportant one. There was not much doubt as to where we were going. We had all heard of the landings at Helles and Anzac, and the claims of Constantinople as a winter resort were critically discussed. The Battalion strategists worked out plans for the invasion of Austria by way of the Balkans, and if the situation was, perhaps, not correctly appreciated in all it a pects, still the thought that we were going to take part in warfare on the grand scale was intensely stimulating and had its effect on the moral of all ranks. At any rate we were going to shake off at last what was beginning to be considered the stigma of Home Service, and many hearts beat high as we formed up on our Battalion parade ground in St. Albans in the evening hours of July 21st and moved about midnight through the slumbering city and entrained for Plymouth. The one fly in the ointment was that the transport personnel and all animals were to be left behind. We consoled poor old Tompson, the transport officer, and his men, with the assurance that we should want them before long, but they were the saddest men in the Battalion that night.

Noon on the 22nd brought us to Plymouth Docks. Without delay we boarded the good ship "Grampian," of the Allan Line, which lay alongside. We were fortunate in our ship and its officers. Captain John Williams, Chief Officer G. H. Simpson, and all under their command did everything to make us comfortable, and our memories of the voyage in the "Grampian" are some of the pleasantest of the war.

The final medical examination had weeded out some temporarily "unfits" and young soldiers not considered sufficiently seasoned for service in a hot climate, and this reduction, together with the loss of the transport section, left us at a strength of 29 officers and 649 other ranks.

The Officers of the 161st Brigade on board the "Grampian" were:—

HEADQUARTERS:

Brigadier-General F. F. W. Daniell (Commanding).
Major H. Fargus, D.S.O. (Brigade Major).
Capt. F. G. Bright (Staff Captain).
Lieut. L. P. Pacey (Brigade Signals).

*And the following Officers of the 1/5th Essex.*

Lieut.-Col. J. M. Welch, T.D., Commanding.

Major T. Gibbons and Major J. M. Heron.

Capt. and Adjt. H. C. Bridges.

Captains W. E. Wilson, H. T. Argent, F. W. Bacon, A. Denton, and C. A. Gould. Capt. K. S. Storrs (M.O.)

Lieutenants E. B. Deakin, T. G. N. Franklin, W. H. Brooks, G. W. F. Bellward, E. Mackenzie Taylor, H. L. Yonge, B. Carlyon-Hughes and H. Mavor. Lieut. and Quartermaster G. M. Nobbs.

2nd Lieutenants H. K. Chester, L. D. Womersley, C. Portway, J. L. French, R. S. Horton, A. Colvin, J. F. Finn, A. E. Sheldon and R. Turner.

Chaplain, Rev. A. J. Sacré, C.F.

At 8 a.m. on the 23rd, in dull threatening weather, we steamed slowly out by the winding channel which has been the starting point of so many brave adventures, to the sound of a hearty send-off from all the ships in the harbour—cheers from the decks and "cockadoodle-doos" all in different pitches, from the deep hoot of the big liners to the shrill screech of the steam pinnaces. Womersley remarked that "there was more Plymouth Sound than usual to-day." (He was not thrown overboard. He was the Signalling Officer, and indispensable.)

Plymouth is a beautiful place from the sea. As it slowly faded from view one thought of Drake in his cockleshell setting forth to circle the world, of the Pilgrim Fathers in the "Mayflower," of Napoleon, arriving in the "Bellerophon," just a hundred years ago, and one felt how great was our privilege that day to be thought worthy to sail those historic waters on England's business. The beautiful Devon and Cornwall coasts on either side seemed like the two arms of the dear Motherland, stretched forth in a farewell embrace, and the thought must have come to many of us:—Would she ever beckon us back with those arms, to take us to her heart again?

It was blowing hard. Two destroyers were waiting for us outside to escort us, falling into their stations on either side and a little ahead. Wicked looking little craft, going clean through, not over, the seas; visible tokens of the sea power which was destined to throttle our foes in its relentless grip. When after a few hours they turned and left us to our fate, we felt lonely. The crew made some rather rude remarks about "those little fellers," "might as well have stayed at home," etc., but the danger of submarines must have been negligible to us in that sea. Many of us indeed, began to feel that we had little interest in submarines or anything else just then, though the number of good sailors was surprising. Among the officers, Storrs, the Padre, H. L. Yonge, and Denton were almost aggressively good. Bright, Bacon, Turner and Nobbs also did credit to their seafaring race. Of the rest the less said the better, though of some less than others, of course. However, things got better, and after the first day there were few of us who could not do justice to the fare for which the Allan Line is famous. The men were well fed too, but rather crowded, and their quarters were very hot. The "Grampian" was not equipped with fans or other hot weather contrivances, and the troop decks became almost unbearable before the voyage was over. But there was no grousing. The fact is that the British soldier doesn't grouse when things are unbearable, he just bears them. When he *does* grouse is—but I will leave that trouble until we come to it!

Things kept improving, and Sunday was a beautiful day on deck. At church parade the Padre preached about bad language, and gave *illustrations* too, I remember, which, pronounced somewhat forcibly, gave the Captain (who was busy on the bridge and perhaps hadn't heard the context) quite a shock, old sailor as he was. He remarked at lunch "You were giving it to 'em rather strong this morning, weren't you?"

In the evening the men gathered in the dying light and sang hymns. It took our thoughts back home again. . . .

The next day we sighted Cape St. Vincent, a grand promontory on the distant horizon, and about 10.30 at night we saw Gibraltar, looming almost on the top of us. A fine sight in the moonlight was the huge black rock, set in brilliants round its base, and with others twinkling from its sides. The undulating outline of the African shore was visible for some miles, with the lights of Tangier and Ceuta nestling in the hollows. Then a hissing grey streak in the water shot by us, a torpedo-boat, suspiciously taking stock of us, it seemed. Presently she came alongside and our engines stopped. A conversation on megaphones ensued. "Are you stopping at Gibraltar?" "No, my orders are to go straight on." "Have you any mails?" "Yes, one bag." The bag was duly transferred, and the conversation resumed. "Anything to report?" "No, Sir." "Seen any submarines?" "No, or I shouldn't be here." "Good-night, Captain." "Good-night, Sir," and the Royal Navy slipped off like a snake into the night and the old "Grampian" got slowly under way again.

The following day we ran into what I think they call a "Sirrocco." (I heard it called other names by the troops.) A very hot wind, with, on this occasion, banks of thick fog at intervals, which made everything wet and clammy. The "Grampian" evidently felt the heat, and one of the dining tables in the saloon protested by curling itself up into a sort of switchback. The night was almost unbearable, nobody allowed to sleep on deck, and all portholes closed. Phew!

Awakening before sunrise on July 30th and looking out, I was rewarded with a beautiful sight. In the glow of the dawn to the north-east stood in clear silhouette the high smoking cone of a volcano; it must have been Etna, and the distance could hardly have been less than 150 miles. But it was perfectly distinct until the sun topped the horizon, when it disappeared. Of course, nothing could have been seen at that distance without the light behind and below it, and the opportunity could only have been a fleeting one. During the forenoon we were in Valetta Harbour. Everyone was interested in the novel sights of Malta. It was our first glimpse of the East, and the hours passed pleasantly enough watching the boys dive for coins, and in buying Maltese lace, fruit, etc., which were pulled up in a basket on a string.

We got off some home letters here, and were soon under way again, the sea like glass in the wonderful clear moonlight. The appearance of a submarine caused some excitement, but she turned out to be French. The monotony of the next day was only relieved by a practice fire alarm. The orders were for every man to fall in at his post in *any* dress, with lifebelt on. One man caused some amusement by falling in with his life-belt *only*. He was having a bath when the fog-horn blew, and paraded with perfect sang-froid. Yes, sang-froid is the word. He was the coolest man on deck.

The next day was Sunday, terribly hot, with a following wind. Church parade at 10.30. The Padre was mercifully brief.

On the morning of August 2nd we were in Alexandria harbour. It was a busy scene, great liners jostling with hospital ships and troopers, constantly coming and going, and everything in a feverish state of bustle. The hospital ships looked beautiful at night. They had a row of brilliant green lights from end to end, with a huge illuminated red cross in the centre.

Next morning we moved to the quayside and unshipped all our heavy baggage, including the men's kit bags. We were evidently going "light," whatever our destination. The quay was a swarm of colour and a very babel of voices. The efforts of the native policemen to keep order were more entertaining than effective, in spite of their sticks which they used pretty freely. One swarthy little urchin was singing "Tipperary," another drilling with a dummy rifle, performing each movement with admirable precision. His arms drill was perfection, and the only order which nunplussed him was "Pile arms." The next day we coaled, and the Battalion did a short route march. It was hot, but it was better than being aboard on coaling day. In the afternoon all who could get leave did so. It was the first visit of most of us to an Eastern City and needless to say was full of interest.

After another day's delay through coaling, we left Alexandria on August 6th and on the 7th arrived in the magnificent natural harbour of Mudros, in the island of Lemnos. The sight which met our gaze there left no doubt that there was verily "something doing"; British, French and Russian battleships, destroyers, submarines, giant liners and every type of craft under the sun were gathered in this magnificent haven. The biggest ship afloat was there, and apparently there was room for fifty more like her. Ashore there was a huge base, with enormous dumps of stores and many camps and hospitals. It was the first jumping off place for the Peninsula. Here we provided ourselves with water in 2-gallon cans with lids, and were given to understand that it was precious; in fact that we should probably have to fight for the refilling of those cans. It was no secret now that a new landing was to take place (in fact it had already taken place) and that the water supply was an unknown quantity; but I doubt if the ghastly possibility of being without water on that inhospitable shore worried any of us. "Hope springs eternal in the human breast" and there was an undefinable feeling that everything must come right. Those who had landed at Helles and Anzac had found water somehow, and it must be confessed that the water cans were looked upon as a bit of a nuisance.

On the 9th we left our luxurious quarters on the "Grampian" with genuine regret, and boarded the "Hazel," quite a small vessell but with a turn of speed which had done her good service on patrol in the Irish Sea. She claimed to do 26 knots, and had lately been engaged in sprinting across the Ægean with troops. We were packed like sardines, and they could hardly have squeezed another man, or even another water-can, into her. Her bridge was sandbagged; she had been under rifle and shrapnel fire. It began to look like business. We lay alongside the "Grampian" until dark, when hurried orders came to move at once. A hasty "good-bye" and "good-luck" from the big ship, and we were off. Pitch dark and not a light shewing, the "Hazel" picked her way through the crowd, and made for the open sea. The absence of moonlight was part of the scheme. As Sir Ian Hamilton put it "It was necessary to eliminate the moon" in order to keep secret the large concentration of troops that was going on. A few hours' sleep on deck, lulled by the rush of waters, and in the early hours we were feeling our way into Imbros. The Captain had long before the war retired from his seafaring life, and had been farming in Devonshire; and as we groped in the darkness into the little cove at Imbros, taking soundings every few minutes, I thought of of what this man was doing for his country, and what he had given up voluntarily in her hour of need. With all the danger and the heavy responsibility on his shoulders, there he was in those dark unknown waters, with his packed human freight, "carrying on" in the most matter-of-fact, business-like way imaginable. Cool, brave, unassuming man of the sea; I hope he lives to enjoy his well-earned rest, his fireside, and his farm in lovely Devon.

We were all very much awake when we dropped anchor at 5 a.m. Heavy firing was distinctly heard, and puffs of smoke could be clearly seen as the shells burst on the distant shores of the Peninsula. Though we did not know it at the time, a keen struggle was taking place, the 53rd Division, supported by the 11th, making a final attempt to capture Ismail Oglu Tepe (afterwards known as " W Hill," from its peculiar formation) and the ridge of Anafarta Sagir. There was also fierce fighting going on at Anzac. The Turks were launching more than a whole Division to the attack of Chunuk Bair, held by those two devoted Battalions the 6th Loyal North Lancashires and the 5th Wiltshires, who were practically annihilated; while at Lone Pine the gallant 1st Australian Brigade were still withstanding the heavy counter-attacks which the Turks continued to launch against that position, which the same Brigade had taken by a brilliant assault at dawn on the 7th. The firing continued all the morning. Why couldn't they put us in? Were they waiting for the decisive moment and the decisive point? We could only conjecture. At last about noon the " Hazel " weighed her anchor, shook herself, and sped to the sound of the guns. We felt that our chance had come.

As we approached, the barking of the cruisers lying off the shore became louder, and we could see the flashes as they knocked bits off the heights. One almost expected to see gaps in the skyline as the result of those hellish looking bursts, but as the smoke cleared it looked much the same. During the morning hours, however, the naval gunners had been having the time of their lives, their target being the swarms of Turks who in successive lines were topping the crests of Chunuk Bair and pouring down the sides. Such opportunities are rare, and from all accounts both the sailors and the field artillery made the most of this one.

We lost no time in landing. When the " Hazel " could get no further we crowded into flat-bottom steam lighters and were soon at quite a respectable pier, with our feet at last on enemy soil. A few shells were bursting on the beach, and an occasional spurt in the water marked the advent of a Mauser bullet, but as far as the Battalion was concerned we got ashore without a casualty. The enemy was indeed too much taken up with events on his immediate front to have much time for us. We were in fact effecting a landing under cover of an infantry attack. We landed at " A " beach, Suvla Bay, and rendezvoused a short distance inland. Concealment was almost out of the question. The heights of Sari Bair overlooked the whole beach, though from a considerable distance. Tekke Tepe was also a good point for enemy observation, but was fully occupied with the battle in progress. The ridge of Kiretch Tepe Sirt was closer, but could be avoided to some extent by taking the cover of the foothills. In any case, the smoke of battle and of blazing scrub must have made observation difficult, and we were not subjected to any aimed fire. No orders were received for an advance, and we settled down into our bivouac.

The country was of the most difficult description. Owing to the thick scrub, chiefly composed of a stunted, stiff and prickly oak, it was impossible to move far except in winding columns in single file. This method was very slow, and the keeping of touch and direction, particularly at night, was very difficult.

At 10 p.m. we were suddenly ordered to move, leaving our packs behind, and were led by a circuitous route to another position, in reserve to troops in front, who, it was understood, were going to attack the next day. The 11th and 12th however, passed without incident as far as we were concerned. We buried several Turks.

On the night of the 12th we moved again, being led by a guide from the 163rd Brigade. The column, being in single file, was a long one, and the difficulty of keeping touch was extreme. It was impossible to see more than about three yards in the inky darkness, and men frequently stumbled and fell in the terribly rough going. The result of each little incident of this kind, of course, immediately left a gap and called for the utmost care on the part of all ranks to avoid losing touch with the front. There is no doubt that enemy spies were prowling about in the darkness, doing their utmost to spread confusion—that most deadly enemy in a night advance. Inexplicable orders kept coming from the front. On one occasion "Retire at the double" was passed back, and many men actually turned about and pressed upon those in rear. At last it was reported that connection had been broken. This turned out on investigation to be quite true. The Battalion in front of us was in two parts, the leading half going on with the guides, the remainder going blindly on, they knew not whither. It was an awkward moment. Unless we were to lose our way entirely, the only thing to do was to retrace our steps and get a fresh guide. It was quite a short distance, but it went to shew the extraordinary care and alertness required of every single soldier in a night movement in such a country.

On returning to Brigade Headquarters the Brigadier undertook to guide us himself. We were formed up ready to start when a staff officer came up to Womersley, who was with Battalion Headquarters, and asked where we wanted to go and whether we required a guide. If we did he would be pleased to direct us. Womersley replied that the Brigadier, who was just in front, was going to guide us himself. The staff officer, curiously enough, did not wish to see the Brigadier; in fact he turned back without a word and disappeared into the darkness. Who the staff officer was who was so willing to guide us to any destination in that intricate country remains a mystery to this day. Eventually we came up with the rest of the Brigade.

The spot we had reached was anything but a comfortable one. A steady succession of "overs" kept whistling close, very close, above our heads. It behoved us to hug the ground pretty tightly, and it was the hardest thing we had ever hugged. The field we were in (for we were in one of the few open spaces to be found), was roughly cultivated, and the clods were composed of the stiff Gallipoli soil with which we were later to become painfully and laboriously acquainted. When dry, as it was then, it was as hard as a brick. When wet it is like glue.

When day broke we found we had a slight bank on the edge of the field towards the enemy and this gave some protection, while another slight bank provided some cover in rear. The Battalion was therefore formed into two lines and ordered to keep concealed as much as possible. Enemy snipers were busy, and this and occasional shrapnel fire shewed that the enemy knew quite well where we were. It was quite impossible to avoid this. A Battalion cannot lie on its stomach all day, and we were completely overlooked. The casualties, however, were very light, a few men wounded, chiefly by snipers, and we found rather to our pleased surprise, that it was quite possible to be under fire all day without "stopping one." On the whole the experience gave confidence, and acted as a sort of inoculation against shell-shyness.

The original idea was for the Division to make a night march and at dawn on the 13th to attack the heights of Kavak Tepe and Tekke Tepe. In the afternoon of the 12th, the 163rd Infantry Brigade had advanced across the Anafarta Plain (Kuchuk Anafarta Ova) to make good this ground for the movement of the remainder of the Division the same night. The advance was successfully carried out, but in the face of strong opposition. The Turks had indeed been heavily reinforced, and the Commander-in-Chief in his report estimated their strength at three times what it was on the 7th. This was, of course, not known to us, but those of us who had learnt to write "information" paragraphs in operation orders had a very shrewd suspicion that everything was not going well. It is a sound rule to withhold bad news, and the absence of information as to the enemy meant that the information would not do us any good if we had it. However, as far as we could see, the 163rd Brigade had driven back the enemy. How two companies of the 1/5th Norfolks pushed too far and were swallowed up in the scrubby slopes of Tekke Tepe, never to be seen again, is graphically described in the Commander-in-Chief's historic despatch. Although the objective was made good and held, the dawn attack was abandoned by General Headquarters, owing to the declared impossibility of sustaining the Division in food and water in the event of their gaining the heights. However, General Birdwood intended to make another attack from Anzac, and would want us to co-operate by attacking W Hill. So we stayed where we were.

On the 13th the Rev. Pierrepont Edwards, C.F., came round and asked for volunteers to collect wounded of the 163rd Brigade who had been out all night. Enemy snipers were very busy and apparently treated all alike who came within their observation. But the gallant Chaplain resolved to make an effort to bring in these poor fellows, and a volunteer party of 24 from the 5th Essex was soon made up and set out unarmed, with stretchers and a large Red-Cross flag. The G.O.C. 163rd Brigade afterwards wrote his thanks to the N.C.O.'s and men who undertook this voluntary duty, and stated that he had mentioned their names in his report. They did not, however, appear in despatches as they deserved to have done.

On the 14th we were ordered to advance to the relief of the 163rd Brigade, who were holding on to the ground they had won but were having rather a bad time. Colvin, with a small patrol, made an excellent reconnaissance of the ground to be covered, whilst Mackenzie Taylor, with his platoon, made good a small hillock to our left front, which was occupied by enemy snipers. Colvin's party in particular were sniped nearly all the way out and back, but brought some good information as to the ground.

At 4 p.m. the advance commenced. The distance to be covered was a little over a mile, for the most part on the level plain which was thickly covered with prickly scrub. The formation was lines of platoons in single file. The moment the leading platoons came into the open heavy shrapnel fire commenced. Rifle fire was also opened from the heights in front, also from the plain on our left. The latter could have only been from snipers who were behind the forward line held by our own troops, but the volume was considerable. It sounds hardly credible that many of these troublesome individuals could continue to exist behind our line but it must be remembered that this line was by no means continuous for the first few days after the landing; this constant sniping was a regular thing, and it was some time before the pests were all disposed of. Australian sharpshooters would set forth in pairs, as if they were going to shoot rabbits, with haversacks, waterbottles, and ammunition, and would be out the whole day, taking on the Turk at his own game, and beating him at it. But it was slow work. The cover was thick, the quarry knew how to use it, and they got busy on that afternoon of our advance over the plain. We could not, of course, return the fire for fear of hitting the troops in front, and there was nothing to do but walk past it, though it was anything but pleasant when it began to come from the left rear. Everyone was carrying something, water-cans, camp kettles, tools, machine guns, etc., and it was hot work, with the sun still blazing. The men were absolutely steady. Direction was not perfectly kept, but this was not surprising, considering the nature of the country and the fact that we had to change direction twice to avoid going over the crest of a hill. However, the majority of the Battalion reached the line occupied by the 5th Norfolks and 8th Hants. Some platoons on the right of the Battalion struck the line held by a Brigade of the 53rd Division, between whom and the 163rd Brigade there was a considerable gap. The detached platoons found the Battalion about dusk, after a somewhat trying movement across the enemy's front, feeling for the open flank, and the gap was eventually filled by the 7th Essex, making a thin but continuous line. 14 N.C.O.'s and men of the Battalion were killed and about 30 wounded in the advance. It was our baptism of fire. The movement was in full view of the enemy, whose shrapnel fire was very accurate. It was also seen by the Australian troops on the left of the Anzac position (which by this time was extended considerably in our direction) and some of them told me afterwards that it was a really good show to watch, and expressed surprise that our casualties were not much heavier. There was one amusing incident. Jam was served out, one tin to every four men, so one had to carry it for the four. Two brothers were in the advance and one fell wounded. They told the other. "Lumme!" he exclaimed, "He's got *our jam*!"

At dark there was a considerable uncertainty as to the situation on our right and the patrol work was particularly difficult. One patrol was unfortunately ambushed, and 2/Lieut. Turner, the leader, and Sergt. Rice were killed, but two men made their way back under a heavy fire. Turner was an old "Artists" Rifleman. He had served in France and had not been with us long, but had made himself deservedly popular. Rice was an old comrade and the steadiest of N.C.O.'s. During the night the relief took place and the battle-worn 163rd got out of the line without incident.

There was little sleep for anybody that night. Our predecessors had been unable to do much in the way of digging in, owing to the exhaustion of the men and shortage of tools, and the night was spent in strengthening the position, a work which continued all the next day in the face of continual fire from the unseen enemy in front. Whilst superintending the work of his Company Captain Denton was shot through the head and killed instantly. Poor "Bar" Denton. He was the keenest of us all, and none was better loved by his men or by his brother officers.

Most of the line held by the Battalion consisted of a lane, with a very small bank and thin hedge on each side, which gave some cover from view, but practically none from fire. The bank was used as a parapet and a trench dug behind it. But the men were very tired from lack of sleep, work proceeded but slowly, and it was some time before any means of getting along the line other than crawling was possible. The nights were decidedly chilly and the days very hot. The absence of blankets for warmth at night and shade by day was severely felt.

In one thing we were extraordinarily and unexpectedly fortunate. There was a well just in rear of the lane, near the junction of ourselves and the 7th Essex. This was a very godsend. It was, however, well marked by the Turkish sharpshooters, and several men were killed and wounded while getting water from it for their platoons and for the wounded, who lay in a dressing station in the skeleton of an old stone building close by, in charge of Capt. Storrs. Our excellent Medical Officer worked untiringly, attending the cases by day and getting them away by night. Neither physical fatigue nor constant danger could damp his ardour or quench his cheery spirit.

There was heavy fighting all day on the left, some Battalions of the 10th Division making an advance and capturing the crest of Kiretch Tepe Sirt, known to us afterwards as the "Razorback." The sound of heavy rifle fire at a distance is difficult to describe, it wasn't a "roar," and it wasn't exactly a "crackle." It gave the impression of a high wind blowing, through which could be heard the incessant and monotonously distinct Pup-up-up-up of the machine guns. The enemy were evidently being rapidly reinforced and made a spirited counter-attack on the salient we were holding. The men showed their first signs of excitement as at last they saw live moving "running man" targets to fire at. At one time we were outflanked on the left, and there was some talk of a retirement. But no such thought entered the heads of the men of the 5th or of the 6th Essex on our left, and the attack was successfully driven back by steady and well-controlled fire. One enemy aeroplane dropped bombs on the 6th. The peculiar sound of bombs dropping through the air was a novel one to most of us. We saw the Irishmen of the 10th Division cheering and waving their helmets on the crest of the Razorback, which they had won, though at a heavy cost. They were obliged, however, to withdraw during the night to their old line a short distance behind the culminating point, at a place called "Jephson's Post," after the gallant Major Jephson of the 6th Munsters, who was killed at the very post which had been named after him when he had captured it with his men a week before.

That night was an anxious one for officers. The men were dog-tired and no sense of danger could overcome the overpowering demands of sleep. Sentries were posted, but they had to lie down, a position which made it trebly difficult to keep them alert, and it was only by constantly passing messages down the line and ordering them to fire that they could be kept awake. They had had very little sleep for a week. They were quite oblivious to the continuous rifle fire at close range to which they were subjected. There were some stone walls near the wells behind us and the bullets struck these with spurts of flame and loud reports which led to allegations of explosive bullets. The fearful nature of some of the wounds also lent colour to this idea, but I believe both were the result of ordinary fire at very close range. The enemy had been reinforced by fresh troops, small parties of whom crept up through the scrub. Colonel Welch shot two of them himself within 10 yards of the lane, and one of them crawled into our line the next morning badly wounded. The next day we received the welcome news that we were to be relieved by a Welsh Battalion. Our casualties in the lane had not been heavy but the killed included Sergt. Wass and Sergt. Ogg, two good non-commissioned officers who could ill be spared.

Midnight came, but still no sign of the relieving troops. If they did not soon arrive we should be caught by the daylight—and there were no communication trenches; all movements had to be done on the top in full view of the enemy. It looked as if getting out was going to be a worse job than getting in. At 3 a.m. the relieving Battalion arrived and at 3.30 we began to file out, again led by those excellent Australian guides who by this time seemed to know every track in that intricate country. It was broad daylight by the time we reached the clearing in which we had bivouacked on the night of the 11th. It was an old Turkish Headquarters and well-known to the enemy. There was a water cart there, and some stores from which we drew rations. We were shelled systematically, and the Battalion had to split up to escape heavy casualties. Distribution of rations and water necessarily entailed some movement, and two platoons suffered severely.

Again we pushed on, this time towards the Razorback to relieve the Munsters. Moving in small columns we made our way up the slope. It is an annoying experience, moving under shell fire and having nothing to shoot back at, but the men plodded steadily on, and by midday we had reached the northern slope of the ridge. We lost Capt. Argent going up, wounded by shrapnel, and several men. Others, including two or three officers, completely gave out and had to be taken to the beach for a rest. It had been a trying ordeal for men who had no previous experience of war; the want of sleep and fresh food, the constant strain, the blazing heat, the black plague of flies, the dirt and squalor of it all, and perhaps more than anything else the all pervading smell of death, had proved too much for others more hardened than they, and it was no disgrace that the ordeal had proved too severe for a time for some sorely tried natures to bear.

We stayed at our new position long enough for some of us to get a bathe in the sea. The luxury of it after the unwashed experiences of the past week cannot be described. A night's rest would have completed the picture, but it was not to be. The Munsters urgently required—and deserved—relief; and at night we moved forward along the rough rocky ridge and took over Jephson's Post and a roughly prepared line running down the northern slope towards the sea. The right of the line ran back along the ridge for some distance. Jephson's Post itself was not exactly a Gibraltar. The rock was nearly bare, and all that had been possible to do was to scrape out the fissures into something like trenches and fill up the gaps with sandbags. All movement by day had to be on hands and knees in most parts of the redoubt.

During the night everyone was busy strengthening the position as far as possible, but it was killing work. The enemy were busy doing the same thing about 300 yards to our front. Between us the dead lay thick, friend and foe, and burying was an impossibility. It was unpleasant work for the patrols and covering parties.

A destroyer lay close in at night and helped us very considerably by keeping her eye (in the form of a searchlight) upon the enemy. Relentless and unsleeping, that beam of vivid light kept the crest of the hill in a luminosity which must have been very annoying for "Johnny Turk," or "Abdul," as he was familiarly called by the men. They put their snipers on to that light and they fired all night at it, but they never hit it. A searchlight at an unknown range and 700 feet below the firer is not an easy night target. During the day they shelled her persistently, but I only saw her hit once, plump on her after-deck, but the damage, if any, was not apparent. She went on with her "bending" until the enemy was tired, then she ran close in and fired back. Truly a sight for the gods! And if old Father Neptune had been sitting, as of old—

"In Samothracia, on the mountain's brow"—*

he would surely have felt a thrill of pride for his children.

On the following day we lost Colonel Welch, sick. Never the possessor of robust health the strain of the past week had proved too much for him, as we all feared who had noted him day after day cheerfully carrying on without a complaint but in obvious suffering. He went with a cheery "Au revoir," quite expecting, or hoping, to be back with us in a few days, and it was a great disappointment to him and to us when he was invalided to England.

By August 21st the 2nd Mounted Division had arrived from Egypt, also the "incomparable 29th" (as they were deservedly called), from Helles, and the Commander-in-Chief, disappointed in the further reinforcements which he had asked for, had decided to make another effort with the means at his disposal to obtain possession of W Hill. The scheme was for the 53rd and 54th Divisions to hold the enemy along the whole of the Suvla front, while the 29th and 11th Divisions attacked the hill. We moved up at 2.15 p.m. and filled every crevice of the redoubt in readiness to advance when the word was given. A fairly thick mist hampered the preliminary bombardment, but the attack of the two Divisions started at 3 p.m. and once more the rifles and machine guns got deadly busy. As we lay waiting we

*Iliad, Book XIII.

could see the battle all along the line, and although it was difficult to follow exactly what was taking place it was soon evident that considerable progress was being made. Whilst this fighting was going on the 2nd Mounted Division advanced across the dry bed of the Salt Lake to take up a position in rear of Chocolate Hill. It reminded us of our own advance across the Anafarta Plain on the 14th. Again there was no cover from the steady rain of shrapnel fire, and we noted with admiration how the English Yeomen carried out their advance in perfect order, though it was only too evident that they were suffering heavy casualties. Anxiously we waited for news that W Hill had fallen, making it possible for the whole line to advance.

But we were disappointed. After remaining in our cramped position until nearly 7 p.m. normal dispositions were resumed and we knew that the attack had failed. It was afterwards known that Turkish positions had been taken at several points by the 29th Division and the Yeomen. Indeed the latter thought themselves that they were on the top of W Hill, but it turned out to be a knoll which would have been impossible to hold, and they were withdrawn during the night. The 29th Division had had nearly 5,000 casualties.

Meanwhile on the Anzac front General Cox had taken and held important positions on the slopes of Kaiajik Aghala (known afterwards as " Hill 60 "), but the completion of its capture had to be postponed until the line between Suvla and Anzac should be established, as it was becoming increasingly clear that our offensive was temporarily at a standstill. Not only were the fighting casualties very heavy but sickness had broken out and spread with alarming rapidity.

Next day the enemy gave Jephson's Post his special attention. As fast as we got sandbags into position in the attempt to make the position habitable the Turkish " whizz-bangs " knocked them off by direct hits, and the whole of the crest became very " unhealthy," particularly from the post itself to the right of the line, which was completely enfiladed. Down the northern slope for some distance it was so steep that it gave cover from shell fire, the shells which did not catch the crest bursting far below on the other side. The enemy did not appear to have any batteries on the northern side as they would have been exposed to direct fire from the destroyers, but a continual rifle fire was kept up.

This continual rifle fire was a feature of the Peninsula fighting. Day and night and all the time it went steadily on. The enemy realized that there was a possible billet for every bullet which found its way into our back areas. This put a premium on high firing, and their fire was generally high, more so, of course, by night. Thus it was that the troops in the front line, particularly at Anzac, had more cover than those in rear, except in special localities like Jephson's Post where there was no cover worthy of the name, and could not be, without blasting.

Still, officers and men worked gamely on with their sandbags, covering them with scrub and hiding them as much as possible. Poor Sheldon was badly wounded in the head while working on the parapet with a party of men, and he died the same night. He also was comparatively a newcomer to the Battalion. He had proved his worth, however, and had set a great example to his men.

The peculiar form of dysentery which had shewn itself the last few days laid its grip on many men. They carried on like heroes, but they were getting badly used up. On the 23rd we were relieved, and moved back along the north side of the ridge for a short rest. Lieut.-General Sir Julian (now General Lord) Byng took over the Suvla Command on the 24th. He walked round to see us, enquiring most kindly after the 5th, who had been in his old Division before the War. I hope we convinced him that the Terriers' tails were up, albeit some of their *beards* were just a bit down!

Bathing in the sea was again our greatest joy, and was well worth the 600 feet climb back to the bivouac. It was not without its thrills, as there were many bullets that found their way to the sea. Someone discovered a small spring half-way up, which gave the most delicious water. Shelling continued and Sergt. H. Stone of "C" Company was killed. He was a real loss to the Battalion.

On the 28th we moved to Lala Baba Hill, between "B" beach and the Salt Lake, preliminary to joining the Australian and New Zealand Army Corps ("Anzac") to which we belonged thenceforth to the evacuation. Lala Baba was persistently shelled, but we dug in well on the western side which gave good cover; casualties, however, were unavoidable, the 7th Battalion suffering the most, one shell knocking out nearly a whole platoon and several mules. We stayed here until the 30th. During this time General Cox had completed the capture of Hill 60, an important tactical point, the possession of which added 400 acres to the territory of Anzac, and gave a good view of the valley to the north of it which runs up to Biyuk Anafarta. It was a brilliant affair, in which Indians, Australians, New Zealanders, 4th South Wales Borderers, and 5th Connaught Rangers took part.

On the night of the 30th we moved forward to a gully in rear of the 4th Australian Brigade. Major Heron (who had become 2nd in command when I took over the Battalion from Col. Welch on the 19th) and several men were wounded by "overs" on the way up. It was a wild night. Much of the scrub which had been fired by high explosive shells in the recent fighting was still burning fiercely in places, and caused some trouble with the mules.

Our Brigade Headquarters (161st) took over from the 4th Australian Brigade commanded by Brigadier-General Monash (who afterwards as General Sir John Monash commanded the

ANZAC COVE.

*To face page* 17.

Australian Army in France), and on September 1st we relieved the 13th Battalion of this Brigade who had taken part in the recent capture of Hill 60 and held the ridge afterwards known to us as Norfolk Street. The Australians had been on the Peninsula since April, and knew all about trench warfare, which we did not; and it was a wise arrangement which allowed them to leave a considerable detachment in the trenches with us, to imbue us with the spirit and the points of the game. They were very kind to our men and quickly became great favourites with them. They were inveterate souvenir hunters, and it is feared that many Essex cap badges and buttons found their way to Australia (where they really shouldn't have been) in exchange for packets of "fags" and other luxuries which had been denied us for some time. Organization at Anzac had had time to get into working order, and there was a marked increase in comforts of all kinds. The Australian and New Zealand Governments looked after their troops well, and, it may be added, no troops knew better how to look after themselves.

There was much to be done. The new trenches were necessarily in an unfinished state, and a long communication had to be dug under a very close and continuous fire, to connect up with Hill 60, which was on our left and slightly advanced. Daylight digging was impossible and all work had to be done at night. If we could have slept by day this would not have mattered, but the intense heat and the flies made it a fitful business, and men got very little rest. The enemy had some good shots, picked men, who fired at anything they could see—there were many places still which gave no cover from view—and their sniping was only kept down by the accurate fire of our own snipers. Any relaxation of observation and careful shooting was immediately followed by heavier sniping—or more accurately sharpshooting—from the enemy's trenches, which were only 60 yards from ours on Norfolk Street. Periscopes were indispensable, and luckily the Australians had some, also some periscopic rifles, which proved very useful. At night the enemy kept up a continuous fire, and any reply from us increased its intensity to rapid fire, which was deafening, but did little damage. The enemy was evidently very nervous and expected us to attack again every night. Unfortunately we had no troops to attack with; all were now required to hold the line. Eventually we decided to let him alone at night, except when he left off firing, then we manned the parapet. As long as he was firing from his trenches we knew he wasn't attacking. When he was quiet, which was very seldom, we suspected him and cleared for action. We now know that he was as little capable of attacking as we were. He had suffered enormous casualties and was wasting daily from dysentery like ourselves. The whole position including Hill 60 was a marked salient and was enfiladed from the Koja-Chemen Tepe—Chunuk Bair ridge, but we soon got some good dugouts made.

The enemy had bombs but he dare not leave his trenches and could not throw 60 yards, so they burst in " No Man's Land," adding to the din. We managed to make a few with jam pots. They had to be lighted with a match. The bomb had not then become as important an infantry weapon as it afterwards became, but our jam pots were quite successful on Hill 60, where we were only separated from the enemy by trench blocks, and bombs were thrown as fast as they could be produced. The casualties in *blankets* were heavy. They were used to smother bombs which found their way in. The trenches were extremely narrow, and very careful arrangements had to be made for relieving companies at night, to prevent them from becoming blocked.

On September 5th we were relieved by the 4th Norfolks (who gave their name to the sector), and moved into a gully of " Australia Valley " which was occupied by Brigade Headquarters. The " rest " period was fully occupied in digging saps and communication trenches and in Divisional and Brigade fatigues. We were only about 400 yards behind the front line, but were at least out of reach of that awful stench of old battlefield which still pervaded the trenches.

By the 18th our strength was reduced to 11 officers and 281 other ranks. I had lost my second in command and my Adjutant (Bridges) and other valuable officers, but I still had Deakin, equable and cheery as ever, who acted as Adjutant, and Womersley, who gave invaluable support, fighting against sickness all the time.

On September 23rd we took over a new piece of line from the 4th Essex. It ran for the most part along the crest of the steep southern slope of the Kaiajik Dere and covered the head of another deep Dere on the right. The enemy lined the opposite side of the Dere. At the head of the Kaiajik we had 200 yards of scrubby level ground between us. We called this point " Laindon Hill." I had my Headquarters on its reverse slope. What remained of the 1/8th Hampshire Regiment was attached to us for tactical purposes and right well we worked together—Major (now Lt.-Colonel) Harrison Marsh, his Adjutant, Capt. Charles Seeley, and all their officers and men did their full share of the work, and a fast friendship was established between the two Battalions, which outlived the war and will always be a pleasant and valued memory.

The entrant of the Dere on our right was a difficult position, completely commanded by a spur of Chunuk Bair which the enemy had fortified by a double tier of trenches. On its further side we joined up with the 162nd Brigade ; if we could be said to " join up " when our right post was separated from their left by about 200 feet of inaccessible rock. However, we made a small post some way up the side, which gave an excellent view and provided a good nest for our snipers, who worried the enemy

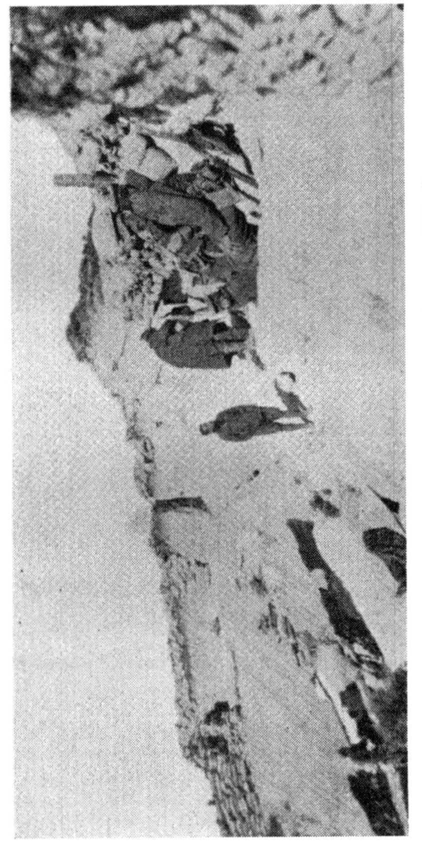

THE FRONT LINE ON LAINDON HILL, ANZAC

*To face page* 18.

to such an extent that on September 30th their little eyrie was subjected to a regular bombardment—without more result than its temporary evacuation by the said snipers, who soon returned to their work, highly pleased with the impression they had made.

The near side of the Dere was not so steep, and a trench was made with difficulty down its slope and slightly "refused" which effectually covered the entrant, while the bed of the stream, now dry, was closed by a barbed wire entanglement and a short trench. This portion of the line was in the hands of Colvin, who organized and maintained, with his slender garrison, a good system for the defence of this danger point.

There was a false crest in front of the centre of our line which hid the bottom of Kaiajik from view, and we started on forward saps with a view to advancing our line to it. Scrub had also to be cleared in front of the line. This was laborious work and had to be done under continuous fire. Attempts to burn it were not very successful.

Trench warfare is not very interesting, especially when one is condemned, as we were, for the most part, to a passive attitude. We simply had not the men to spare for those minor enterprises which do so much to keep up the offensive spirit and wear down the enemy. A large proportion of N.C.O.s and men were on duty as sentries, patrols, and listening posts every night, getting what sleep they could by day. Officers were necessarily overworked. There was a steady, though not heavy, drain of casualties, and sickness continued to take toll of us. When should we get any reinforcements? Had the Authorities at home forgotten all about us? A welcome addition to our strength in officers arrived on October 7th. Compton and Archer (1/5th) Conway, Gray and Beard (2/5th), Brown, Coates and Calverley (12th), eight in all, but still no men.

There was a violent storm on October 8th, which reminded us that the rainy season might soon be expected. It was not pleasant to reflect what our position would be like when the rain got into our stiff clay trenches and the Deres ran in flood. In many cases the natural beds of the latter were our only means of covered communication.

The storm was accompanied by heavy rain and a gale of wind, The thunder was deafening, and I never saw such lightning. It seemed to upset the Turk, who added to the scenic effect by sending up hundreds of flares all along the line. It was a weird and awe-inspiring sight. As we looked back towards the sea, every flash lit up all the ships lying off the coast, and even the hills of Imbros and the distant peaks of Samothrace leapt into view and left their outlines photographed on the after blackness.

The enemy's artillery had a great advantage throughout. Their observation posts gave them a comprehensive view, not only of our lines but of a great part of our back areas, including most of the shore. Added to this was the complete command which was afforded by their positions on the heights. Our batteries had to be sited in low gullies, and observation was practically impossible except from the front line trenches, and even these had a limited view. Nevertheless the howitzers in particular, did good work and the effect of their 4-5 and 5" high explosives on the enemy's front line afforded an inspiriting sight to our tired eyes.

The enemy must have been poorly supplied with howitzers. This was a lucky thing for us, living in the deep and rather narrow gullies. As it was, his "whizz-bangs," either knocked a bit off the parapet or burst on the opposite wall, quite close, but comparatively harmless. He used very little high explosive another fortunate circumstance for us. His long-range guns confined their attention principally to the ration dumps and refilling points. The shells sounded very "tired" as they passed high above our heads. Sometimes at night we could see the fuses, like dim shooting stars.

On October 11th we had more rain. I thought Essex clay was stiff and holding, but it is not in it with Gallipoli glue.

We were relieved at dawn by the 4th Essex and remained in "Hatfield Park" in reserve until the 20th. Parties of men are allowed to go back to the sea to bathe. It did them good and was much appreciated; but it had to be paid for. We lost a good non-commissioned officer in Sergt. R. W. Miller, of C Company, who was killed by a bullet just as he was walking out of the water.

Four more officers arrived on the 18th, Rubens, Capron, Tompson (the younger) and Bateman. Against them we had to set off Colvin and Finn, who had succumbed to the inevitable sickness. Heron rejoined, also Oscar Wilson, who had only been to the Hospital on the beach.

The weather got more and more unsettled, but Anzac was getting more or less prepared for it, as well as for the heavier shelling which we knew must come with the entry of Bulgaria into the war. The steep reverse slopes of the Anzac Hills were a wonderful sight. Tier after tier of dug-outs covered every inch of space. Mule lines were made in terraces in the same way. The roads across the plains were now dug deep into the ground with high banks on each side. Very little of our little strip of newly acquired territory was uninhabited, and it behoved everybody to dig in,—above the water level if possible.

Great flocks of geese and storks flew over every day going west. Both sides fired at them with rifles, without effect, except to increase the "overs." We could have done with a goose. The Turks even tried their "Archies" (anti-aircraft guns) at them, but still no result.

Mining was carried on by both sides. The labour was very great. The Turks did not strike one as good miners, although they are well-known to be wonderful diggers. They fired a mine on our left while we were in the line, but only succeeded in blowing up a bit of their own trench. On our side the Welsh Horse could give them points. They had many real miners in their ranks, and the way they used the light entrenching implement (which Essex men pronounced "no good") was a revelation. Of course they had other tools as well.

About this time a catapult was used for propelling bombs. In this, I believe, we were in front of the enemy, for one night a huge Turk tumbled into the British lines and inquired for the man who threw the "big bombs." He considered himself the champion bomb-thrower on the other side, but admitted that on this occasion he had found his master. I cannot personally vouch for the truth of this story, but it was told me on good authority and it is too good to be lost in oblivion.

The feast of Bairam commenced on the 18th. It commemorates the offering of Ishmael (not Isaac the Turks say) by Abraham on Mount Moria, and they celebrate it by making abundant sacrifices of sheep and goats. Prisoners said they were promised by Enver that they should celebrate it at home that year, as they would have driven us into the sea by then and the war would be over. (Now Enver was an optimist . . . .)

About this time we first made the acquaintance of B. K. Bond, C.F., kindest, keenest and best of Padres, who was shortly afterwards attached to the Battalion, not to leave it until two years later, when promotion robbed us of his services and his pleasant company. He conducted a service in the gully on October 17th when his discourse was punctuated by shrapnel fire. We finished the service, including a celebration of the Holy Communion. Only one man was slightly wounded.

The moon was very bright for the first few nights in the line and we effectually prevented the enemy from doing some repairs in front of his trenches. It was quite easy to read ordinary print by the light of the moon.

Time passed with little incident beyond an occasional spasmodic bombardment by the enemy and the explosion by our engineers of a good mine, which blew up an enemy bombing sap, which had been some trouble and annoyance to the respectable inhabitants of Norfolk Street.

Things became noticeably quieter except for artillery fire, and even this did not come up to expectations. Our working parties and patrols had occasional casualties and incautious shewing of heads above the parapet too often caused the loss of comrades.

In those quiet times sniping became a more or less popular pastime and I became quite bitten by it myself. We worked in pairs, the firer with his rifle, the observer with his telescope. Womersley was an excellent observer and gave me several hits. The target was almost invariably a sandbag loophole which the observer watched. When he saw a "face at the window," he said, "fire," and the firer, who was aiming at the spot though he could not see the face, pulled the trigger. Sometimes one could see an enemy sniper who would "take us on." In this case, when the enemy was seen to poke his rifle through the loop-hole, the observer would say, "Come down." The firer would then put his head out of danger. The observer would watch the actual discharge of the rifle, duck his head at once, and then resume his watch. The firer would again get on to his aiming mark and wait for the next order. The observer was really the brains of the pair. The firer had nothing to do but hold and press the trigger. Observing called for good judgment, a thorough knowledge of the telescope, and facility in describing targets. Some people have doubted the possibility of watching a man fire at you and "bobbing" in time, but at 500 yards it takes the bullet more than three-quarters of a second to reach you, whereas the "bobbing" can be almost simultaneous with the discharge.

Regtl.-Sergt.-Major (now Lieut.) Fry and I used to work together also, and found it very interesting. Fry was a good shot whom I had often shot with at rifle meetings. I would observe for him and vice versa. We had one contrivance which enabled one to observe for oneself at close range, and this was the "Wallaby Rifle." It was really a rifle holder, and could be fixed in any position. Having aligned the sights on the enemy loophole, the firer looked through his telescope and pressed the trigger when he saw the target appear, thus firing the rifle and observing the shot without taking his eye from the glass. The drawback was that eventually it was generally spotted by the enemy, through firing so much from one place. It was a heavy thing and required fixing firmly in the parapet. It was much more suitable for night firing, as targets could be registered by day and shot at by night, by means of scales marked on the stand.

There was a fascinating target at 1100 yards which it was difficult to leave alone. A short length of wide deep sap, one of the enemy's main communications, lay open to view from Laindon Hill. At this range it was possible to wait for a party of Turks to appear in the field of the telescope, then to fire, and then to watch the strike of the bullet—generally on the wall of the sap. The three-seconds flight of the bullet gave plenty of time to transfer the eye from the aim to the telescope. I didn't often hit anybody, but it was most amusing to watch the astonishment of "Johnny" as he jumped aside and seemed to say "Where did that one come from, Abdul?" After a time it was not considered wise to continue this game, as the Turk would certainly have screened such an unhealthy spot, and some useful observation would have been lost.

On one occasion I had to acknowledge defeat. Womersley and I had discovered a new enemy machine gun emplacement, sited to enfilade their front, and only visible from a forward sap of ours, which gave a view of a good deal of the Dere which was invisible from the immediate front. The 8th Hants had christened the sap "Carisbrook Castle," and our machine gunners had put a gun position in it as the only possible counter position, though much too high and prominent. I was shooting from here on November 5th when I saw the enemy bring his machine gun into action in the new emplacement. We started with our usual deliberate methods—and the Turk fired first. Something struck me on the side of the neck with a blow like a sledge hammer and knocked me off the parapet. Hugging the place, which was very painful, I went back to my dugout and discovered that the bullet had not penetrated far, but had burnt a large hole in the surface of my neck. It had glanced off a sandbag and hit me sideways. I had to go to the ambulance and get it seen to, but it did not necessitate my leaving the Battalion. It stopped my sniping for a time though, and it was two months before the wound healed up.

We had a magnificent view from Laindon Hill (it was well named) across the sea to the westward, and the sunsets were the finest I have ever seen. Hardly an evening passed without one of these superb spectacles. The rugged heights of Samothrace were a beautiful sight, and sometimes the distant peak of Mt. Athos, in Greece, could be seen.

A frequent visitor to the front line was General Sir William Birdwood, "the soul of Anzac." He passed a cheery word with all the men and the effect of his encouraging presence was visible on many a tired, drawn face. He was up to every trick and dodge of trench warfare and his keenness on every detail was infectious. He was a bit of a botanist too, and frequently stopped to pluck berries and small flowers from the shrubs, of which there were many interesting and beautiful varieties on the Peninsula.

The story of the General and the Australian sentry is worth repeating. "And who are you?" he said to the sentry, who was comfortably leaning against the parapet. "Oh, I'm a bit of a sentry; who are you?" "Oh, I'm a bit of a General." "Are you? Wait till I get my rifle" (it was some distance away) "and I'll give you a bit of a salute!"

Time had wrought great changes in our organization, and we were now getting fairly regular supplies of fresh meat and bread once or twice a week. Water had still to be strictly husbanded as it all had to be brought up on mules. Rum was almost a daily issue and the men appreciated it highly, for the nights were getting very cold and this increased the strain of night duty. Talking of mules, it must be stated that these much maligned animals served us well, as they have all through the war. No draft or pack animal will do its work so well under all conditions of terrain, weather, and subsistence, as the mule. The breed used on the Peninsula were small, wiry, and extraordinarily handy when properly managed. The drivers and leaders were almost exclusively Indians, who seemed to possess the "mule-sense" to a remarkable degree. The animals were invariably linked in threes, one behind the other, with one leader to the three; and the way they untied themselves in difficult situations was wonderful to behold. To all appearances the leader's method was to "leave well alone," but it must have been a sort of sympathy between man and beast which could overcome the serious obstacles of the rough winding hill tracks, indefinable to the ordinary human eye, and quite invisible at night. The Turkish gunners evinced a remarkable partiality for mules. They appreciated their value to us, and most of the convoys had to move by night; but it was very seldom that they let us down. "Johnny," the mule leader, was a most patient and enduring friend to the British Army and was a favourite with all ranks.

The close fighting on Hill 60 went on night after night. The Turks realised the importance of the position and continually put fresh troops into this most uncomfortable spot, but they never regained the ground they had lost. It was a horrible place. The ground was not so stiff as in most parts of the line, which made the work doubly difficult, and both sides existed under appalling conditions of dust and filth. Not an atom of scrub was left and the surface suggested a large rabbit warren on an outcrop of chalk, practically the whole of the hill having been turned by spade or mine, scarred by innumerable bombs and ploughed by shell fire.

The 7th Essex bore a most honourable share in the maintenance of Hill 60, being attached to the Brigade in whose sector it was included, doing excellent work and suffering the inevitable casualties. On October 9th, Pelly, of the 7th, came round to our line to get better observation of some of the Turkish trenches in front of his Battalion. We showed him what he wanted to see and he started back with his information. Unfortunately he could not resist the temptation to have another look on his way home from a different part of the line, and he was shot through the head and killed instantly.

There was a spur running forward from our ridge, at the forward end of which, by heavy labour, we succeeded in making a tunnel big enough to hold an 18-pounder. The gun was brought up in parts and put together in the chamber at the end of the tunnel, known as "The Lion's Den." It was intended to be used in an attack on the enemy on Hill 60, but owing to shortness of men the enterprise was never carried out. Although within 200 yards of the enemy they never, I think, discovered it.

SICK AND WOUNDED ARRIVING AT THE HOSPITAL SHIP.

*To face page 25.*

By the end of October our strength was 21 officers and 191 other ranks. There was continual bickering on Rhododendron Spur, and other parts of the Anzac line. On the night of November 4th, there was violent activity in the neighbourhood of Lone Pine. The Battalion stood to in readiness for an attack and special patrols were sent out, but it proved to be only a local affair.

The Anzac trenches in the wild hilly country on the right (the original Anzac line) were models of what trenches should be, and monuments of strenuous labour and skill. The earth there was absolutely perfect for trenches—the stiffest and toughest stoneless earth imaginable. No revetment was required and the trenches were many of them simply tunnels running along under the crests, with fire positions leading forward from them and breaking through the forward slope. Traverses in the trenches themselves were unnecessary, as they were completely covered in, and thus formed absolutely free lateral communications for the movements of men, ammunitions and supplies. The walls of the tunnels were as smooth as stone. There were no flies. There was nothing for them to live on. Every particle of food was removed after each meal and every spot of moisture dusted over. Flies cannot live without moisture. One notice on the wall struck me :—" Smile, you beggar, smile ! " Deep wisdom in those words.

Some of the trenches were very close. One underground sap opened up within 5 yards of the enemy's parapet. As you looked through, the Turkish sandbags were almost on the top of you. An officer with a revolver and a man with a rifle sat on each side of the opening. They spoke in whispers without taking their eyes off the hole. Why they were not bombed out I don't know, and forgot to ask. Not a Turk dared look over his parapet, and possibly they didn't know the hole was there.

The capacity of the Australians for digging was extraordinary. In one of their forward moves they had dug an assault trench 50 yards forward, leaving the merest shell of earth and fibre on the top, carrying the whole of the excavated earth in sandbags back through several saps to the gully in rear. Then they assembled in the trench, broke through at a given signal, and had their bayonets into the Turks before they had recovered from their surprise.

On November 9th we discovered that the enemy had anticipated us on the false crest to which allusion has already been made. Our saps had proceeded with painful slowness, while the enemy had no need to sap, as he had dead ground by which to approach the crest. I was surprised that he had not occupied it earlier, although our patrols had given him anything but an undisturbed time. He had now established some sort of small post about 100 yards from our line from which he observed with a periscope. We could easily have advanced our line to this crest but we were already on a salient, which an advance would have made more pronounced, and we were subject to artillery fire from the front and both flanks. The position could not have been held without trenches and covered communications, and we simply had not the men to do this extensive work. So we went slowly, very slowly, on with our saps, in the meantime devising other methods of making the enemy's forward post uncomfortable. The most effective method seemed to be artificially propelled bombs, and our catapult threw a cricket-ball bomb with rather surprising accuracy. This kept the enemy quiet by day, but the post was still rather a thorn in our side by night. Our parapet ran along the highest crest, which gave a clear skyline to the enemy from his forward post. Consequently our patrols, emerging from this part of the line, were severely handicapped and casualties frequently occurred as they were going out or coming in. Once out they could use the ground, but over that fatal skyline they had to go. Why didn't we raid this post? The only answer is that we were holding a long line with a terribly attenuated garrison, a great part of whom were too ill for any enterprise. The enemy himself was evidently in no mind to attack us, and as long as this was the case I was opposed to inducing a period of Hill 60 warfare on that spot. If the reader is disposed to convict me of "want of initiative" or of being "lacking in the offensive spirit," it is because I have failed to convey to him the true state of affairs. We were literally hanging on by our eyebrows to those hills, and there was nothing which could be called a position between our slender front line and the sea. We were fully resolved to hold what we had got, to the last, but we were not looking for trouble. Rather a humiliating confession? Yes! But not through any fault of ours, and I was determined to save the men all I could.

A deserter, who crawled into our listening post near the Lion's Den, was dressed in new winter clothing, including heavy great-coat. He said his regiment had 12 machine guns mounted by day and night, besides many more in reserve. He had not heard anything said about attacking, but the Turks thought we might attack. They were evidently not making the mistake of under-rating their enemy. The prisoner added that they had much sickness.

Brigadier-General Daniell, commanding 161st Brigade, and his Brigade-Major, Fargus, were in the front line trenches almost every day, advising and encouraging. Fargus was particularly taken with the catapult and proved a good shot with that somewhat archaic looking weapon. The enemy's sharpshooters on Chunuk Bair could see right into our line where it was open in rear, and although it was 1500 yards away I was always a bit anxious that this daily "conducted party" would form a too attractive target. On one occasion a bullet struck the ground within inches of the Brigadier's feet; evidently an aimed shot, and a good one too. After that I induced them to take a more covered route. The Brigade staff were very helpful and kind. Captain F. G. Bright of the 5th, made an excellent Staff Captain, and never spared himself in any effort to make us as comfortable as possible.

On November 15th, after a month in the trenches, we were relieved by the 4th Essex at "Stand-to," and went into Brigade reserve in "Inglenook," a gully near Brigade Headquarters. I again lost my Adjutant the next day, Deakin being obliged to leave, sick. Womersley was appointed in his place, still continuing his good work as Intelligence Officer. A small quantity of galvanized iron arrived and we began to make ourselves some cover against the weather, which was becoming steadily worse. Sandbags were badly needed, but they were very scarce.

On the 23rd we were back in the line again. We were weaker than ever and most of the Battalion were continuously in their fire positions. The enemy was very quiet. He was probably as busy as we were, getting into winter quarters.

In the afternoon of the 26th, we were suddenly informed that we were being sent to Mudros for a rest. All baggage was sent to the beach that evening in readiness to embark the following night.

And after that the deluge. It began to rain about 6 p.m. and the storm raged all night. The men in some of the posts were soon up to their knees in water, those in the bed of the Dere were literally washed out of their trenches, and all alike were wet to the skin. At six the next morning we were relieved by a Battalion of the New Zealand Mounted Rifles and moved into a shallow valley, called "East Ham Gully," and bivouacked in the open. The spot had not previously been occupied and there were no dug-outs. It rained and rained. Never mind. We should soon, we said, be away from this rotten peninsula. At 4 p.m., wet and draggled and cold, but happy, we started for the beach. About half-way there we were ordered back. We could not embark. All the piers had been washed away, ships had dragged their anchors and sought safety in the open sea. There was nothing to do but return to our inhospitable bivouac. The wind increased in violence and the rain changed to snow and sleet. The men cleared the snow and top soil in patches to get a dry spot and huddled together in groups. Some with great difficulty got fires lighted but they could not be kept going. In the morning the sleeping Battalion was literally buried in snow. The gale continued and a biting frost set in, but the snow ceased to fall. Fires were more successful and the men walked about all day and most of the night to keep warm. When things were as bad as they could be they sang the latest songs, and roared with laughter at anything ridiculous (and we were a comical looking crowd). That is the way with the British private soldier, he is fearfully and wonderfully made.*

The next afternoon we moved into a "better 'ole." "Taylor's Gully," as it was called, had been occupied by New Zealand troops who had put in some good work, *and* by some extraordinary chance had failed to remove every scrap of wood and iron. The result was comparative comfort. I shared a wonderful dug-out with several other officers, a real cave, dug right into the side of the gully. We hung a blanket over the opening and lit a fire inside. We had to lie flat to avoid being choked, but we kept warm, and slept like tops. Oscar Wilson was the stoker, and kept the smoke at a minimum by feeding the fire on the "little and often" principle, keeping it comparatively clear. For three bitter nights we had slept in the open and our appetite for fresh air was, at any rate temporarily, appeased.

The next day we did some close-order drill. The sun shone brightly and the ground was hard and clean; the snow blew about in the gale like sand. The next day, December 1st, we were ordered to move into Waterfall Gully; anything but a comfortable spot, and swept, moreover, by steady streams of nearly spent bullets. Movement had to be reduced to a minimum. Three men were wounded during the day. In the evening I was returning with Womersley from a visit to our good friends, the New Zealand gunners, who had regaled us with some excellent tinned herring, when Womersley fell with a bullet in his thigh, which just failed to penetrate, although I could see the point trying to push its way through. There was a Field Ambulance near by, where he was attended to and got off to a hospital ship the next day. It was really a bit of luck for him, but I was left adjutantless again. Capron filled the breach.

The next morning we were allowed to bring up some of the baggage from Anzac Cove, and the second blanket was welcomed with acclamation. And the next day it went back again; the 54th Division was to embark in the night. As soon as the baggage had gone the move was officially cancelled. A really good joke this. But it was followed by a better, for at 6.30

*Mr. G. Ward Price, in his graphic articles in the Press, describes those latter days with an abler pen than mine. He says:—

"Never probably, since Crimean days, have British forces in the field had to endure such cold as the last days of November brought to our men at the Dardanelles."

"Frozen, buffeted by wind and sleet with hardly the possibility of motion to keep the circulation alive, the men endured agonies. Sentries watching through the loopholes in the parapet were found dead at their posts when their turn came to be relieved, frozen rigid, their stiff fingers still clutching the rifle in an ironfast grip, the blackened face still leaning, under its sackcloth curtain, against the loopholes. . . . The Turks . . . suffered even worse . . . Down the gullies, turned into raging torrents by the cloudburst that preceded the blizzard, their bodies came washing along with the carcases of mules and all sorts of equipment. Their trenches too, were so completely flooded that they had to get out of them and lie about in the open, being actively shot down by our men, though some of the latter were frozen too stiff to pull the trigger, and almost dead with cold, had not strength enough to raise their rifles, but stood there and, as one officer told me, 'could only grin at the Turks.'"

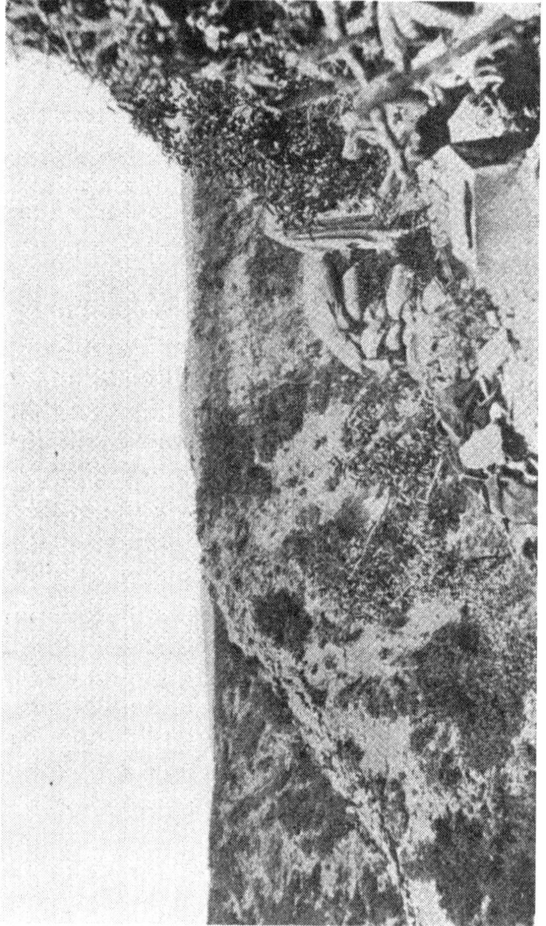

WALKER'S RIDGE, ANZAC.

*To face page* 29.

we were ordered to march for the beach at 7. We were punctual. A spirited strafe was going on in the front line, and "overs" were dropping thick, but by doubling across the bad places we got out of the gully into a sap without a casualty. It was very dark, but nobody lost touch that night. The sea had gone down as suddenly as it had risen and the re-built piers were functioning well. Lighters took us off, packed as thickly as we could stand, The "overs" followed us, and Bateman lost a few of the short hairs behind his ear by a bullet, when we were well out to sea. It was Johnny Turk's parting shot.

At midnight we boarded the good ship "Ermine." Our strength was 13 officers and 141 other ranks. Six officers and over 100 other ranks had "stuck it" all the time, viz., 17 weeks. A doctor told me that the average length of stay for the whole of the troops on the peninsula for each man was 25 days.

Most of the Brigade were on the "Ermine." She was not a floating palace, but she gave us a warm welcome, and shelter from the cauld, cauld blast. We all felt horribly reckless, as Alfred Lester would say, and I confess to making myself ill with Skipper sardines.

We had taken our last glimpse of Anzac with mixed feelings. The terraces twinkled with lights. It might have been Torquay or Ventnor at a distance. But our thoughts just then were not of these things. Our vision went beyond those star-spangled slopes, and lingered in fancy on many a dark hill and valley beyond, where rested our comrades, who slept beneath the ground they had won. Anzac would one day become dark again, as it was in the beginning. But *their* light would still shine with a steady fire, to guide our feet into the way of duty.

The Battalion played no heroic or spectacular rôle on the peninsula, and we took no part in any general action, nor did we get the chance of an assault on an enemy position. It was just a steady grind under every conceivable discomfort. There was no getting back to comfortable billets after a rough time in the trenches; and there was no getting away from shell and rifle fire. No conditions could have been more unfavourable for maintaining the fighting spirit of all ranks, but the Battalion never lost heart and gave a good account of itself on all occasions. The advance across the Anafarta Plain on August 14th was a good augury for the future and a credit to any Battalion. Our casualties on the peninsula were 27 killed or died of wounds, 10 died of disease, and 133 wounded.

CHAPTER II.

# THE LAND OF EGYPT.

T noon on December 4th, in lovely weather, the "Ermine" reached Mudros. We had a three-mile march to camp, and it was a very weary crowd that toiled slowly up the hill. The men were as weak as rats and could barely struggle on under the load of their equipment, but they were as cheery as ever. When we reached camp they were told off to bell tents, a luxury they had not enjoyed for many a long day. In peace time a bell tent would be considered hardly adequate accommodation for 15 men; but that number got into each of those tents and slept the sleep of the just.

The weather at Mudros was decidedly warmer than the peninsula, although the island had had a good share of the blizzard. The next day was spent in cleaning up rifles and equipment and in endeavouring to smarten up personal appearances. The water supply was limited to a gallon a day per man for all purposes, but this was but a trifling inconvenience to people who were used to taking their "tub" in their shaving water.

We spent a pleasant week at Mudros playing football, donkey-riding, and indulging in other rural delights. In the evenings we had sing-songs, organized by that indefatigable padre, Bond. The latter and I rode out about 6 miles on donkeys to a place called "Therma," where there were some natural hot springs, and enjoyed the indescribable luxury of a hot bath. The natural temperature was just the correct one, and there was quite a decent bathhouse with soap and clean towels provided. It was evidently a very ancient establishment but I could not find out anything about the history of it. The inhabitants, who were mostly Greeks, charged exorbitant prices for everything, except the aforesaid baths, for which there was not apparently much demand.

The relief from continuous duties and from the strain of being constantly in close touch with the enemy soon worked wonders on the men. It was rather amusing, though, to note how some failed for some days to throw off entirely the "trench stoop."

There were nursing sisters at the hospitals and we often walked out of our way to have a look at one. I hope they didn't think us rude, but it was good to see a woman again—and an English woman too.

We received our first reinforcements at Mudros—three officers, Coleman, Godhard and Scragg, and 45 other ranks. They were very disappointed that they never reached the peninsula, a feeling in which we shared. On the 13th we sailed for Alexandria on H.M.T. "Marathon," a most comfortable ship in every way. The Brigade staff came with us. The men enjoyed the excellent food they gave us. Potatoes were a great luxury:—and the men groused because they weren't hot enough! They will forgive me for referring to this incident, but it struck me as characteristic. They hadn't tasted a potato since they left the "Grampian" and I had hardly heard a murmur for the same period.

It was a delightful three days' voyage dodging among the picturesque islands of the Grecian Archipelago, arriving at Alexandria on the night of the 16th. The following day we disembarked and marched to Mex Camp, a sunny spot on the edge of the desert. We spent a pleasant ten days there, getting fit with close order drill, route marches and sea bathing. Several officers and men who had been wounded or had gone sick on the peninsula, rejoined. Leave was given freely to Alexandria, which was reached by donkey and train.

On Christmas Day we had football, Officers' and Sergeants' messes exchanged calls, etc., and Alexandria produced a very respectable bill of fare for the Battalion Christmas dinner. Two days afterwards we were warned for an early move. The Senussi Arabs were on the war path. They had overpowered the Egyptian coastguard and captured the crew of an English ship which had been wrecked at Sollum. Troops had already been sent to deal with them, including some English Yeomanry regiments, and rumour said that a battle had already been fought, in which the enemy was found to be well-equipped with artillery and machine guns, and to be well organized and led. They were under the command of Nuri Bey, a brother of the notorious Enver. If this rising had taken place in early 1915, when the Turks were attacking the Suez Canal, and if at the same time there had been a rising in Egypt, things might have been serious. As we now know, this was the programme arranged in Berlin, although General Ludendorff in his "War Memories" naively observes, "these were Utopian ideas." The fact was that in spite of all their efforts neither Germany nor Turkey had sufficient influence in the East to bring about a co-ordinated effort, and the three events were only brought off at wide intervals of time. Moreover the dates at which they severally materialized were probably those we should have chosen ourselves. At the same time there was a danger that Turkey would be successful in raising a Holy War in Tripoli and the Lybian desert, and events were watched with considerable interest.

The 161st Brigade was detailed to guard the Khedivial Railway line, running west from Alexandria to Dabaa, and to prevent communication between the desert and the coast. They were also to prevent arms, ammunition and supplies from reaching the Senussi from the East. On the enemy side German U boats maintained connection with Turkey and helped to keep the Arabs supplied with arms.

The move was made by train, and the Battalion was told off to garrison the village and station of El Hammam, about 40 miles from Alexandria. It was an important place, with several good wells, a large market, and a railway pumping station. The natives were engaged in a very primitive form of agriculture, and managed to grow a certain amount of barley, which depended entirely on the winter rains; the country also supported a few flocks of sheep and goats.

We had the help of about a dozen native policemen, who were very useful in making our orders known to the population. The latter probably sympathized with their co-religionists. The Senussi were a strict sect, with a high reputation for asceticism and were looked upon as very holy men. The local sympathizers were unarmed, and outwardly, at any rate, our relations were mutually friendly. They were fine looking men, much finer than the Egyptian fellaheen, who indeed were frightened of them and looked to us for protection from them. We had an armoured train, two aeroplanes, 35 fast trotting camels, a squadron of Yeomanry, and a few days later some light armoured cars, at the post. The camels were used for patrolling, a fact which made patrolling a more popular duty with the British infantry soldier than it usually is. In fact all ranks were delighted with the camels and soon rode them well. They were specially trained for fast, light work, having been used by the coastguard.

We were kept busy for some time providing for the defence of the railway station and the aerodrome and hangars. Plenty of sandbags and barbed wire now, and the place was soon both comfortable and strong. There were daily and nightly patrols along the line and, of course, outposts by night, but the men got regular rest and were getting stronger every day. Some slept in the buildings and some in tents outside, but inside the defences; the latter consisted of an outer line of trenches, while the pumping station and a wall, which we built of large stones formed a sort of central keep.

Officers and sergeants both had messes in the station buildings. Rubens made an excellent P.M.C.

Machine guns were posted on the roof as well as in ground emplacements. The water tower provided an excellent observation and command post. I need hardly say there was an alternative one in case the enemy should turn out to be too horribly modern in his methods and armament. The aeroplanes made daily flights, and the armoured train patrolled the line. The train garrison consisted of Colvin and Scragg with 80 men; also

COMING TO MARKET, EL HAMMAM.

*To face page* 33.

some Egyptian gunners with two old Krupp guns in which they took a great pride. Detached duties are always popular with the men, and the armoured train "stunt" was no exception. The garrison lived on the train and made themselves very comfortable.

Incidentally, they soon had an opportunity of doing us good service, not against our new enemy, but one of our old ones—the weather. A very heavy rain on January 2nd had washed away a considerable length of the line between us and our base at Alexandria. Our railway communication was thereby interrupted and our reserve rations of bully and biscuit had to be broken into. But only for two days. The armoured train went as far as the line was intact on our side, the supply train from Alexandria drew up on the other side of the gap; the A.T. men man-handled the rations across and we again enjoyed the luxuries of civilisation.

We had left Mavor behind on the Peninsula, as a military landing officer, and he rejoined us on the 9th. He was one of the last to leave Anzac.

On the 12th Carlyon-Hughes, Calverley and myself with 50 other ranks pushed out some distance into the desert as support to a squadron of Herts Yeomanry, who were carrying out a reconnaissance to Zawiet Sidi Abdel-Ati, where an enemy gathering 1,200 strong had been reported. The Yeomanry reached the place to find the gathering had dispersed, and they had to be content with reading and posting a proclamation, which I hope had the desired effect.

The market at Hammam was an interesting sight. Hundreds of natives appeared in all directions apparently from nowhere, with corn, camels, sheep and goats. Greeks and Jews from Alexandria attended, and there was some lively bargaining in stuffs and ornaments in exchange for produce. Camels occasionally changed hands and the methods were really not very different from a horse fair at home. The same knowing-looking dealers and cautious buyers, the same haggling over price, the same hand-strike to clinch the bargain, and the same crowd of curious onlookers. The natives were poor, but the women wore large quantities of jewellery, chiefly of silver set with stones and coral. The ladies frequently paid for the highly coloured silks and cotton goods with silver ornaments, home-made from silver money in more prosperous times.

On January 24th two of the Duke of Westminster's armoured cars arrived and on the 26th the squadron of Dorset Yeomanry (who had replaced the Herts Yeomanry) left for Mersa Matruh. Both afterwards took part in a very successful battle near Sollum, where the enemy was routed and the Arab leaders captured, Nuri was reported killed but this turned out to be incorrect. The Dorsets made a fine charge and the armoured cars proved a great success, working great havoc with their machine guns.

Our station was five miles from the sea, across fairly hard sand and a considerable expanse of "saltings," which made very good going, with two high sandbanks, evidently washed up by successive sea levels in ages gone by. The one nearest the sea was not properly speaking sand at all. It was entirely composed of minute fragments of shell. It was brilliantly white, and made a beautiful contrast with the intensely blue sea beyond. This blueness of the sea was indeed remarkable. It seemed to have no relation to the blue sky overhead, as I had always thought. There were all shades of blue in it, and when the sky was black with clouds the sea was a brighter blue than ever. This march to the sea for a bathe, and back, was an excellent thing for the battalion. The allowance of firewood was extremely limited and we found the wreckage which strewed the beach very useful.

We frequently had visitors, by air, rail and desert, and this relieved the monotony of life. On February 5th a column of 120 Bikaneer (Indian) Camel Corps, under Lt.-Col. Rawlinson, Indian Army, arrived from a long trek in the desert. They looked most picturesque as they appeared in the distance in open desert formation. They were fully mobile, carrying everything on their camels, which were of a much larger breed than ours. They had with them an Egyptian Machine Gun Section. They pitched their camp near the station. On the 11th they left for Moghara, a small oasis, about 40 miles to the south-west, where the situation was uncertain. They were followed during the morning by an armoured car and another car of the ubiquitous "Ford" breed—and later by an aeroplane, whose special job was to reconnoitre for the column. When well out in the desert, after dropping a message to the camel corps, and while manœuvring to do the same to the armoured cars, which were about five miles in rear, part of one of the planes of the machine broke away and it crashed to earth, killing both pilot and observer. The poor fellows' remains were brought into camp the same night, terribly smashed up. This sad accident cast a gloom over the whole station. The observer, a mere boy, was making his first duty flight. The pilot was an experienced airman, who had served in other theatres of war, and there was nothing known to account for the accident. Captain Van Ryneveld, M.C.,* who was in charge of the air detachment at Hammam, was a Dutchman of the Transvaal, who, as a boy, had used a rifle against us in the South African war. He was a fine sportsman and an intrepid flyer, as was also his second in command, Captain Stent, and their "stunts" were much admired by all the garrison.

The next day news was received that a convoy of 50 laden camels was going to try and slip by between us and the sea

*Now Col. Sir N. H. Van Ryneveld, K.B.E., D.S.O., M.C., famous as the first airman to fly from Cairo to Capetown. I am proud to remember that my first flight in the air was made in company with such a distinguished pilot.

with provisions for the enemy. With the help of the Yeomanry we established a line of outposts across the five miles to the sea, but the convoy never appeared. Perhaps they had chosen another route after all, or perhaps, more likely still, they had never existed.

There was a track running more or less parallel to the railway which was known as the Khedivial road, and this was about this time made practicable, by the efforts of the infantry, for motors, and road communication established to Dabaa and beyond. It was not an easy road to find, even by daylight, but the going was fairly good, and the Fords simply romped over it. These Fords were wonderful on this stony desert, and in the hands of a good driver it was extraordinary the ground they could get over, even off the road, and I enjoyed several very interesting trips in them, under the skilful pilotage of Captain Russell Wells, 15th Hussars, who was in command of the detachment. One trip was to Abu Sir, an ancient stronghold on the coast about 12 miles distant. It was very rough going and one steep rocky ridge was to all appearances quite impracticable, but we got over it somehow. It was amusing to watch the native women and children flying for their lives when they saw us coming. One Arab, who shewed us the best track, actually laughed outright (a rare thing for the solemn Bedouin) when he saw his wives and kiddies bolt into their tent screaming in terror. We stuck in some marshy ground about a mile from the place, so we left the car there and walked on. A man who accompanied us was carrying his rifle, and a very old Arab, who saw us coming, was evidently very scared. He kept taking cover behind rocks and shifting about as we moved, to keep out of sight, and peering at us over the top like a wild animal, until we satisfied him that we were not going to shoot him. The ruins were evidently of quite a considerable town, more than half-buried, with a great keep, or citadel, whose walls, 30ft. thick, had at one time been washed by the sea. There were the remains of a temple with a semi-circular altar, also of several houses under the ground level. One of the rooms was full of little hairy bats, hanging on the vaulted ceiling ; they wriggled and blinked their bright little eyes as we threw the light on to them. Two circular rooms were evidently bath rooms, with a hole in the roof to let out the steam. They had seats all round with recesses (for clothes ?) above them. Some small rooms quite deep down were cut out of the solid rock and showed the marks of the tools clearly. In one there were bushels of small bones which proved to be all bones of birds. Were they sacred birds which had been buried ? Some antiquarian reader may know. Near by were two large quarries. The stones were for the most part cut about 4ft. by 2ft. by 2ft. The whole place was evidently Greek, or Roman, not Egyptian. There were the remains of a fine Roman lighthouse near by, built of brick and stone. These materials were also used in other buildings, in layers, shewing red and grey stripes. There was a large oven, practically complete, made entirely of brick. Some of the stone staircases to small chambers in the thickness of the citadel walls were in good preservation.

The only carving I saw was a statue, very much decayed, of a lion, or a sphinx, a fragment of a frieze, and some remains of fluted columns. No excavations appeared to have been made. Coming home in the glow of the setting sun we met a fine looking Arab on a magnificent horse, with his gaily dressed little son up in front of him. The horse shied violently at the car but the man sat like a statue and the boy was more frightened of the motor than of the horse. They made a charming picture.

Some much finer ruins were visited on another day, about the same distance away, but inland; an enormous cathedral, with monastic buildings, and quite a little town clustering round them. What this establishment was doing there out in the wild it is hard to conjecture. But probably the climate has changed since it was built, and it may then have been a fertile country. The place was called Abou Mena, after Saint Menas, a Roman soldier and Christian martyr, who was beheaded for his faith in A.D. 296. Tradition says that his co-religionists were carrying his body on a camel to bury it in Egypt, and when they arrived at this spot the camel stopped and refused to go any further. This was construed as a sign of divine will that the saint should be buried there. This was done, and the story goes that a spring of sweet water appeared which had miraculous healing properties. A shrine was erected, around which arose a church. At a later period (about A.D. 400) a magnificent basilica was added. Although now completely in ruins, its remains give a clear idea of its former glories. It was nearly 400ft. long. The columns were all of marble, but the bases only remain, over 50 of them, the columns having been transported to Germany and other places. The capitals were beautifully carved, and they lay about among the thousands of other fragments which strewed the whole area. There was an enormous well, 16ft. in diameter, but the spring had apparently dried up. The old church was underneath a part of the later one, the original altar directly underneath the great altar of the latter. It also contained the tomb of the saint, a lofty chamber cut in the rock. The Germans had done the excavations and done them very well, too. Where all the superstructure went to I don't know; probably to Alexandria to build mosques, and houses for the children of conquering Islam. But now that the valuable part has been used up, it will probably remain out there in the desert solitudes until the end of the world, an indestructible monument to that Roman "Tommy" who died for his faith.

El Hammam made an excellent training ground and the Battalion was put through a musketry, including field firing, course, and a bombing course, besides carrying out small tactical schemes and close order drill. There were two good football grounds. All the surrounding Arabs were gradually concentrated in a huge camp close to the post. The natives did not relish being packed so closely together ; they did not take kindly to " town " life and there was a good deal of bickering and quarreling among them, particularly the ladies. They were very poor and had to be provided with food, but the women still wore quite a large quantity of jewellery which they were loth to part with. We managed, however, to purchase some interesting articles through the native men, who removed the said articles from their wives and daughters, not without violent protestations and tears from the dispossessed females. Captain Walker, of the Brigade Machine Gun Company, had occasion to earn the gratitude of one of the Arabs in the " town," who thereupon invited him to his tent. Captain Walker graciously accepted the invitation, and the Arab, after thanking him for the service he had rendered him (probably let him have some firewood or given him some old clothes) offered to give him his daughter as a slight token of his esteem. Walker was somewhat taken aback, but thought the proper thing to do was to hand the simpering damsel back to papa, which he did. But I heard afterwards that the gift was seriously meant and the family felt somewhat slighted, besides being annoyed at the failure to get their daughter off their hands.

A wife of one of the Senussi chiefs wandered into the post one day, nearly starved. She was given food and shelter and the next day produced a fine baby. Two days afterwards she was out and about as if nothing had happened and the young Senussi recruit was flourishing exceedingly when we left a month later.

There is probably more rain in this district than at any other place in Egypt, and storms were fairly frequent, but didn't last long. They were often accompanied by thunder and very vivid lightning. Meteors were common, and some of them were very brilliant. Sentries at night more than once reported " Star shells " in the distance and there was every excuse for this mistake. " A bright light in the desert " was also frequently reported, but generally turned out to be Sirius or perhaps Jupiter rising out of the sand. In England the heavenly bodies are seldom seen until well above the horizon, owing to the vapours in the atmosphere. In Egypt they can be seen actually to appear from the skyline itself.

Sandstorms were much more unpleasant than the rain storms. The sand reached an enormous height and blotted out the sun. Those of us who lived within stone walls had a great advantage over the tent dwellers on these occasions.

During our stay at El Hammam, one of our most interesting visitors was Jennings Bramly Bey, an Englishman with a complete knowledge of the Arab and his ways, and of his country, the desert. He was accompanied by a party of friendly Bedouins, who had volunteered their services, horses and all, without pay, purely from attachment to the English in general, and Jennings Bramly in particular. They were armed with rifles and rode very good Arab ponies, which they had no objection to lend to any officer who was sportingly inclined, and we used to ride races with them. Although very quiet and reserved, the sporting instinct was strong upon them, and a race was the occasion of much shouting and excitement. They rode with a loose rein, with one hand high in the air, leaning well forward in the stirrups and shouting into the horse's ear. Their long robes flew behind them as they rode and made a most picturesque effect.

Jennings Bramly had done a good deal of exploring, and was in the habit of dressing as an Arab and living their life while on his long journeys. He loved the desert and could tell some good yarns about it. One felt that here was a man upon whom the East had cast its spell. It would be a good thing for the East if it cast its spell on many more like him.

On February 27th, we received news of the complete rout of the Senussi near Sollum. The campaign was evidently over. The aeroplanes left us for good on March 3rd. On the 5th the Battalion left by train for Mena Camp near Cairo, where the division, less the 161st Brigade, had been quartered for some time. The journey through the Delta to Cairo was full of interest. The fertile country, crowded with the industrious fellaheen, was a great contrast to the aridity of Hammam and fully explained the veneration in which all Egyptians hold that most wonderful of all rivers, the Nile. Detraining at 8.30 we were able, through the kindness of some of the English residents, to obtain good refreshment at Abu Ela Station, and marched about ten miles by moonlight through Cairo and by the wonderful Gizeh causeway, to the camp, which was practically overshadowed by the Pyramids. The huge bulk of these most ancient of the world's buildings was immensely impressive. We got in at 1.30 a.m. and put the men into large rush huts, where they slept comfortably. The officers had tents. It was a well laid out camp, but on very soft sand, which made training very laborious, and the climate was much warmer than on the North Coast. Captain Tompson joined us here after being kept in England in charge of the Divisional Transport, much to his disgust. About three weeks were spent at Mena Camp, which gave us time to see the sights of Cairo (to which place there was an excellent tram service), and to visit the Pyramids and the wonderful tombs and antiquities of Sakkhara and other places.

THE BATTALION ARRIVES AT SHALLUFA (SUEZ CANAL).

*To face page* 39.

## CHAPTER III.

# THE WILDERNESS.

HE Turks had by no means given up the idea of an advance on the Suez Canal, and were known to be preparing an expedition, under German guidance and leadership, for that purpose. The protection of the Canal had become therefore of vital and increasing importance, and Sir Archibald Murray was working out an extensive and elaborate plan for its defence. On March 30th the Battalion moved to Shallufa on the Suez Canal, crossed the Canal by a pontoon bridge and bivouacked on the Eastern bank.

On April 1st we took over one of the chain of fortified posts, already in course of construction by the 42nd Division. They were named after different towns in Lancashire, by the Manchester and Lancashire troops who started them. The one we took over was about three miles from the Canal and was called Manchester post. We relieved the 1/8th Lancashire Fusiliers. A detachment of R.E., under Lieut. Dixon, was attached to the post, and superintended the construction of the defences, which consisted of a series of strong posts dug in the sand, the whole surrounded by barbed wire. The other desert posts were all constructed on the same principle, and some were ten miles or more from the Canal. They averaged about four or five miles apart.

Thus began a very laborious and tedious sojourn in the wilderness for the Battalion, lasting for nine months. The whole story of that period is one of monotony and vexation of spirit. The year 1916 was the hottest known in Egypt for many years, the temperature on several occasions reaching 117 in the shade. There was an appalling amount of work to be done. An ordinary trench, six feet deep and three feet wide, requires an enormous excavation before the revetment can be put in, owing to the extreme fineness of the sand, which runs like water, and will not stand for a moment at a less angle than 45 degrees. Often during a night the wind would fill up the work of days and the job had to be begun all over again. Luckily we got the assistance of the Egyptian Labour Corps, that wonderful organization which stood us in such good stead right up to the end of the war. The "Gyppies" were extraordinarily good at their work and most cheerful and well behaved, and the British Army owes them a big debt of gratitude. They moved the sand in baskets, carrying it well away from the sides of the trench, a superior method to throwing it from a shovel. The latter method employed at the bottom of a trench would bring the sand pouring back again and a lot more with it. Against the wind it was practically impossible. The trenches were revetted with hurdles, lined with canvas, or sometimes close-boarded. When placed in position they had to be securely anchored with very long wires, to take the great strain of the fluid sand. A couple of courses of sandbags completed the parapet and parados. Even the sandbags had to be used double, one inside the other, or they would be empty in a very short time, so fine was the sand. A good trench could be made entirely with sandbags, but this was very costly and required more than twice the digging.

In addition to the fire-trenches huge excavations had to be made for water storage, command posts, dressing stations, etc. Communication trenches six feet deep, with overhead cover had to be provided. Without overhead cover it would have taken the whole garrison all their time to prevent these trenches from getting filled up.

This digging and wiring was the daily task of all who were not on duty, and it seemed a hopeless task at that. The annoying part of it was that there was no enemy within 100 miles of us and there seemed no hope or chance that the trenches would ever be used. It has been the lot of armies all through the war to dig, and dig, and dig, and then leave their work unused; but not such trenches as these.

There was little chance of the ordinary forms of recreation at these desert posts. Football was a farce. But the men kicked the ball about as British soldiers will do on any sort of ground and in any sort of climate. A canteen was started and this was a great boon. The Y.M.C.A. established themselves at the posts on the Canal itself, and at some of the posts further forward; but they could not be expected to be everywhere. Concert parties began to be formed, and their visits were very welcome. Padre Bond got a legless piano which was easy to carry about and did splendid service.

The sand of the Sinai peninsula is surely the finest in the world. It got into everything, one's hair, eyes and ears were full of it. So was the food. It got in between the layers of the soles of one's boots, gradually forming a lump inside as hard as stone. It stopped every watch in the camp. It was constantly on the move in the daytime, blown along by a wind which got up just before the sun and went down with it. When it blew hard, as it frequently did, it would remove all the sand from the windward side of the tents, while the "floor" inside would gradually rise. Great ranges of sand dunes stretched over the desert, and their formation marked the direction of the prevailing winds. Their leeward sides were very steep. They were constantly changing in height and shape and sometimes the landscape would undergo considerable modification in a single night. Some of these great dunes were really imposing mountains, several hundred feet high, with deep gullies scooped out by the wind eddies round their bases.

The nights were magnificent ; the air was so clear, and the stars shone like diamonds. On moonlight nights the helio was frequently used for signalling at long distances. The dews were very heavy and sentries could wring the water out of their great coats in the morning. It got cold quickly after the sun went down and the sand, which was too hot to bear the hand on in the daytime, was stone cold an hour after sunset.

The amount of animal life in the desert is surprising. The sand swarms with huge black ants, and the scarab beetle was everywhere. Scorpions were fairly common, also a small sand viper which had an evil reputation. Foxes and jackals were plentiful wherever there was a patch of hardened sand in which they could make an earth. Most of the foxes were sandy in colour and small, but I have seen, near the Canal, fine red foxes that would have done credit to the Shires. Foxes at home are reputed to live upon chickens, ducks and pheasants, with an occasional newborn lamb thrown in ; but their worst enemy could not accuse these foxes of enjoying such fare. They probably got a living by hunting the jerboa rats, and eating them, with beetles and other insects as a condiment. There was no fresh water and they must have depended for moisture on the heavy dews. The jerboa above-mentioned, was a sand-coloured rodent with a bushy tail. The sand mice were charming little creatures and became very tame in one's tent. The canvas water bucket was the great attraction. They made boldly for it and licked it with evident satisfaction.

The chameleon was plentiful in some parts and was a great favourite. Watching him catch flies in a bunch of scrub tied to the tent pole was quite a popular amusement on warm afternoons. It involved no exertion, and the rapidity with which our enemies the flies were taken by that lightning tongue, at any range up to seven inches, and conveyed into those capacious "chops," there to be masticated with every sign of enjoyment, was fascinating to behold.

For the first month or two all food and water had to be brought on camels. The water was carried in copper or tin "fanatis" holding about 15 gallons each, which by the time they arrived were too hot to bear the hand on. It will be readily understood that the water was not very palatable. Most of it was made into tea, of which we drank large quantities, without, as far as I could observe, any ill effects. Later on, conditions improved greatly, as pipes were laid under the sand to most of the posts, which plan, besides saving much labour of men and camels, meant also a much larger allowance. Baths were made of sandbag walls and tarpaulins, and were a great boon to all ranks. Metalled roads were also laid down to all posts. Signboards mocked the exile from home with such inscriptions as "To Manchester," "To Oldham," "To Salford." Light railways were an additional communication with several posts and were very useful, particularly for carrying the huge quantities of R.E. material required for the defences. The railways have of course been taken up and salved, but the roads doubtless remain, and will remain, until the sea again washes the sands of Sinai.

We had a good deal of trouble with wrist-watches, which appeared to object to the climate or the sand, or both. Anyhow most of them refused to go, and the shortage of time-tellers was severely felt, especially by officers and N.C.O.'s on outpost duty, who had to post sentries and send out patrols at stated times. It occurred to me that by observing the position of certain stars in the Northern hemisphere at a known time at dusk, an indication of the time could be obtained by taking their positions during the night, by means of a simple dial with a hole in the centre through which to get the Pole Star, and a plummet attached. I entrusted the making of some such device to Calverley, who was somewhat scientifically and mechanically inclined. In doing so I overlooked a fact of which I should have been aware, viz., that once you have started Calverley's brain working nothing on earth can stop it. He would not be satisfied with anything short of perfection, with the result that he eventually produced a most wonderful instrument, a thing of many strings, weights, springs, figures, balances, and levels which I can well believe could be made to do anything under the sun—except perhaps, speak Arabic—if you only knew how to work it. I strongly advised against the inventor's suggestion that he should take out a patent for it, one reason being that it would be impossible to produce it at the price of a decent watch, and the other being that nobody could work it except himself. Calverley has forgiven me, I am sure, for suggesting that he should submit the whole thing to Mr. Heath Robinson for hints as to further improvements. It was really very clever and gave him something to do; no small benefit to anyone in those dull days.

Talking of Calverley reminds me that he returned one day from a ramble in the desert with a pocket full of flints, which he maintained against the opinion of the large majority of the mess, were Palæolithic implements. And the experts at the Cairo Museum said he was right, too. These implements and flint chips were found at one spot about four miles from the Canal. They all lay on the surface of a patch of hard sand.

During our stay in the desert the men were trained to do long marches on the soft sand in marching order, frequently covering fifteen miles in the day over virgin sand, no mean feat of endurance with the thermometer at anything from 100 to 110 in the shade (and it must be borne in mind that there was no shade). The two secrets of marching in these conditions

A HALT IN THE DESERT.—BREAKFAST.

*To face page* 43.

are a slow pace and open formations. Two miles in three quarters of an hour with a halt for the remainder of the hour was found to be the best method. The formation usually adopted was lines of platoons in fours, with the fours opened out to one pace interval between men, and with no two platoons marching in the same track. Sand is much heavier where it has been churned up by marching. This formation, besides causing less fatigue, had the advantage of being easily adapted to tactical requirements. By marching with wide intervals and distances between platoons, a firing front could be instantly formed in any direction, with supports and reserves in position. At the mid-day halt bivouacs were quickly put up, consisting of blankets and rifles with butts buried in the sand, and provided excellent protection against the sun. Strict water discipline was observed, no water being touched until after three hours' marching, and then only at stated times by order of the commander of the column. Correct covering and dressing were insisted upon. Only by doing so could each man get his necessary amount of air.

Amongst other qualities of the sand was its extraordinary power of resistance to rifle fire and H. E. shell. A single "stretcher" sandbag was impenetrable even by machine gun fire until the fabric was worn away and let the sand out. A few shovels-ful of sand thrown in a heap would stop anything in the shape of a bullet at any range. I have seen a 5-9 shell pitch plump on top of a timber dug-out with but three feet of sand overhead, and do no damage to the dug-out itself. There is no such thing as "loose" or "rammed" sand. A trench filled up by the wind is as solid as if it were hydraulically pressed; you cannot put any more in; you cannot tread it down.

Outpost work was a tedious business. Sentries listened all night in a silence that could be felt—there is no silence like that of the desert. The chief interest of patrolling lay in the uncertainty of finding your way back. Patrols at first frequently lost their way, until they learnt something about the stars. It was amusing to follow their tracks the next morning, before they became obliterated by the wind. It seemed a little unfair to check the records of night patrols by following their tracks by daylight; but it was instructive.

On May 15th Colvin rejoined, with Scragg and the garrison ot the armoured train. They had had a most interesting time in the Fayoum and came back very fit.

On May 26th the Battalion moved to Salford and Oldham posts, about three miles apart and both about six from the Canal. Both were in a very unfinished state and entailed heavy labour. A large draft of three officers and 286 other ranks arrived from England on June 20th. They were unacclimatized and suffered severely from the heat. On the same day Brigadier-General Daniell issued his farewell order. We had had nothing but kindness and help from our Brigadier on service, and we were very sorry to lose him.

On the following day our new Brigade commander, General Marriott Dodington arrived and inspected the post. He had been on the staff at Anzac H.Q., but we had not met him before. He won our hearts at once. He had ideas about training, responsibility of Company Commanders, etc., which were destined to bear good fruit and his tenure of command was a glorious one for the Brigade.

On June 24th the Commander-in-Chief, General Sir Archibald Murray, inspected the post. He arrived by the light railway at 5.15 a.m., his horses having been sent on, had a quick look round, and after a quarter of an hour galloped off in a cloud of sand to visit Ashton (occupied by the 1/4 Essex) and Oldham Posts. He was keen to know our views as to our ability to hold the post against attack. We could only sigh and wish we had the opportunity of demonstrating the same. He was also very keen on us getting more water, and four days after 500 gallons arrived through the new pipe line.

On the 26th Capt. P. C. Yonge, with 2nd Lts. Moller and Cook and a Battery and a half of Stokes Guns, with personnel, left Salford Post for Salonika.

On July 5th the Battalion was relieved by the 6th Essex and had a spell on the banks of the Canal at Geneffe, the Canal Station at the south end of the Little Bitter Lake. It was a delightful change to see the blue band of the Canal and the steamers gliding through with passengers on their decks. Occasionally a Trooper would pass and greeting would be exchanged with the usual chaff. A good many ships came through by night, and they made a pleasing picture with their searchlight at the bows and all lights on.

We got as close to the water as we could and there was daily bathing for all ranks. The water in the Canal is extremely buoyant, and it required no effort to stand in it in an upright position with head out of the water. Many men spent hours in the water daily and their skin got the colour of copper. Passengers in the ships frequently threw them tins of "fags" and other luxuries. "B" Company was about ten miles to the north, opposite Kabrit Station, between the Great and Little Bitter Lakes, where lay also a British Gunboat. They had a good time bathing and fishing, and football matches were arranged with the crew of the Gunboat.

Brigade Headquarters were at Geneffe, and the garrison included the Middlesex Hussars, and a Brigade of R.F.A, a Field Company of R.E., detachments of Imperial Camel Corps, and Camel Transport Corps, Works Company, and other details. The perimeter of the camp was a large one and the Yeomanry had to be called on for outpost duties. Regular leave was granted to Cairo and Alexandria. At Sid Bishr, near the latter, was a large rest camp on the seashore, and parties of 50 from the Brigade proceeded there about every eight days. Camel patrols kept up communication with Kabrit daily by the banks of the lake and inspected the "swept track." The latter was made by a sort of flat sand-plough, which marked a wide ribbon of smooth sand a short distance from and parallel with the bank. The Turks had once managed to convey a mine, and floated it in the Bitter Lake, and the object of the swept track was to detect any evilly disposed persons who might bring in similar contrivances across the desert, and do damage to the Canal. It will be remembered that this vitally important waterway is 100 miles long and extremely vulnerable at any point. A ship sunk in the Canal would have held up the traffic for a long time and possibly affected seriously the course of the war. It was, therefore necessary to patrol both banks constantly, day and night. The watching of the western bank was done by native Indian Cavalry.

We made a good rifle range at Geneffe and the whole Battalion was put through a course of musketry, including Lewis gun firing. We had had these new weapons since April. Maxwell Browne was our Lewis gun officer, and he had trained some good sections, who became very keen on their work.

The Canal was full of fish, and must have been a wonderful feeding ground, from the large number of vessels which came through every day. A contract was made with native fishermen by which fish breakfasts for the whole Battalion were provided pretty frequently. Flying fish were common.

On July 28th orders were received at 1.15 p.m. to be ready to move at once. There were indications that there was something doing further north. Indeed it was known that the Turks were advancing in considerable force towards the Canal by the old coast route, and that their advanced troops had surprised the Yeomanry near Katia about 35 miles east of the Canal. The order was therefore a welcome one, and there was soon a "move on." The tents were all struck by 2.15 and at 2.30 "C" and "D" Companies marched out, en route for Shallufa, the nearest bridge. "A" and "B" followed at 4 p.m. The whole Battalion with baggage was across the Canal by the Shallufa Bridge by 5 o'clock, well in front of time, as the train for the north did not leave until 7.30. Opportunity was taken to bathe and fill up with portable refreshments from the Canteen. At 7.45 we drew out of Shallufa Station, strength 26 officers, 841 other ranks, detrained at Ballah at 1.30 a.m., and relieved the 1/5th Lancashire Fusiliers. The relief was completed by 5.30 a.m. The posts were widely scattered, one being four miles away, and we had a busy time of it. The next day we had to send reinforcements to "Ballybunion," a railhead about eight miles out in the desert, and eventually about half the battalion found its way there and was attached to the 1/7th Essex.

I noticed that one of the stations on the way up was called "Goshen," a reminder that we were now in that once fertile land. It must be confessed that its present day appearance belied its ancient character. It was nothing but a sandy waste, except on the fringe of the "Sweet water Canal" on the west side, which now ran parallel to the Suez Canal, and which supported a few trees and rank grasses. But in ancient times an important arm of the Nile, called the Pelusiac branch, flowed this way, crossing the present Canal, probably between Ballah and Ismailia, and discharging into the sea at Pelusium, more than twenty miles to the east of the present Canal. It has now completely disappeared, but the low ground to the east of Ballah is in many cases of a swampy character, and further north it has been flooded with salt water by breaching the banks of the present Canal, thus forming an effective barrier against attack.

On August 4th guns were distinctly heard, from the early morning until well into the day, and a battle was reported to be in progress near Hod el Enna, west of Katia. Aeroplanes were very active all day. The position was uncertain, and we half hoped that the Turks might work round and endeavour to reach the Canal, in which case we could have fallen upon their left flank; but no orders came, not even a "Stand to," and all was quiet in the evening.

On the following day, August 5th, definite news was received of the defeat of the Turks at Romani, about 25 miles east of Kantara. Our old machine gunners, under Brooks and Coleman, now formed with the other Battalion sections into a Brigade M.G. Company, were present throughout and had several casualties, the post occupied by them being subjected to a determined attack. Sergt. Herbert gained a well deserved D.C.M., and Sergt. Parker the M.M. Several train loads of Turkish prisoners came through Ballah during the next day, looking very done in. Their advance had been a really wonderful performance and they had attacked with the greatest bravery at Romani. They accepted their fate philosophically, and in reply to questions as to details, merely shrugged their shoulders and said, "" Turkey finish."

On this day, Corpl. Cunningham and Pte. T. Knights were mentioned and congratulated in orders for a very plucky piece of life-saving in the Canal.

A welcome addition to the amenities of life was received on August 7th in the shape of a gramophone, presented and sent out by the inhabitants of Little Waltham, and accompanied by a very kind letter from our good friend and former C.O., Col. W. Neville Tufnell, D.L.

On the 9th the name of Sergt. W. Chapman (of Thaxted), appeared in orders as having been mentioned in despatches.

The 14th was the anniversary of the advance at Suvla and was observed as a holiday. A capital day's sports were arranged, including aquatic sports in the Canal.

Although the Turks had retreated we were not allowed to slack in the matter of defences, and three days a week were given to digging, the other three being devoted to training.

On the 23rd we handed over Ballah post to the 2/10th Middlesex Regiment, and Ballybunion was taken over by the 1/4th Royal Sussex Regiment. We crossed the Canal to the west side and bivouacked, awaiting orders. In the evening the 1/7th Essex arrived and bivouacked close by. No more orders came and we pitched a camp the next morning before old Sol became too aggressive. The next day we received orders to entrain. We thought we might be going north, but were disappointed. Our destination was Shallufa, which we had fondly hoped we should never see again, and it could not justly be called a "cheery crowd" that struck camp at 2 o'clock in the afternoon. We left Ballah at 9 p.m. and had another horribly bumpy journey through that absolutely rotten land of Goshen. Arrived at Shallufa, we fell in at 2.30 a.m., and marched out to Salford and Oldham once more. A dismal march, only relieved by an early cup of tea from the travelling kitchens en route. The men stuck it grimly with their heavy packs, and their heavier hearts, and by 8 o'clock had relieved the 1/5th Bedfordshire and the 1/11th Londons at Salford and Oldham posts respectively. Battalion Headquarters was at Salford, Wilson being in command at Oldham. Once more the dull daily round began. It was a most trying time for all ranks, the worst time of the whole war. Some of the home papers wrote sneeringly of the 54th Division "kicking its heels" in Egypt, while others were doing the fighting. It was true, but it was not very kind to remind us poor wretches of it.

The Commander-in-Chief again visited the posts on October 28th. His visit was followed by a reinforcement of the Egyptian Labour Corps at Salford, which was an enormous place and looked as if it would never be finished. Oldham, which was more moderate in size, was complete, and the G.O.C.-in-C. complimented Wilson and his garrison on its organization and the good work which had been put into it.

Route marches on the desert were dull affairs, but excellent training, both in march and water discipline, which afterwards stood us in good stead. Falling out on a route march was looked upon as an indication that the stragglers required further training, and they were sent on an extra trip to Oldham and back the next day. The party, which was never a large one, was known as the "Oldham Athletic" and came in for a good deal of chaff, which probably did as much as anything towards reducing casualties on route marches.

The "Gyppies" gave us an entertainment on November 5th, which was rather interesting. They played the most weird and primitive instruments, with very little sound, and that only on two or three notes. There were songs, with very little tune, but (I was informed) with very improper words, which were greeted with loud applause by the rest of the company, who sat round in a square (*can* you sit round in a square ?) and clapped the time of the song and joined in the refrain. There were also dances and juggling tricks of a sort. The dances were mostly of the " can-can " variety with a good deal of swaying and twisting of the body and very little leg movement, typical of the East, and I have noticed not without imitators in the drawing-rooms of Cairo, and in England too. Others were in the tragic manner, done with knives in each hand, going through the pleasing motions of stabbing oneself all over and bleeding to death in great agony, lifelike, or deathlike in the extreme. Some of the men were very good at a kind of quarter-staff play with long poles, which was a genuine battle and some hefty blows were given and taken, apparently in good part. The wrestling was also pretty severe. There were no rules as to where they grabbed each other and some of them looked rather sick after it.

The show finished, by request, with a " Zikr," a sort of rhythmic religious exercise, performed by about 20 of the natives, specially selected for their sanctity, measured in terms of their ability to keep up the exercise for a long time. They formed themselves into two rows facing each other, and the thing started. In consists of a swinging motion of the upper part of the body, the head describing a half circle with its lowest point about in line with the knees, and at the same a chanting of the words, " La ilaha illa-llah " (" There is no God but God "), or simply, " Allah, Allah, Allah," to the sound of a pipe. This went on for perhaps about twenty minutes, and then one by one they dropped to the sand exhausted and apparently in some cases in convulsions, until only about half a dozen were left. They, we were informed, were the holiest men of the company. The native onlookers seemed to take it in a spirit of amused curiosity, and the performers were apparently not at all averse to going through their strenuous ritual for the amusement of a crowd of unbelieving Tommies.

On November 16th the long stay at Salford and Oldham came to an end and the Battalion moved to Ferry Post Bridgehead, opposite Ismailia, at the northern end of Lake Timsah. " B " and " D " Companies, less two platoons, went to Ferry Post Railhead, about seven miles out, the remaining platoons occupying two other small posts on the Canal Bank, called Bench Mark and Ridge Post, two and three miles respectively from Ferry Post. It was near these posts that the Turks had reached the Canal in the early part of 1915. They were most uncomfortable places on the high embankment and were infested with rats; the only compensation was the fishing, which was excellent. The front line was some five miles beyond the Railhead, among huge sand dunes, and consisted of a series of small posts. These were on much higher ground and the air was delightful. Australian

Light Horse formed part of the garrison at Railhead and made daily patrols into the desert.

"B" Company was sent out to two of these front line posts, named Round Hill 1 and Round Hill 2, which they took over from the 1/5th Suffolk Regiment on November 28th, and "D" Company was stationed as a mobile reserve a little in rear, at a place rejoicing in the name of Hagley Park. It was not particularly park-like. There were fortnightly reliefs, Battalion Headquarters remaining on the Canal, where the thatched huts were fairly comfortable, though somewhat out of repair.

H.M. Cruiser "Eurylas" and the old French battle-ship the "Requin" lay in Lake Timsah; also some small monitors. Officers of the cruiser were frequent visitors to the mess, and the return visits to their ward room were always very enjoyable. The "Eurylas cocktail" was very popular and was introduced into our mess by Willmott, our excellent P.M.C., as a permanent institution. The officers of the "Requin" also called on us and l'entente cordiale was kept fully alive.

On December 30th the Battalion marched up to Railhead in relief of the 6th Essex, with two companies still in the front line. The 12th Australian Light Horse were most hospitable and kind, and the relations between officers and men alike were most friendly. We played them at "rugger," which was their game, and at "soccer" which was ours, and each proved victorious at their own game. We had some difficulty in raising a rugger XV., but they gave quite a good account of themselves. Tent pegging was another sport we learnt from the Australians.

We had some violent storms of wind and rain at Railhead and it was a difficult matter sometimes to keep the tents standing in the gale.

Before Christmas we were back at Ferry Post Bridgehead again. We spent as happy a Christmas as possible, and managed a good dinner and sports for the Battalion. Another successful feature was a Christmas pantomime, in which the two Wilsons, Bacon, Heron, Wink, Bartley, Beard, Archer, Portway, Kinnersley, Bateman, and others distinguished themselves. Bacon was a general officer, Beard was his wife, and Jack Bartley their charming daughter. Wink was a German spy, and John Portway, our heavy-weight boxer, made a dainty little Fairy Queen. The show was repeated a few nights after for the benefit of the outlying companies who had been relieved. It was a priceless performance, and a happy memory of many of the caste who afterwards fell, worthily playing their parts in the great drama of battle at Gaza.—"All the world's a stage . . . "

The month was also memorable for the visit of Miss Lena Ashwell's concert party, who gave an excellent show at the Y.M.C.A. to all the troops at Ferry Post. It was the first occasion on which ladies had been permitted to cross the Canal and

E

their presence was much appreciated. The whole party came to supper in the mess afterwards.

Soon afterwards we crossed the Canal and the whole Division went into camp at Moascar, near Ismailia, for final training and re-fitting in preparation for our march to the Promised Land. The Commander-in-Chief had decided on an advance, and the Desert Column had already been formed, covering the laying of a railway, which was progressing at a wonderful rate along the old coast route which connects Egypt with Asia, about which I shall have more to say in another chapter. While at Moascar, Capron, my Adjutant, and I had some good shooting on the back-waters of Lake Timsah, where duck, teal, snipe and coote were plentiful. A French official of the Canal company used to lend us his little steam launch and run the party, and we had some very enjoyable sport.

At last on January 31st we began our march. The first stage was to El Ferdan, 15 miles on a hard road, and the Brigade passed General Sir Charles Dobell, K.C.B., a mile or two out from Ismailia, in column of route. The hard road was a great change from the soft sand of the desert we had been acquainted with for so long. It made marching easier and increased the pace, but there were many blistered feet, and the care of these important parts of the infantry soldier's anatomy called for all the resources of the company commanders. We bivouacked for the night and marched early next day for Kantara, which was the base of operations for the invading Army. Full marching order was carried, with iron rations, waterproof sheets and two sandbags per man.

Kantara was a very large tent town, though not such a huge city as it afterwards became. We marched right through and bivouacked about four miles from the Canal—13 or 14 miles march altogether. On the following day we reached Gilban. Here the hard road ceased and thenceforward we marched almost entirely on the "wire road." This consisted of five widths of about 1½ inch mesh wire netting, laid flat on the sand and fastened down. It was one of the discoveries of the war. The going on it was excellent and the amount of foot traffic it stood was enormous. It gave a firm foothold with less jar than a metalled road. No animals or vehicles were allowed on it, and only staff motor cars and urgent despatch riders. We marched in three columns abreast, the companies on the wire road, the pack mule transport alongside, the camels forming the third column. No wheeled transport was taken by the infantry. The triple column arrangement not only reduced the length of the column and facilitated control, but overcame difficulties connected with camel and mule transport moving at different paces. The camels of course, lost ground during the spells of marching, but made it up during the halts, and were never very far behind at the end of the day's march.

This was fortunate for us, as they carried the day's water, other than that carried in water bottles on the men. The latter supply was strictly controlled, as we had practised in training, and men had to look upon their water bottles as a platoon supply and not a personal one.

Pelusium Siding was reached on February 4th and on the following day we marched into Romani, the scene of the last defeat of the Turks. We stayed five days here and had an opportunity of inspecting the battlefield and visiting the graves of three men of our old machine gun section, who had fallen there. Incidentally we buried a good number of Turks who had been killed in the attack. Several we found were lying, each behind his little sand hill which he had used for cover, and in most cases surrounded by large numbers of cartridge cases. Some had

THE WIRE ROAD.

pushed on almost to the barbed wire. They were brave fellows and our men gave them the honours of war and buried them decently. In most cases the graves were marked with crosses, with the simple inscription "Turk at rest." It was the men's own idea and it struck me as a very fitting inscription. The cross was perhaps incongruous; but what of that? It was a Christian's tribute to his enemy and, perhaps, not so out of place after all. Romani covered a large area and the defensive posts were in most cases prominent sandhills entrenched in the same way as our Canal posts. They appeared to have stood the shell-fire well on the whole. One or two rather over-prominent and obvious observation posts had been roughly treated. Camouflage is very difficult in smooth, clean, unbroken sand; indeed, it is impossible. But open trenches can be made quite invisible on the forward slope of a sand hill, provided the parapet is slightly higher than the parados, thus eliminating shadow. From the air of course they are very distinctly visible. Overhead cover is easy, provided materials can be got, but this implies loop-holes in a fire trench, and these are very conspicuous in sand.

On February 10th the march was resumed to Rabah, on the 11th to Khirba, on the 12th to Bir el Abd, on the 13th to Salmana, on the 14th to Tilul, and on the 15th to Mazar. All were easy stages and were usually made after an early mid-day meal, thus saving carriage of rations and enabling a large reserve of water to be taken. The later start also gave time to get dry after a wet night. Hot tea was always going soon after arrival. Officers bivouacked in a row with a canvas screen on the windward side. The nights were cold and it rained pretty frequently. Camel loads had to be carefully worked out, and kits were strictly limited to 30 lb. per officer. One extra blanket per

A SHORT HALT.

man was carried on the camels. One camel only was available for officers' mess utensils and stores.

On February 22nd the 1/4th Essex and ourselves took over the garrisoning of Mazar from two Battalions of the Royal Welsh Fusiliers. Wilson was sent on to take over Bardawil, and Finn with his platoon garrisoned Maardan. Bardawil is a corruption of Baldwin, and was a reminder of the crusades. Baldwin, King of Jerusalem, successor to his famous brother Godfrey de Bouillon, had a stronghold on the coast near by, at a place called El Flusiat, in the ruins of which we found the remains of a large church. Below the broken floor of the church we found stone coffins marked with the Cross and still containing bones, probably of early Christian warriors or divines. One pillar had carved upon it an unmistakable crusader's cross. The stronghold was protected on all sides by a morass, which would not bear the weight of a horse, except perhaps on tracks known only to the garrison. On the occasion of our visit we left our horses and got across the soft going on foot, but it was very treacherous.

We started a riding school at Mazar and put up some fences which afforded plenty of amusement.

On March 11th we were relieved at Mazar by a battalion of Indian Imperial Service troops, the Gwalior Rifles, and marched to Maardan. On 12th we resumed our march to Bardawil, and on the 13th we reached El Arish, an ancient town and fortress at the mouth of the Wadi El Arish. It had offered considerable resistance to the mounted troops who had eventually turned it, and the Turks had fallen back on Rafa on the frontier, from which they had also been ejected by brilliant work on the part of the cavalry of the Desert Corps.

We had a pleasant bivouac among some fig trees near the east bank of the Wadi and stayed there eight days, during which we were all inoculated against cholera, did some training to keep the men fit, and generally got things in order " to the last button." We knew the Turks would probably make a stand at Gaza, that scene of so many battles in the world's history. It would not be this time an affair of cavalry, and we all hoped that at last the Essex Brigade would have a chance to prove its mettle in fair fight against the Turk on his own ground and to pay off some old Gallipoli scores.

The route by which we had come gave rise to many reflections, and before we follow the Battalion on its march into the Holy Land, I propose to make it the subject of a fresh chapter.

CHAPTER IV.

# THE OLD ROAD.

EADER, do you know the history of this old desert road? If you do, don't trouble to read this chapter, which is a digression from the doings of the 5th Essex. If you don't, come and sit with me in the twilight on the banks of the Wadi el Arish, the ancient "River of Egypt," the western boundary of the land which was given to Abraham and his seed, and perchance we may see some of the ghosts of the past; kings, prophets, pilgrims, conquerors, mighty armies, fugitives, caravans, and raiding bands—as they cross and recross this old river bed, this way and that, through the mists of time.

How long it has been in use as a great highway none can tell. But the mists of antiquity clear a little in 2200 B.C. or thereabouts. Then we know that the peoples of Western Asia began to be pushed westwards, and there was, along this very road, a constant stream of migration, which peopled the Delta of the Nile with the nomadic Semitic tribes of Edom and Southern Syria, who for centuries had been leading their herds to feed in those fertile lands. The foreigners became so strong in the land that they eventually conquered it and set up a new dynasty, the "Hyksos" or Shepherd Kings, who ruled Egypt for over 400 years. Towards the end of this period we see old father Abraham, with Sarah his wife, driven by famine, taking this same road with his flocks. Then we see the Ishmaelites going down into Egypt, after buying little Joseph for 20 pieces of silver. It was a good bargain for Egypt.

Before long all countries are streaming into Egypt to buy corn during the great famine that the wise Chancellor had foreseen. Jacob, stricken in years, with his "three score and ten souls" trudge their way by this sandy road to the land of Goshen to dwell in the land of his famous son. We see, too, the return of the remains of the patriarch, borne back in state to be buried at Hebron, escorted by "all the servants of Pharoah and the elders of the land of Egypt—chariots and horsemen—a very great company."

Next the old road sees the expulsion of the foreign rulers by Amasis, the founder of the XVIII. Dynasty in 1600 B.C. A few years later we see the great king Thotmes leading an army along this road and waging successful war in Asia. His grandson Thotmes III., the greatest warrior of his race, carried

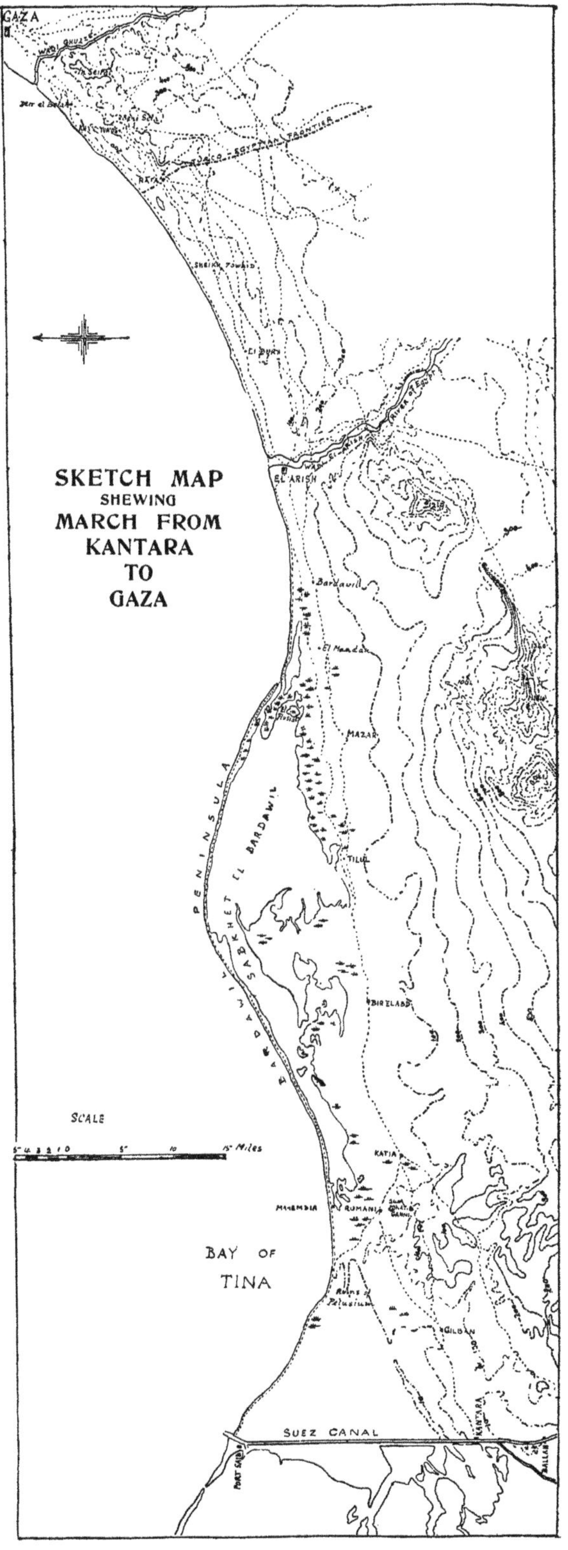


To face Chapter IV.

on ceaseless wars for 50 years. His conquests extended as far north as Karkemish, and Assyria was compelled to pay tribute to Egypt. He and his son Amenophis ruled a mighty empire, extending from Ethiopia to the Euphrates. It was a busy time for the old road in those days. Palestine became a province of Egypt, and many letters have been found which were sent by desert post from the Governors of Palestine cities to the Egyptian kings.

Then came the wars with the rising power of the Syrians, and there was ebb and flow of armies, like the ebb and flow of the sand itself, up and down the historic highway. Rameses I. was hard put to it to hold his own, but his son Seti had more success, and so had his famous grandson Rameses II., who in 1328 B.C. led a mighty host against Khita, King of Syria, and chiefly by his own personal valour turned what looked like being a disaster to the Egyptian Army into a great victory, in which Khita was overcome with great slaughter, and Rameses continued his conquests even to the shores of the Black Sea. A hard man this Rameses, as the children of Israel (who had by this time "multiplied and waxed exceeding mighty; and the land was filled with them") found to their cost. By him they were scattered all over Egypt and put to forced labour upon the public works and upon the building of the "treasure cities Pithon and Raamses." We know how at last they were released from bondage, probably in the reign of Menephthah his son, who so many times "refused to let them go"—but that is another story. They didn't come by this road. Those who flee from the wrath of a king eschew the king's highway.

About 1200 B.C. we see a large force marching westwards to conquer Egypt in the time of Rameses III. This time it was supported by a fleet—Phœnician or Philistine perhaps—and a battle was fought near the old mouth of the Nile (now dry), where Pelusium afterwards stood,—and now is not. The Egyptians defeated the invaders and chased them back along this same old road into Syria again. But the Egyptians did not stop in Syria this time. They feared this new thing in war—sea power—threatening their communications, and besides there were troublous times at home; so we see the victorious army returning to their own country resting content with such loot as Palestine afforded. For a time the road seems to have become less war-like, and the caravans of the Phœnicians and other traders formed the principal traffic. Egypt was busy with a North v. South trouble, which ended in Southern or Upper Egypt becoming a province of Lower Egypt. Thebes fell on evil days and Tanis in the Delta became the capital of the country. Incidentally this shifting of power from south to north made relations with Asia more intimate and the desert route became as important as ever. But as far as we know, for a short time—a mere couple of centuries or so—the road ceased to give footing to armies from either hand, and the peaceful caravans pursued their way. About B.C. 1015 we have the emissaries of King Solomon visiting Egypt and purchasing horses and chariots. The following year it must have been an imposing cavalcade which brought the daughter of Pharoah to the court of Jerusalem, to be the bride—one of the brides—of that much married monarch, Solomon, King of all Israel. Then comes sedition in the land, and Jeroboam, son of Nebat, hurries secretly to Egypt on mischief bent.

A few more years and once more the distant sand cloud betokens the coming of a mighty army. The year 971 B.C. saw—according to Josephus—an army of 60,000 cavalry and 400,000 infantry with 1200 chariots of war, under Shishak, King of Egypt, marching by this road to invade Palestine. The ancient historians were not particular to a few thousands and probably the numbers are exaggerated, but there is the army right enough. Are not the names of 150 cities of Palestine captured by Shishak in this campaign written in stone on the walls of the great hall at Karnak? And even to Jerusalem he came, " and he took away the treasures of the house of the Lord " (1 Kings xiv. 25-26). Thus alone was Rehoboam, King of Judah, able to save his capital. It was a rich convoy that wound its way through the desert passes when they brought back the spoils of the Temple and of the King's palace. But Judah is to be revenged. Yet another large army under King Osorkon, takes the road from Egypt. With high hopes it swings past, singing its battle songs. In a few days, utterly defeated by Asa, King of Judah, at Mareshah, its broken remnants wend their way back towards the setting sun.

For another two centuries or so the road seems to have borne no armies. A new power—the Assyrian—was rising in the east, and Israel and Judah had become tributary to it. Observe those hooked-nosed, bearded men, silently hurrying westward. They are the secret messengers of Hoshea, King of Israel, to " So, King of Egypt " (2 Kings xvii. 4) for help to deliver him from the oppressor. Help was forthcoming, such as it was, and once more Egypt takes the field, only to be defeated at Rafa, not many miles from where we sit, by Sargon, King of Assyria, in 720 B.C. The old road gets busy again. For fifty years there is war between Assyria and Egypt and the armies of both countries cross and recross the desert on its well-worn track. In 701 B.C. the Egyptians once more return, a defeated army at the hands of Sennacharib who had routed them at Altaka in Dan. Sennacharib follows in pursuit and lays siege to Pelusium, leaving Rabshakeh, his general, to destroy Jerusalem. Both projects were unsuccessful. The army had to be drawn off Pelusium, according to Herodotus, because " a multitude of mice gnawed all their bows to pieces in a single night." The Assyrian King returns, only to find

Rabshakeh's army completely broken up by a pestilence—an event which also saved King Hezekiah of Judah from destruction, "And the Angel of the Lord went out, and smote in the camp of the Assyrians an hundred four score and five thousand; and when they arose early in the morning behold they were all dead corpses" (2 Kings xix. 35).

But still the rich land in the west draws the Assyrians like a magnet, and again in 670 B.C.—we see approaching the army of King Esarhaddon, who marches it to Egypt, not to return until he has made the land of the Pharoahs an Assyrian province. Then once more the Egyptians make a strong bid for their freedom, and the next armies we see are moving eastward as of old. First the Assyrians, retreating and fighting, attacked and followed by the Egyptians under Psammetichus, governor of Sais, who for his prowess was made King of Egypt. Nineveh fell in 609 B.C. The Assyrian Empire collapsed like a pack of cards a few years after reaching the zenith of its power, and a new empire was set up in Babylon.

Next we see another Egyptian King, Necho, bringing up fresh armies and continuing the war against the new Babylonian power. This Pharoah Necho, in 608 B.C., wins a great battle at Megiddo, slays Josiah King of Judah, and we see Jehoahaz, the king's son, sent to Egypt, a prisoner along the old road, never to return. And in due time back comes Necho himself, now a fugitive from Nebuchadnezzar of Babylon, who had defeated him on the far Euphrates. Twenty-two years later another Egyptian army crosses into Judea to the assistance of King Zedekiah, who had rebelled against Nebuchadnezzar, and again the Egyptians return, a broken army, pursued by the Babylonians. In 586 B.C. Jerusalem is destroyed and a few years later we see the sorry remnant of Judah flying into Egypt with Jeremiah their prophet. In 581 B.C. Nebuchadnezzar again invades Egypt and brings back the fugitive Jews. The captivity is thus completely accomplished and Judea lies desert for 70 years.

The second Babylonian empire did not last long; Babylon was captured by Cyrus King of Persia about 530 B.C., and a new power was in being to harass the Egyptians. Cambyses the son of Cyrus was the next King to cross the River of Egypt with an invading army, and Herodotus tells us wonderful stories of how this army was supplied with water in camel skins carried on live camels—there were no copper "fantassis" in those days. The wonder-loving old historian even describes how arrangements were made to lay *pipe lines*—there is surely nothing new under the sun—from a river in Arabia called the Corys, distant twelve days' journey, to carry the water into cisterns dug in the desert track to receive it. There were three separate pipes to three separate places, and the pipes were made of "the skins of oxen and other beasts." The Persian R.E. must have been an efficient service. And a permanent supply was afterwards kept up, according to the same authority, by collecting all the wine jars in the country and carrying them to Memphis, where they were filled with water and stored in dumps all along the road to Syria. But this was after the Persians had conquered Egypt. Cambyses, then, took the road, with his camel skins and (perhaps) his pipe lines, and defeated the Egyptians in a great battle near Pelusium. For more than a hundred years Egypt was a province of the Persian empire, and many a draft must have "proceeded by march route" to the occupied territory, their progress made easy by those wine-pot water dumps of theirs. Then followed a brief interval of independence, followed by a re-conquest by Artaxerxes, and so the ebb and flow over the desert track went on. The fourth and last conquest by the Persians was that under Darius.

Then the Persian empire fell in its turn, before Alexander the Great, of Macedon. The latter, after taking Gaza, brought his army by the same road in 332 B.C., occupied Egypt with little opposition, and founded the city bearing his name (irreverently abbreviated by the British army into "Alex") after assuring himself of divine assistance by a visit to the temple of Jupiter Ammon at Siwa in the Lybian desert. After Alexander's death at Babylon in 323 B.C. Ptolemy, one of his generals, led armies into Palestine to fight against Antigonus of Syria for the possession of that country. The Syrians in the end prevailed, and an attempt on their part to invade Egypt was stopped on the road by the Roman Senate. From that time forward Palestine came under the power of Rome and there was a period of quiet for the desert road.

In 49 B.C., according to Plutarch, Cleopatra was banished to Syria but returned disguised, to gain entrance by strategem into the presence, and by her wiles into the heart also, of the great Julius Cæsar at Alexandria.

. . . . . . . . . .

"*When he arose, he took the young child and his mother by night, and departed into Egypt.*" (Matthew ii. 14).

"*But when Herod was dead, behold an Angel of the Lord appeareth in a dream to Joseph in Egypt, saying, Arise and take the young child and his mother and go into the land of Israel, for they are dead which sought the young child's life. And he arose and took the young child and his mother, and came into the land of Israel.*" (Matthew ii. 19-20).

So passed and repassed, obscure and unnoticed, the greatest Captain of them all.

. . . . . . . . . .

The next invaders from the West were the Romans under Titus, in A.D. 70, who utterly destroyed Jerusalem after one of the most terrible sieges in history. In A.D. 268, Zenobia, Queen of Palmyra, brought a large army across the desert and defeated the Romans in the Delta, later returning to her own city, where she was afterwards defeated and captured by the Emperor Aurelian. Roman legions continually tramped the road for nearly 400 years until A.D. 620, when Chosroes, King of Persia marched into Egypt after taking Damascus and Jerusalem, and for ten years it was once more a Persian province. Chosroes met the fate of so many of his predecessors, being defeated by the Emperor Heraclius, and once more the Roman legions resumed their sway, based on Constantinople.

Then came the followers of Mahomet, and Arab governors came to Egypt appointed by the Khalifs at Baghdad. One of these governors, Ahmed ibn Tulun, revolted in A.D. 868 and again an army marched eastward and conquered Palestine. Forty years after, the Khalif Moktafi marched his army westward and re-conquered Egypt. What a military road! Palestine again became a province of (Arab) Egypt and it was a governor appointed from there who was at Jerusalem when Godfrey de Bouillon captured the Holy City in A.D. 1099 and founded the Christian Kingdom of Jerusalem. In 1187 we see the army of Saleh-ed-Din, better known as Saladin, who had made himself Sultan of Egypt and built the citadel in Cairo, marching eastwards, to defeat the Christians and deprive them of the greater part of their kingdom.

In 1251 St. Louis of France (Louis IX.) after surrendering Damietta to the Moslems led an army from Egypt, and repaired the fortresses on the coast and in Palestine, ready for the reception of reinforcements which never came, and in 1291 another Sultan, El-Ashraf Khalil, with yet another army from Egypt, came and finally expelled the Crusaders from the remnant of their kingdom.

And then came the Turks. Sultan Selim I. defeated the Arabs near Aleppo in 1516 and marched into Egypt. The latter became a province of the Ottoman Empire and remained so for four centuries. But during that time another great soldier was to try his luck by the desert route. This was Napoleon I. After his victory at the battle of the Pyramids in 1798 the army of the Mamelukes of Egypt was split in two, one half under Ibrahim Bey, retreating by this road into Syria. In February 1799 Napoleon determined on an invasion of that country and set out from Cairo with a sort of flying column of 12,000 men with 43 guns and 900 cavalry. His object was to strike quickly at the Turks in Syria while their organization was still incomplete, take Acre, and return to Egypt in time to deal with another Turkish army which was expected to land in Egypt from the Island of Rhodes. An ambitious scheme for an army of 12,000 men, especially as he had just lost command of the sea at the hands of one Admiral Nelson, at Aboukir Bay. But Napoleon undertook it, and on February 20th 1799, took this town of El Arish. On June 1st he was back again, having been foiled by Sir Sydney Smith at Acre. In rear of his army the great coastal plain, says the official report, " presented but one blaze of fire." Every village had been destroyed and the crops burnt. Suffering greatly from want of water, his army hurried westward, arrived at Cairo on June 21st, and on July 25th at the second battle of Aboukir utterly defeated the Turkish army which had just arrived from Rhodes.

In 1831, Mahomet Ali, Turkish Governor of Egypt, declared his independence of Turkey. His son Ibrahim Pasha led an Egyptian army into Palestine and gained victories over the Turks, but the European powers intervened and Ibrahim brought his army back. Then we have Turkish forces in the present war, one in 1915 actually reaching the Suez Canal and getting back again ; the other, smashed up at Romani, is the one whose homeward tracks we of the 5th Essex have been following in our march to the Promised Land. Of all the armies that have trodden this road ours is perchance the last. Who knows ?

Such is the story of the old road. Has any other road in the world such a history ? And to-morrow we march eastwards, with hopes as high as any of theirs who went before us through the ages ; our destiny, like theirs, in the hands of an inscrutable Providence.

CHAPTER V.

# THE PROMISED LAND.

N March 20th the Brigade Group, consisting of the 161st Infantry Brigade, 161st M.G. Company, 270th (Essex) Brigade, R.F.A. (under Lieut.-Col. Lawrie), and the 1/3rd (East Anglian) Field Ambulance (under Lieut.-Col. Troup), the whole under the command of Brig.-General Marriott Dodington, marched out of El Arish and reached El Burj. On the following day we marched to Sheikh Zowaid, where we stayed until the morning of the 24th. During our stay the Battalion was given its second dose of cholera inoculation. The frontier was reached on the 24th and we bivouacked that night at Rafa on the border where there had been a Turkish frontier post. The country was now presenting quite a contrast to the sandy desert, and there was some corn, growing green in patches. The green was a delightful relief. The frontier was marked at intervals by marble pillars, evidently taken from some dismantled building, probably a Crusaders' church. The pillars were very similar to the ones we had seen at El Flusiat, and it is quite likely that they came from there. We bivouacked on a sandy rise, the village lying in a hollow between us and the sea. Many of the fields were fenced with cactus hedges—the "prickly pear" with which we afterwards became so familiar. There were a few fig trees, as at El Arish. The 4th Battalion and ourselves were warned for outpost duty on the following night, and Col. Jameson, commanding 4th Essex, and myself set out early in the morning with General Hare and his staff to reconnoitre the line to be taken up. On our way we passed the picturesque village of Khan Yunus, where the G.O.C. 53rd Division had taken up his Headquarters. The village was crowded with troops and natives, the sandy lanes between high cactus hedges being almost choked with watering parties of horses, mules and camels, while the inhabitants watched the proceedings with solemn interest. They looked very dirty and wretched, but apparently lived to a great age. The children of course were having the show of their lives. Some of them I noticed had what would have been quite fair hair (if it had been washed), while some were decidedly red-headed. Some at least were probably descendants of the ancient Philistines, who were settled here in the time of Moses. The red headed ones were perhaps of Phœnician ancestry. There were the ruins of a fine mosque which gave the impression of having been a church, but I did not get the opportunity of exploring it. Khan Yunus came near to being the scene of an important event in the world's history in 1799, when Napoleon and his staff arrived to find it in the hands of the Turks, and narrowly escaped capture. His main body had been misdirected by its guides and had wandered into the desert to the south. Fortunately for him the Turks thought the party were the leading troops of the French army, and retired towards Gaza.

We proceeded along the old Cairo road towards Gaza. Though not metalled, the surface was comparatively hard and the road had a small ditch on each side and a line of telegraph poles along the route.

To the right lay a ridge of rocky hills, to the left a narrow plain, separated from the sea by a sandy ridge. We arrived at In Seirat, a small village hidden away in the clefts of the rocky ridge, and climbed a hill to the north of it to view the country. The hill, which was already crowded with staff officers and commanders, afforded a magnificent view. To our left front lay the fertile plain, green with barley, the old Cairo road stretching on towards Gaza, which lay in a heat haze about six miles to the north. Below us the Wadi Ghuzzi wound its way across our front to the sea on the left, The two domes of Sheikh Nebhan shone white in the surrounding green. The steep cliffs of the Wadi made black shadows on the stony bed, now dry, but recently washed by the rains from the hills. To our left and slightly behind us on the edge of the sand dunes, lay the village of Deir el Belah, the southern outpost of the Crusaders, and beyond, the blue expanse of the sea. Occasional rifle shots indicated that the cavalry were already in touch with the enemy. We could see the horses of the patrols taking cover behind the rocks. Very dimly in the distance could be discerned wheeled traffic moving along the Gaza-Beersheba road. The prominent bluff of Ali el Muntar, crowned with its mosque, commanded the whole plain ; a natural outpost of this land of the Philistines. Well might the early Mohammedans call Gaza " Dehliz el Moulk "—The" Threshold of the Kingdom." In all the countless invasions of Syria from the west, Gaza was the first place which had to be accounted for ; and the green plain before us had been the scene of many a fierce struggle from the earliest times.

Among the old Pharoahs of Egypt, Thotmes, Rameses, and Shishak all had to fight for it. Joshua pushed his conquests up to its gates, but failed to take it. Hezekiah got possession of it, but his tenure was short and uncertain. Tiglath Pileser, King of Nineveh, took it for the Assyrians in 735 B.C. Sargon punished it severely for rebellion, and it remained subject to his successors, Sennacherib and others, until Pharoah Necho wrested it from them in 605 B.C., only to lose it again by his defeat by the Babylonians. When Cambyses, King of Persia, set out to conquer

Egypt, Gaza alone dared to resist him, and was only subdued after a long siege. It also stood a siege for two months against Alexander the Great, who treated its brave defenders with the greatest barbarity. After that world-conqueror's death it became for two centuries a regular cockpit, in which Egyptian, Syrian and Jewish armies settled their quarrels. Twice Antigonus took it from Ptolemy and twice the latter retook it at the edge of the sword. The Syrians again destroyed it in 198 B.C. The Maccabees laid siege to its suburbs and forced the city to sue for terms. Alexander Janneus took it after a year's siege in 96 B.C. Antiochus the Great conquered it for the Romans. It fell to Pompey in A.D. 62. Abu Bekr, the first Caliph, won it for the Moslems in A.D. 634. In the twelfth century the Crusaders found it almost deserted, and Baldwin committed it to the Templars, who fortified it, but after the battle of Hattin it fell to Saladin.

In 1244 Christian and Saracen armies, united for the nonce in a common cause, met with a bloody defeat in the valley at the hands of the Kharismians. In 1516 it saw the final subjection of the Mamelukes by the Turks.

Napoleon took it in his stride during his lightning invasion of Syria, and it passed to Ibrahim Pasha in his invasion of the country, the Turks only regaining it through the intervention of the Great Powers. And now it was apparent that Gaza was going to add another chapter to its history—and ours.

Behind Ali el Muntar and to the left of it lay the town itself, surrounded by fruit gardens hedged with prickly pears. A few red roofs were visible, and several minarets, interpersed with olives and date palms. Tradition says that it was up the hill of Ali el Muntar that Samson carried " the doors of the gate of the city and the two posts " on his shoulders.

The Divisional Commander decided that one Battalion was enough to hold the outpost line. The 4th Essex was detailed, and leaving Colonel Jameson to reconnoitre the line, I rode back to fetch up his company commanders. I found the Brigade resting in the shade at Beni Selah, about eight miles back. I conducted the outpost company commanders to their C.O., and waited at In Seirat, where the Division had fixed its Headquarters, until the Battalion arrived. During the evening we received orders that we were placed under the command of the G.O.C. 53rd Division, General Dallas, who was to attack the Gaza defences on the following day. We were detailed as General Dallas's general reserve. Some disappointment was expressed by the fire-eaters that we were detailed for reserve, " which of course would never be wanted," etc., etc. They were satisfied before another sunset. Some of them, poor fellows, had already seen their last.

C.O.'s and Adjutants met the Brigadier late in the evening, and the latter told us all that was known of the enemy and the intention of the corps commander. The Royal Flying Corps had obtained some photographs on March 17th, showing that the Turks had already fortified the ridge to the S.E. of the town, including the commanding eminence of Ali el Muntar, the saddle to the south of it, afterwards known as the "Warren," another gentle rise of the same ridge which from its verdure was known as the "Green Hill,' and at the most southerly point a sandy hill, which already shewed such a network of trenches that it was dubbed "The Labyrinth." From this point the line ran in a north-westerly direction across the green valley, through the orchards to the S.W. of the town and over the sandy ridge to the sea. It was roughly entrenched, but not continuously —the distance was over three miles—and showed a few hundreds of yards of trench with dugouts or shelters in rear, repeated at intervals. From the Labyrinth trenches ran in a north-easterly direction between the ridge and the south end of the town, and to the north of Ali el Muntar was another trench facing north. Briefly the defences consisted of a fortified locality about 1500 yards long, and 800 yards wide, situated on the feature which formed the natural defence of the town, viz., the ridge to the S.E. of it, while a line was in process of formation connecting this system with the sea, the Labyrinth being at the salient. Within the system itself many other trenches were in course of construction. Eight days had passed since the photographs had been taken, and it would have been a libel on the well known capacity of the Turk for digging and on the skill of his engineers, to doubt that during that period the defensive system had been developed and strengthened. It displayed the same characteristics as all the other field work of the Turks that I have seen, both on the Peninsula and in Palestine. To begin with, the main tactical ground features were dug into complete small trench "systems," then these were connected laterally, afterwards other features were dealt with, often in front of the original works, which then became a strong second line with good observation, while the new front line, sited on lower ground, gave more effect to rifle and machine gun fire and favoured concealment. The last thing the Turks seemed to worry about was a continuous line of fire trenches. Another thing he never dreamt of was to stop digging and say "This work's finished." I firmly believe if he stopped in a place long enough he would lose his army in his own trenches.

But to return to the scheme. The Turks were known to have large reinforcements coming from the north and from Beersheba. The cavalry, consisting of the Anzac Mounted Division and the Imperial Mounted Division, were to cross the Wadi Ghuzzi before dawn and place themselves on the right flank, hold back enemy forces coming from the east, and, if opportunity offered, to attack the town from that quarter or from the north, while the 53rd Division were to attack the defences from the S. and S.E. The 162nd and 163rd Brigades were to follow the cavalry in support, while the 161st (Essex) Brigade was attached to the 53rd Division as general reserve, to confirm its success or to meet eventualities. The 52nd (Lowland) Division was a day's march in rear. All was quiet during the night.

HELPING AN ARMOURED CAR OVER THE WADI GHUZZI,
MARCH 26, 1917.

*To face page 66.*

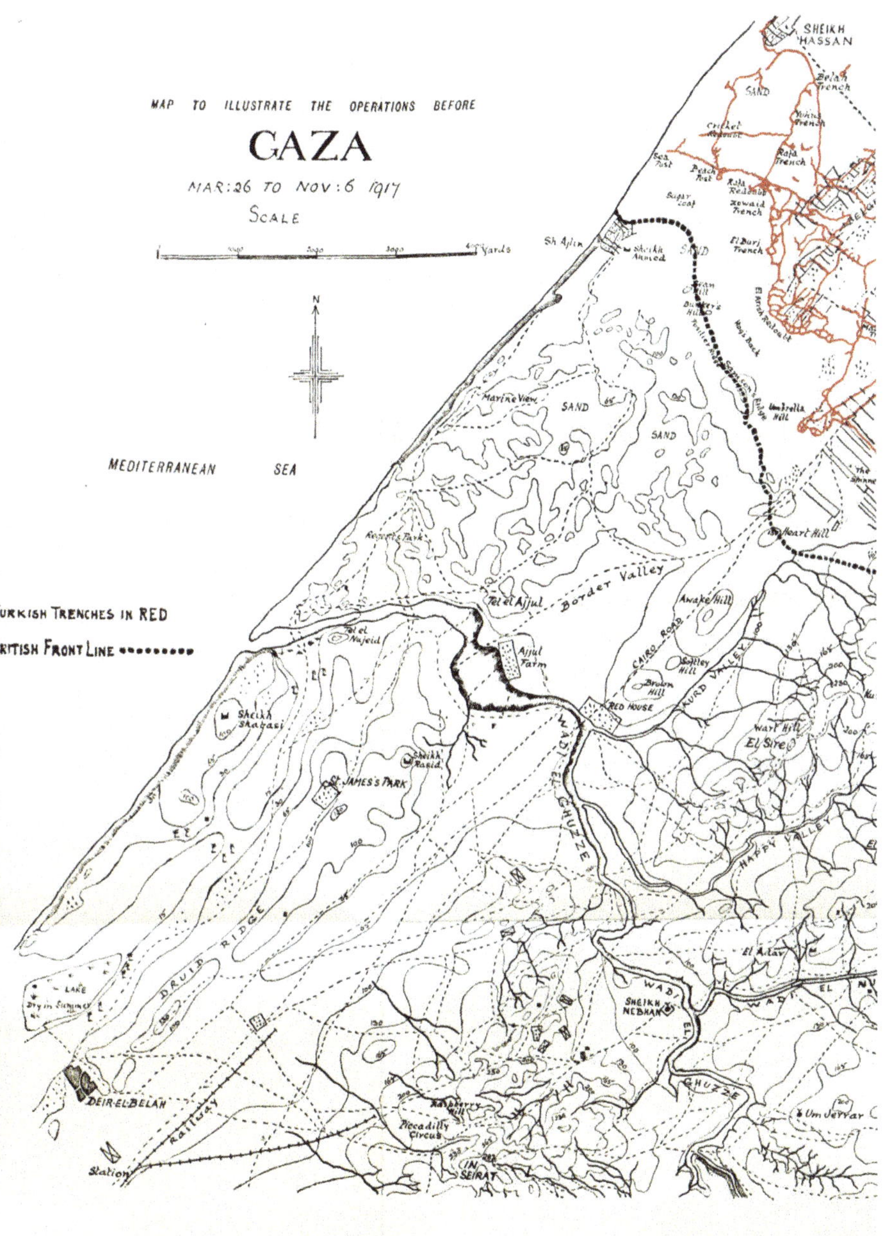
MAP TO ILLUSTRATE THE OPERATIONS BEFORE
GAZA
MAR:26 TO NOV:6 1917
SCALE
Yards
N
MEDITERRANEAN SEA
TURKISH TRENCHES IN RED
BRITISH FRONT LINE
SHEIKH HASSAN
SAND
Sh Ajlin
Sheikh Ahmed
Marine View
Tel el Ajjul
Border Valley
Awake Hill
Ajjul Farm
CAIRO ROAD
RED HOUSE
KURD VALLEY
El Sire
WADI EL GHUZZE
HAPPY VALLEY
Sheikh Shabasi
Sheikh Rasid
St. JAMES'S PARK
DRUID RIDGE
LAKE
Dry in Summer
DEIR-EL-BELAH
Railway
Station
Piccadilly Circus
IN SEIRAT
SHEIKH NEBHAN
El Adar
Um Jerrar
Umbrella Hill
Heart Hill

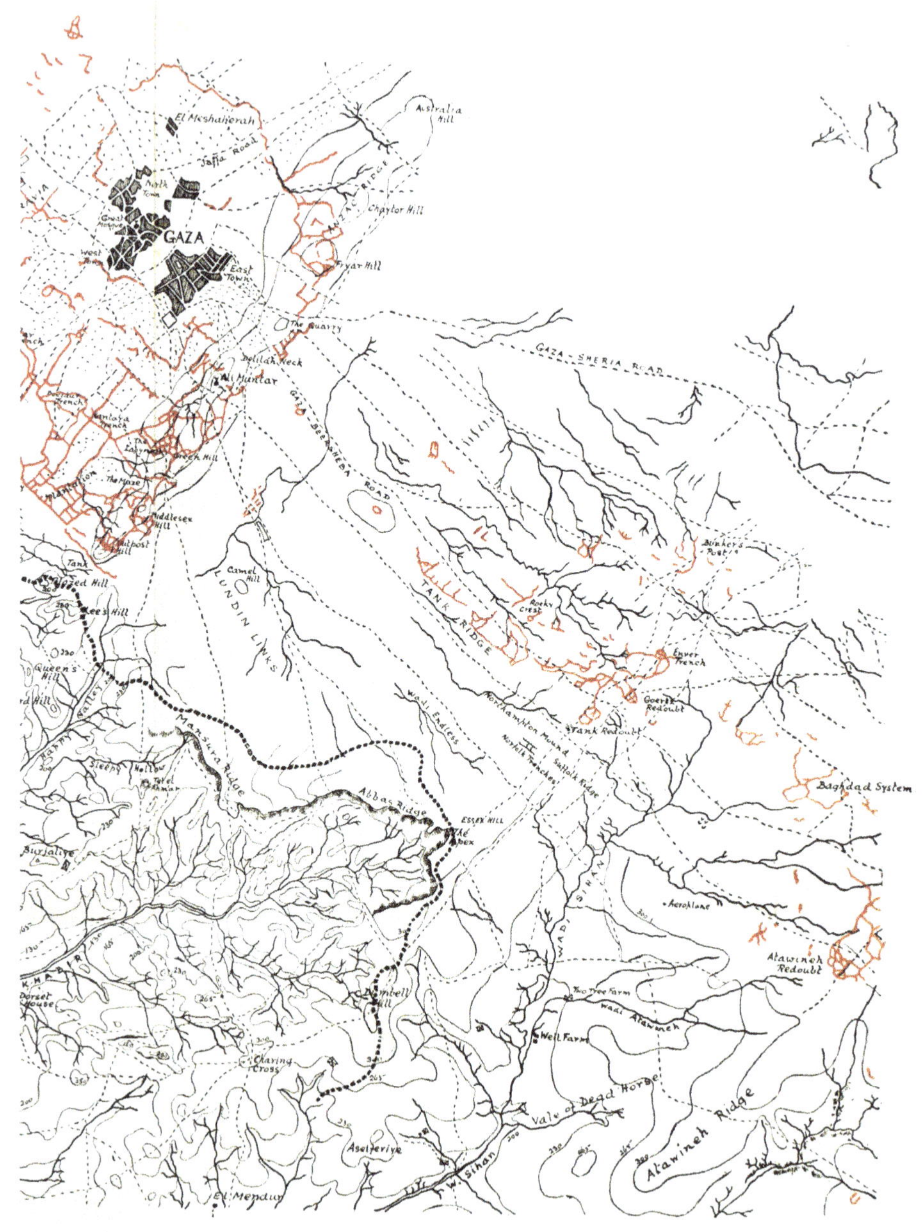


To face Chapter VI.

CHAPTER VI.

# THE FIRST BATTLE OF GAZA.

N the darkness of the early hours of the morning of March 26th, we were awakened by the cavalry making their way, accompanied by their batteries, down the slope towards the Wadi. There was a thick fog, which made their rôle a very difficult one in a country with no roads and broken by deep gullies and rocky hills. After an hour or more the sound of the last hoof and the crunch of the last wheel died away in the fog. Still no sound. Day broke, and it was thicker than ever. We knew that the infantry had started, but it was evident that they had not yet become engaged. We followed the tracks of the cavalry through the green corn and halted in the Wadi near Sheikh Nebhan. The mules enjoyed themselves on the green barley, we on that famous thirst producer, bully beef. Several armoured cars arrived and required some help in getting across the deep sand in the bed of the Wadi, but all were got across and disappeared to the N.E. After a short halt—too short for breakfast—we crossed and followed the Wadi Nukhabir (a branch of the Ghuzzi) in the same direction. It looked like the main attack being from the right, with the Essex Brigade to finish off the job—if the Turks from Beersheba didn't get there first. There was still no sound of a battle. We left the Wadi, turned north and halted on the south side of the El Burjali Ridge.

It was now 10 o'clock and the attack started on our left, on the other side of the ridge. The Turkish gunners got busy. Enemy planes swooped above us though at a considerable height. We appeared to be weak in the air, but our planes were probably busy elsewhere. The enemy searched our slope of the ridge with shrapnel, which burst very high, but made it advisable to get into a gully close by. Here we were just getting tea served out for breakfast when we were ordered to move forward again, still keeping to the right of the ridge. There was still considerable shrapnel fire and we followed the bed of the Nukhabir. It was heavy going in the sand and the heat was intense. There were constant short halts and the hours wore wearily away, but everything appeared to be going well, at any rate the attack was evidently progressing, if slowly. Eventually we came in sight of the steep escarpment of the Mansura Ridge, about a thousand yards to the north. The ridge is really the edge of a level plateau, about 4,000 yards wide, which ran right up to the main enemy position. The battle still raged on our left, but we could see nothing of the fire fight. The enemy continued to shell the Wadi, and we continued on our way by platoons. The leading platoon of "A" Company was caught by a shell which wounded Willmott, the Company Commander, in the head, severely wounded C.S.M. White and Chester, the platoon commander, and caused several other casualties among the rank and file. It also killed several of the Lewis gun mules. The guns and ammunition were off loaded and brought on by hand. Poor Chester died the next day, mourned by officers and men alike. He was never a barrack-square soldier, but probably had more brains than anyone else in the Battalion, having had a brilliant career at Eton, which promised great things—alas, never to be realised. A little hesitating in his manner and careless in his outward appearance, he had nevertheless the heart of a lion and a true sympathy for his men which earned him alike their affection and their esteem.

The Essex gunners were busy behind the ridge, taking on the Turkish batteries with rapid fire and keeping the enemy's heads down; but the range was considerable and visibility poor; as far as I can remember only one battery was in action at this point, and my impression was that we were somewhat weak in artillery on this flank. But a Battalion commander's view of the game is very limited, and doubtless other batteries were "pulling their weight." Certainly this one was wasting no time. General Dallas's headquarters were on the edge of the plateau a few hundred yards in front of the guns, and I could see him anxiously scanning the country to the north through his glasses. With him was Brigadier-General Marriott-Dodington. The Brigade was lying in wait just behind the guns.

About 4 o'clock Wright, the Brigade Major, came galloping back from the ridge. The radiant expression on his face told pretty plainly what his orders were before he delivered them. "The Brigadier wishes to see C.O.'s and Adjutants at once; they are going to put us in."

The orders were very simple. The information was that the 53rd Division's attack only wanted a little additional impetus to complete the capture of the main enemy position. The probability was that the mere threat of attack from this flank by a whole Brigade would make up the enemy's mind to surrender the whole ground. The 4th and 5th Essex were told off for the firing line, each finding their own supports. The 4th were given the right, the 5th the left. The peak of Ali el Muntar marked the limit of the frontage on the right, the sandy hill on which was the "Labyrinth" marked the left; while on the right slope of the "Green Hill" stood a solitary tree which was the point of direction for the inner flanks, dividing the frontage into two equal parts. The exact position of the enemy was unknown and no trenches were visible; they probably ran along the low ground at the foot of the slopes. The distance to the tree was made 4,000 yards. The ground appeared to be perfectly level and open. It was covered as far as could be seen with coarse thin grass. The attack was to be pushed home at the quickest possible pace and the Turks turned out. It was exactly like the "attack" we had practised so many times on Mousehold Heath at Norwich, and the "brecks" at Drayton. The 6th Essex were to follow in support. The 7th was to remain at Divisional Headquarters in reserve.

This sort of scheme didn't require much explaining and no time was lost in getting under way. The Battalion was disposed in four lines—"C" and "D" Companies (Colvin and Wilson) formed the first three lines distributed in depth, "A" and "B" (Gould and Bacon), and Battalion Headquarters making up the fourth. The advance commenced in lines of platoons in fours, the Lewis gun and ammunition mules with their platoons. As soon as the little spurts of dust shewed that we were within long rifle range the mules were off loaded and moved off to the left into some more or less sheltered ground, and the platoons in succession split into sections in file. Then as effective ranges were reached the leading sections extended into lines of skirmishers at three paces interval, covering the whole front—and so on. It was an absolute drill-book attack; and it went like clockwork. Direction, line, and intervals were perfectly kept. Platoon and section commanders gave their orders as coolly as on parade: "Steady on the left," "Keep your three paces." No troops could have been steadier, although the rifle fire was becoming brisk and several casualties occurred. Wink formed an aid post in a hole in ground, and the stretcher bearers, following in rear, lost no time in getting the wounded back.

Then the machine guns started a cross fire from both flanks; men fell thick and fast; and still they went on, utterly regardless of anything else but "getting there." This was all I was destined to see, as I was either picked off or ran into a chance shot at long range. The bullet, which went through my thigh, did not hurt me; but it stopped me, and I could only lie there in the open and watch them as they disappeared in the dust and smoke. The fire became more and more intense. Could they live through it? One thing I knew—they would never turn their heads. Pte. George Buers, my faithful batman, applied the field-dressing and bound up my wound, quite indifferent to the bullets which fell thick around us and whistled and whined past our ears. The 6th Essex came following steadily on. My friend Alexander, their 2nd in command, passed me. "How are the 5th going?" I said. "Oh, top-hole" he replied, and swung on gaily, to meet his death in the open, like the gallant soldier that he was. Corpl. Smith, of the signal section, came back to say the line was all used up and what was he to do? I could only tell him to get on to Brigade H.Q. and ask for more. He walked up again,

BEHIND THE MANSURA RIDGE, MARCH 26, 1917.
THE BRIGADE MOVING UP TO THE ATTACK.

*To face page 68.*

following his wire, very worried about that, but apparently about nothing else. He was reported missing the next day, and I afterwards heard that he was badly wounded and died, poor fellow, in Turkish hands.

The deadly monotony of the machine gun fire went on, but I could hear that our Lewis guns were firing pretty continuously too. At last I heard a cheer—and then another and another,—and I knew that victory was won. Elated as I was by that cheer, it made me feel strangely small when I heard it, as those splendid fellows swept over the barbed wire and into the enemy's trenches—while I lay on the ground with my head in a hole, which I had scooped with my hands to save my poor old carcase. Well, there was nothing else I could do, so Buers and I started on our slow progress back to Brigade H.Q. and the dressing station. It was quite dark before we got back. I saw Wright, the Brigade Major, who told me the position was taken and was being consolidated. Water and ammunition were sent up, and a party of volunteers, consisting of grooms, cooks, and other employed men under Bond, the padré, were working like niggers to get the wounded brought in. The night was so dark and the distance so great that the work was most laborious, but they never stopped until well after daylight. Dear old "Massa" Johnson, the 4th Essex padré, was equally in defatigable, but the supply of stretchers was totally inadequate.

As the wounded began to arrive from the front line I heard the news. My old and tried friend, John Heron, died on the field—the most loyal and unselfish second in command that any C.O. ever had. His faithful batman, Hammond, tended him to the last under a murderous fire. The gallant young Harvey Capron, keenest and helpfulest of adjutants, fell within 20 yards of the position, shot through the heart. "Isn't this magnificent?" he had shouted, in his joy of battle, to Colvin just before he fell. His friend, Maxwell Browne, knowing himself to be mortally wounded, told the stretcher bearers first to get in those there was a chance of saving, and died alone in his glory, out there under the stars. Poor young Jack Bartley, whom I had known from a baby—"Jock" as his pals called him in the mess, where he had so often delighted us with that magnificent voice of his—fell gallantly leading his platoon to victory. Edmunds, of Broomfield, a comparatively recent arrival, met his death in the same way. Of Gould, Beard, and Oscar Wilson nothing was known. They are now known to have been killed. Never again would they set the mess in a roar—"Ticker" Gould with his quaint impersonations, Beard and little Oscar in their inimitable sketches of the "rabbit catcher and his boy." Brave, cheerful spirits! In death they were not divided. . . .

It was a heavy night for me as I lay in that crowded dressing station amidst the cries of sorely wounded men, and thought of all the Battalion had lost. I had not then heard of the heavy toll of those wonderful N.C.O.'s and men who shared fully with their officers the glory of that day. Among them were Sergt. H. E. Kemble, my orderly-room-sergeant, who had begged himself into the front line from the base, exchanging his duties there for the work of the Battalion " Orderly Room " in the field; Sergts H. Hafts, Mann and Jeayes, and Corpls. Rainbird, P. R. Humphries, H. Stock, J. Murray and F. Hart, good section leaders all, and L./Corpl. F. J. Rolph. The total casualties of the Battalion, including a few on the 27th, were 18 officers, and 340 N.C.O.'s and men. The casualties of the 4th Essex on our right were even heavier than ours. Their C.O., Lt.-Col. E. J. Jameson, D.S.O., was got back to the dressing station badly wounded and died the next day. Everyone who had seen him in the action testified to his sublime courage.

Brigade H.Q., who were close by, told me later in the evening that the Battalion was firmly established on the key position.

Early the next morning I was surprised to receive a visit from Wilson, upon whom the command of the Battalion had devolved. He confirmed all I had heard, but added the astounding fact that during the night they had been ordered to evacuate the position. He said the Turks were apparently completely disorganised, and that they could be heard rushing about in Gaza in the greatest confusion. He could not imagine why the Brigade had been ordered back. The Turks had made no attempt to counter attack and patrols had pushed on to the outskirts of the town without encountering opposition. More extraordinary still, the Brigade was going over the same ground again and were starting in about an hour's time. The Battalion was reorganised, the men were " seeing red," and quite convinced of their superiority over the Turk. The higher command evidently were equally convinced; otherwise they would not have committed the Battalion to another engagement after having lost 18 officers (including the whole of Headquarters) and nearly 50 per cent. of its strength in casualties. What happened on March 27th I shall leave Wilson to tell in his own words. I never knew until long afterwards. The whole thing was a mystery to me at the time, and much of it remains so to this day.

The sun crept higher in the heavens and the enemy began to shell the dressing station. This was startling, but what was more startling was the fact that the fire was coming from an entirely new direction—not from Gaza, but from nearly due east.

As I afterwards learned, the enemy were already in occupation of the Skeikh Abbas ridge, from which the remainder of our (54th) Division had withdrawn, according to orders, during the night.

THE BATTALION IN ACTION IN THE ATTACK, MARCH 26, 1917.
Ali El Muntar is the highest point on the horizon; Green Hill is on its left

*To face page 70.*

Casualties were being removed with painful slowness, and all cases who could possibly walk were told to clear as best they could. Evidently it was no good stopping where we were; wounded men were being killed by shrapnel as they lay in the open. The doctors were working heroically through it all, but it seemed only too probable that the enemy before long would be walking into the dressing station. Frank Bacon, with a shattered elbow, and myself, decided that we could do no good by waiting to be knocked out or taken prisoners, and we started on our painful journey on foot to the Wadi Ghuzzi, where, we were told, there were some field ambulances. To cut a long story short we eventually found the 2/1 F. A. (East Anglian) where Lt.-Col. Watson did all he could for us. It was slow progress, but we got there before dark, and were sent back to Deir el Belah, I in a "sand cart" ambulance, Bacon on a "Camel cacolet." The latter told me afterwards that after the camel following his had had a nibble or two at his broken arm, the one he was on fell and shot him on to the ground He finished the journey on foot.

What happened to us during the next five days which elapsed before we got into comfortable beds in Cairo, is not of general interest.

Padré Bond came to see us at Deir el Belah on the 28th and told us that the Battalion was back at In Seirat, and that the whole force was withdrawn behind the Wadi Ghuzzi. The dressing station had been captured by the enemy. A New Zealand officer I met at the Field Ambulance told me that their squadrons had watered their horses near Gaza on the 26th and had completely surrounded the city. He could not imagine why they had been recalled and was quite sure that if they had been allowed to remain and if the remainder of the infantry could have been put in on March 27th, we could all have walked into the town. There is little doubt that he was right.

I recollect the first part of the journey in closed iron trucks, which were more like ovens than anything I had previously been in. I have a vivid recollection of Indian troops with kindly looks and gestures, bringing us water at one of the stops; and shall I *ever* forget the whisky and soda provided by Mavor, of the 5th, who was R.T.O. at Khan Yunus? It was the warmest whisky and soda I have ever consumed, but it was the best.

Now, while I am spending a more or less "cushy" time in Cairo, let Wilson tell the story of how the gallant 5th bore the heat and burden of the day.

CHAPTER VII.

# MARCH 26 and 27, 1917.

(BY MAJOR W. E. WILSON, D.S.O.)

E reached Mansura a few minutes before four p.m. Within a few minutes of our arrival orders came to move companies with all speed towards the place of debouchment from the basin. At the same time .Company Commanders went quickly forward to meet the Colonel, who with the Brigadier, was at the top of the ridge. To everyone's surprise orders were immediately given to carry out an attack forthwith on the Turkish positions, covering Gaza from the south-east.

The objectives, carefully pointed out by the Brigadier and the Colonel were about two miles distant. The ground from start to finish seemed smooth as a billiard table, with a gentle rise all the way—truly a *glacis* slope. There did not appear to be an inch of cover; just the short grass, still green. "C" Company (Capt. Colvin) and my Company "D" were detailed to lead the Battalion's attack.. We received our orders simultaneously with the move into position; little resistance was expected and our mission was to "put the lid on it." The advance was carried out in perfect order; never had the Battalion worked more faultlessly when in training.

Some 2,000 yards must have been traversed in this formation, when, above the sound of desultory rifle fire, the deadly "pop-pop" of machine guns was heard and the leading platoons were seen to break into lines of sections and very shortly afterwards into extended order. The hostile machine gun fire now increased in intensity and it was quickly realized that we had to advance through a severe machine gun barrage. The nature of the ground gave the Turks a perfect field of fire, of which they took full advantage. Casualties amongst our men were becoming heavy; no time, however, was wasted in searching for cover, where none was to be found. The Companies pushed on at a brisk pace, but without haste or confusion, and their bearing was faultless. It was this steady advance that saved the Battalion from complete annihilation.

"A" and "C" Companies eventually captured the Green Hill position at the point of the bayonet. "B" and "D" Companies established themselves further to the left, the major portion finding themselves at the Brown Hill, later known as the Labyrinth. When the latter two companies reached their objective it was found that the Royal Sussex, of the 53rd

Division, were holding an exposed position on the western (Gaza) side, and that they had suffered severe casualties.

A few seconds after the whole of " B " and " D " Companies were up, the Turks opened a heavy fire with 5.9's on the position. This fire came a little too late and the range was over-estimated; consequently the damage done was not great, the greatest trouble being that it destroyed all the signal wires, thus isolating " B " and " D " Companies from Battalion and Brigade Headquarters. The signallers gallantly braved the Turkish gunfire, but unfortunately could not regain touch, owing to the fact that practically all the Battalion signallers were out of action.

Communication being thus cut off, Cpl. A. E. Ruffle volunteered to get into touch with Headquarters—a deed which required no little pluck, in view of the fact that the Turk's artillery and machine gun fire were intense. He returned some two hours later, with the news that Capt. Colvin was established on the Green Hill to our right and that he could not find Battalion Headquarters. As dusk approached " B " and " D " Companies took over the line held by the Royal Sussex, which Regiment had suffered very seriously, having lost amongst others its Commanding Officer.

Not having received any information and being quite in the dark with regard to the movements of Headquarters, Bateman and I went back to Brigade Headquarters, collecting all possible stray mules, etc., in order to return with water and ammunition. On arrival at Brigade Headquarters about 9 p.m. I was informed of the heavy casualties the Battalion had suffered. The Colonel had been wounded and I was informed that I was temporarily in command, and that I must meet the Brigadier on the Green Hill at midnight, to discuss the best means of withdrawal, which seemed already to have been decided upon. On my way back I visited Colvin on the Green Hill position and I then saw what a strong one it was, the Turks, in addition to the ordinary wire entanglements, having still further protected the position by pits some four feet deep by six feet wide, filled with barbed wire. " A " and " C " Companies must have wrought havoc with the bayonet, the ground being literally covered with Turkish corpses, their white uniforms shewing up strongly in the moonlight. Undoubtedly " A " and " C " Companies had borne the brunt of the attack. I then returned to " B " and " D " Companies, placed Deakin in command, and informed them of the decision to retire, which caused intense disappointment. I also met Finn, who, with his platoon, had advanced up to a stone hut, which was midway between the Green Hill and the Labyrinth, and up to which a rough track led from Mansura. He and his batman were the only two left with a whole skin. This will shew the intensity of the Turkish machine gun fire.

It was pretty evident that we had the Turks beat ; standing on the Brown Hill we could plainly hear the rumble of wheels and the hub-bub of excitement rising from the town. The Turks were undoubtedly withdrawing with all the speed they could, and our patrols encountered no opposition, although they penetrated almost to the town itself. At midnight the Brigadier, Colonel Bowker (of the 6th), and I met on the Green Hill, and orders were given for the withdrawal to start immediately, the withdrawing troops being ordered to collect the wounded and bring them back with them.

The latter proved an enormous task, but the men naturally worked like lions to help recover their wounded comrades.

On withdrawing from the Labyrinth it was found that the Sussex were so reduced in numbers that it was quite impossible for them to handle their own casualties. It was here that Capt. Deakin collected a party of 50 men and was responsible for bringing many of their men to safety.

The work of recovery went on all night; difficult at the best of times, it was the more so because the night was dark and the ground flat, without any recognizable feature. Worst of all, there was hardly a stretcher to be had, the wounded in nearly every case having to be carried in waterproof sheets.

It was past dawn by the time the remnants of the Battalion returned behind the outposts of the 7th Essex to Mansura.

About 6 a.m. the Brigadier sent for me and informed me that another advance would be made on the position which had been evacuated some hours before. He promised that the Battalion would be this time in reserve, that I might be able to collect my remnants.

However, our respite was short-lived, and by nine o'clock I was informed that the 4th and 5th would take up a line facing (if I remember rightly) north-east, from Mansura Ridge to Queen's Hill.

The 4th Battalion took up a short line with their right on Mansura, the 5th, being slightly stronger, continued to the left, with their left on Queen's Hill. By this time the strength of the Battalion was somewhere about 250, and I re-organised them into three companies :—

(1) "B" under Archer.

(2) "C" (and part of "D") under Colvin.

(3) "D" (remainder of "D" remnants of "A" and H.Q. details), Carlyon-Hughes.

Colvin's and Archer's Companies furnished the front line, Colvin being on the right, Archer on the left. Deakin, being now second in command, was in command of the front line.

Some 300 yards to the rear about 40 men with some Lewis guns were in support. Another few hundred yards away, I kept the remaining men, oddments of H.Q., "A" Co., etc., about 30 to 40 men in all.

Throughout the day, except for desultory Turkish shrapnel fire, things were more or less peaceful. During the forenoon many stragglers found their way through the line, amongst them men of the 6th and 7th Essex, who had been captured and released by the Turks, who had deprived them of footwear and clothing.

During the morning I felt uncertain as to the whereabouts of troops on my left. Although some troops of the 53rd Division had certainly been there earlier in the day, I could get no reliable information as to their movements, and I felt uneasy as to the wide gap between my flank and the sea. As the afternoon wore on, it became apparent that the Battalion's flank was in the air, and, realising this to be the weak spot in my line, I ordered my supports, with their Lewis guns, to move there about 5 p.m.

From that hour until dark perfect stillness reigned—it seemed almost unreal. It must have been between 7 and 8 that a terrific fire was suddenly opened on our left, the exposed flank, and along the whole front. This continued for some ten minutes and then died down.

This attack on the Battalion's left was delivered by a considerable number of Turks—it was estimated at about 200. They approached to within calling distance of our line, and were at first mistaken for some of our own troops who had found some difficulty in withdrawing earlier in the day. Many were dressed in our service dress, evidently robbed from our dead.

These Turks were calling out repeatedly "Essex, Essex!" and it was a lucky chance that one of their number, evidently over anxious to impress, called "Royal Essex!" This confirmed our suspicions, and without more ado we opened fire. Without cover and also at short range, the Turks had no chance, and they turned and ran, leaving over 100 casualties.

When the attack started I was talking to the Brigadier, whose Headquarters were hard by. On hearing the fire he ordered me to move immediately, and, if possible, to counter-attack with the bayonet. In a few moments I had my remaining men under way, and we dashed forward towards our left. The firing was very heavy, and the Turks opened up a hot fire along our front, with the evident intention of supporting their attack on the left.

Owing to the darkness the Turkish fire was high, and it was only due to this fact that we reached the front line without casualties.

By the time we reached the front line the short and sharp engagement was practically over. I met Deakin, who reported the cause of the firing, and returned and reported to the Brigadier.

It was then that he confirmed the rumour which I had previously heard, that the whole attacking force was to withdraw to the other side of the Wadi Ghuzzi that night and I received orders that the Battalion should withdraw from their present line about 10.30 and be ready to move with Brigade at 11 o'clock.

I returned and issued the necessary orders for withdrawal, and at the appointed hour we moved from our position and collected together at Mansura. Major Wright supervised our withdrawal; his help was most invaluable and will be remembered by those who had the conduct of the Battalion.

The withdrawal to the place of concentration (Mansura), was without note, except that a battalion somewhere to the left opened rapid fire, to which, as far as our front was concerned, the Turks did not reply.

It must have been about midnight when we started on our march back to In Seirat. As might be expected, the march was slow, owing to the difficult country to be traversed, the halts were many, and on these occasions it was hard to keep the men awake.

Some two hours must have gone by when the column came to a halt for some minutes. I regarded it as one of the many which had already taken place; but as the moments went by I wondered what the cause might be, and went forward to find out. I got as far as the 4th Essex, only to find that their rear company had lost touch, and that we were quite left behind.

I was not certain of the direction of the Brigade's line of march, nor even of the whereabouts of our position, and after careful consideration I decided that it would be best to halt till dawn.

A few minutes reconnaissance showed that we were close by the Wadi Ghuzzi. I moved all the detached column into it, and waited till daylight.

By daylight I found that we were close to Sheikh Nebhan, almost at the same spot from which we had started so lightheartedly 48 hours before.

At once I got the Battalion and other details on the move, and after a weary march across the hills we found ourselves with the Brigade once more, much to the relief of the Brigadier.

On arrival I found that Finn with about 20 men was missing, but after an anxious two hours he marched in.

. . . . . . . .

During the operations above described and the subsequent re-organisation, Wilson commanded the Battalion, with Deakin as second in command. Finn was appointed Adjutant, a position he held and filled with success until the end of the campaign, and the companies were commanded by Carlyon-Hughes, Leonard Gray, Portway and Colvin, the latter retaining his old company—my old company too, I am proud to say—which had sustained the heaviest casualties of any.

The immediate awards for the first battle of Gaza were :—D.S.O. : Capt. (temp. Major) W. E. Wilson ; M.C. : 2nd Lieut. (temp. Capt.) A. Colvin and Lieut. H. S. Calverley ; D.C.M. : Sergt. W. Cooper, C.Q.M S. J. E. V. Coote, Sergt. H. Reed, and Corpl. T. C. Main (R.A.M.C. attached) ; M.M. : Sergt. E. White and Pte. E. A. G. Jordan. Subsequent awards appeared in the *Gazette* for services in the same action :—M.C. : Capt. E. B. Deakin, 2/Lieut. J. F. Finn ; Mentioned in Dispatches : 2/Lieut. J. L. French. The awards were well deserved, and were much too limited to allow of many acts of gallantry being officially recognised.

Wilson was left in command in very difficult and critical circumstances, and the way in which he conducted the operations of the 27th, particularly the retirement during the ensuing night, displayed rare powers of leadership. Colvin shewed splendid dash and resolution in the attack and how he escaped unhurt was little short of a miracle.

Calverley fought like a young lion. Although wounded in the leg he carried on with his Lewis guns until the position was taken, afterwards organising his guns for the consolidation and busying himself with the wounded, some of whom he saved from prowling Bedouins, making three of the latter prisoners. He only left for the Dressing Station when ordered to do so by his company commander.

French also did excellent work in a very hot part of the line, afterwards doing a very useful reconnaissance in advance of the captured works, and on the 27th successfully beating off a Turkish counter-attack.

Finn displayed great coolness and initiative throughout the two days' fighting. He sent in an extremely valuable report on the situation to the Brigade Commander after the attack on the first day, and on the second day gave Wilson great assistance.

Deakin shewed complete disregard of danger in the attack, and after the withdrawal went back and was responsible for bringing in many wounded. His leadership and resource were also conspicuous on the second day.

Womersley did splendid work directing signal communications, under the most difficult conditions imaginable, and in spite of being wounded in two places.

Pte. William Fell shewed great gallantry in going out on a flank alone and locating an enemy machine gun which was temporarily holding up the advance of his company. The Lewis guns engaged the enemy and covered the further advance. Fell afterwards died of his wounds.

Pte. Tom Davidson, when his platoon was held up by machine gun fire from a hut on his flank, got the fire of his section on to the loopholes and continued to cover the advance of his platoon and to encourage those around him after being wounded severely himself. He was left on the field and was not among those brought back during the night.

Lance-Corpl. A. E. Ruffle's good work has already been referred to. He also made several journeys forward to bring back wounded after the position had been evacuated.

Sergt. H. N. Rand, on the 27th, was in command of an escort to some machine guns which were covering the withdrawal. After the guns had withdrawn he was captured by the oncoming Turks. He bayoneted two of them, but was knocked unconscious by a third. Afterwards recovering consciousness he succeeded in making his escape in the dark, and in reaching the Battalion. Curiously enough, when in command of a patrol some three months after, he picked up his own notebook, which had been taken from his pocket by the Turks.

Pte. Oscar Rand, during the advance, was detailed to bring up ammunition to his Lewis gun across the open and kept it supplied single handed by tying the end of one of his puttees to the canvas carriers and pulling them along the ground. The gun was eventually knocked out, but he recovered it after dark.

Lance-Corpl. Bert Fenner continued to fight his Lewis gun after being hit three times in the arms, eventually collapsing from loss of blood.

Pte. Edward Jemson displayed great courage in crossing a beaten zone several times and getting many wounded to a place of safety.

Corpl. N. C. Cunningham, of the Signal Section, succeeded in laying a fresh line to Brigade Headquarters and in establishing a Battalion office under continuous machine gun fire.

The above are only a few instances, brought to notice by superiors, of the gallantry and resource shewn by all ranks in this battle. A far greater number will never be recorded.

A wire from Divisional Headquarters on the 29th contained the following :—

" Following from C.G.S. begins—Chief wishes you to convey to all ranks under your command his great appreciation of their gallant conduct during the operations of the last two days. He wishes to congratulate 53rd Division and General Dodington's Brigade on the courage and determination with which the attack on the Ali Muntar position was carried out."

The Brigadier circulated a copy of the following letter from the G.O.C., 53rd Division, to whom we were attached for the operations :

MY DEAR DODINGTON,

A line to thank you and all your Brigade for the gallant part you and they played in completing the capture of the Ali Muntar position on the 26th inst., in holding it and effecting the retirement. It was great work, and the pity is the unavoidable evacuation of what he had won on the 26th.

Yours very sincerely,

A. G. DALLAS.

THE TOP OF THE HILL, ALI EL MUNTAR.
(Taken on March 26, 1917.)

To face page 78.

The Brigadier issued the following Order on the 28th:—"Message to all ranks of 161st Infantry Brigade and 161st M.G. Coy.—I desire to express to you all my respectful and most grateful thanks for your conduct in the operations which have just taken place. (Sgd.) M. Dodington, Brigadier-General, Commanding 161st Infantry Brigade."

A letter I received from General Dodington on April 4th touches a more personal and intimate note, but I am permitted to publish the following extracts from it:—

MY DEAR GIBBONS,

You don't know how delighted I was to get your letter. Yes, Wilson will be retained in command and he is doing so well. The regiment is fit and ready again and when you come back you will find it the same as when you took it into action on the 26th March. I tried to reach Officers and men with my message and I have since been round to each unit and told them the true unvarnished tale of the whole two days. You do not know what I have felt about the Brigade; the attack on the 26th was absolutely beautiful, such precision, such drill, and yet such dash. Will you do me a great favour? You will doubtless see a lot of our wounded, both officers and men, while you are away, and if you would give them my message I should be so grateful. My fear is that they should not know that all they did was appreciated. I cannot say enough for the Brigade. . . . How I wish I could have seen the wounded myself, but, of course, except those I came across on the field I had no opportunity. What surprised me more than anything else the other day was the resource and skill of the officers, and in *very* many cases the N.C.O.'s. Some day when you come back (the sooner the better), I will tell you many things which I cannot now. I can tell you, however, that we had the Turks *stone cold* in Gaza on the night of the 26th and could have bagged the lot if only those higher placed had known as we knew. We had them too on the 27th if only certain action had been taken. . . . You don't know how I long to thank you all personally, you and all the others who have worked and helped to make the Brigade what it was the other day, and is still, despite its losses. I trust and hope you and very many others will come back soon to us; we want you all. There was much work done by the Brigade on the two days besides the attack on the Green Hill. Please remember me to all my officers and men, all those you see who fought so well, and who have done so much. When making some recommendations the other day I felt inclined to throw them all out, as how can one select when *all* did so well? . . . Come back soon.

Yours sincerely,
M. DODINGTON.

The letter was thoroughly characteristic of our beloved Brigadier. Who wouldn't want to "come back soon" to such a commander?

A full account of the battle of March 26th and 27th is given in Sir A. Murray's official despatch, from which I may be forgiven for quoting the following extracts:—"The G.O.C. 53rd Division called on the Brigade of the 54th Division (Brigadier-General W. Marriott Dodington) which had been placed at his disposal, to take this position. The Brigade responded with the greatest gallantry in face of a heavy fire and after hard fighting it pushed home its attack with complete success, so that when darkness fell the whole of Ali Muntar position had been carried and a footing gained on the ridge to a point about 1,200 yards north-east of that position."

Of the 27th the C. in C. writes :—"From this point they directed artillery fire on the rear of our positions on the Mansura Ridge. Our positions were also exposed to heavy artillery fire from the north. Nevertheless, though tired and ill-supplied with water, the 53rd and 54th Divisions remained throughout the day staunch and cheerful, and perfectly capable of repulsing with heavy losses to the enemy any Turkish counter-attacks."

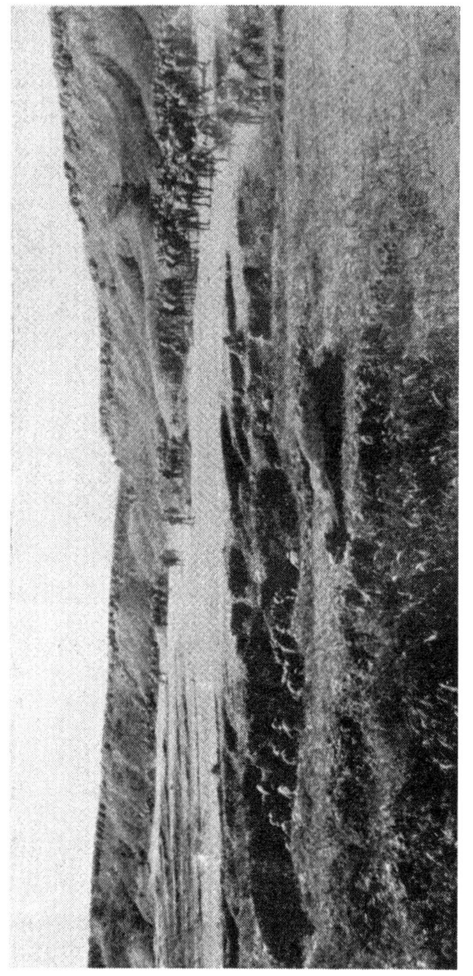

BEHIND THE SHEIKH ABBAS RIDGE, 2nd BATTLE OF GAZA,
APRIL 19, 1917.

*To face page 81.*

CHAPTER VIII.

# THE SECOND BATTLE OF GAZA.

HEN I got back to the front on April 19th, I found a big engagement in progress. Everybody had high hopes that the cruel luck of the 26th March was going to be reversed. More guns had been sent up, Tanks were being used for the first time, and it was evident that a determined bid was being made for the possession of Gaza.

The Battalion had left a "nucleus" at In Seirat consisting of Deakin, Portway, Miller and Kinnersley with 69 other ranks. The battle had begun on the 17th when the Sheikh Abbas–Mausura–Kurd Hill position was taken by the 52nd and 54th Divisions with very little opposition. The position was consolidated on the following day and on the morning of the 19th I found the Battalion dug in on the Sheikh Abbas Ridge. It was very weak but fit and cheery as usual. Wilson was in command and the Brigadier wouldn't hear of my relieving him until the battle was over—in fact he ordered me, politely but firmly, back to In Seirat.

The Turks had received heavy reinforcements and had immensely strengthened their positions, especially to the south-east, in which direction a strong series of work covered the Gaza–Beersheba Road. If the cavalry were to envelop Gaza as they had done on March 26th, the infantry would have to break through that line first. This was the heavy task imposed upon the 54th Division, with the cavalry of the Desert Column and the Imperial Camel Corps protecting its right flank. On its left was the 52nd Division, attacking along the ridge. Still further to the left the 53rd Division advanced along the sandy country to take the Samson Ridge–Sheikh Ajlin line extending to the sea. This position was taken in face of considerable opposition; and the 52nd Division had made good Lees Hill, and had also taken, and retaken, after it had been recaptured by the enemy—Outpost Hill, but it could get no further. The 54th had progressed considerably in their attack on the Tank Ridge position to the south-east of the town, enfiladed by very heavy fire from Kh. Sihan—where the Camel Corps were held up—and from Middlesex Hill, which had defied the efforts of the 52nd Division on our left. Of the few tanks, one had been knocked out in the first advance, another on Outpost Hill, and another on the "Tank Redoubt" in which the 8th Hampshires had actually gained a footing, suffering enormous casualties, as also did the 4th Northamptonshires and the Norfolks. The Commander-in-Chief in his official despatch, says "The 54th Division, on the right of the main attack, had progressed, in spite of determined opposition and heavy casualties, as far as was possible until a further advance of the 52nd Division should prevent the exposure of its left flank. Reports received from the 54th Division stated that the situation was satisfactory and that no help was required in order to enable the ground gained to be held until further progress by the 52nd Division should render practicable a renewal of the advance." He adds "I should like to state here my appreciation of the great skill with which General Hare handled his fine Division throughout the day."

In the evening the Brigade on Outpost Hill was forced to evacuate the Hill. Orders were received to consolidate the ground won during the day in readiness for a resumption of the attack at dawn. The total casualties had amounted to some 7,000.

The Higher Command decided that night that the projected attack on the following day did not offer sufficient chances of success to justify the very heavy casualties which would be involved, and that the only thing to do was to entrench on the line now held and wait for a more favourable opportunity; an opportunity which could hardly arise until the army had been substantially reinforced.

The enemy made no general counter-attack and all his local attacks were easily repulsed.

So for the second time the luck had been against us, and the gallant efforts of the troops failed to reap the reward they deserved. But although we had had to taste defeat, it was consoling to know that we had earned the good opinion of our chief. Sir Archibald Murray's concluding remarks in his despatch contain these words. "In conclusion I should like to place on record my appreciation of the magnificent work done by all the fighting troops before Gaza. No praise can be too high for the gallantry and stedfastness of the cavalry, infantry, artillery, Royal Flying Corps, and all other units which took part in the two battles. Particular commendation is due to the infantry. The 52nd, 53rd, and 54th Divisions, though actively engaged for over a year in the Sinai Peninsula, had not, since their re-organisation after the operations in the Dardanelles, been able to show how they had improved out of all knowledge in training and discipline and in all that goes to make up an excellent fighting organisation. Under severe trial they have now given ample proof of the finest soldierly qualities."

CHAPTER IX.

# TRENCH WARFARE.

HE position consolidated extended from the sea near Sheikh Ajlin, over Samson's Ridge, across the Happy Valley, in front of "Blazed" and "Lees" Hills, and along the edge of the plateau by Mansura to the apex at Sheikh Abbas, a frontage of about 14,000 yards. From there it turned south to "Dumbell Hill," and beyond.

I took over the command on the 21st, on which day the nucleus also joined up and the 6th Essex took over the right sector of our line. On the 22nd the relief was completed by the 5th Bedfordshires taking over the left sector and the Battalion moved at night to Dumbell Hill, where we relieved the 3rd Battalion of the Imperial Camel Corps, which had suffered heavy casualties. In rear of the hill were several deep gullies which formed a veritable network of covered communications, all now quite dry with sandy beds, by which pack animals could move with ease, though the tortuous courses of the gullies made the journey from the dumps a long one and the many branches and tributory gullies made it easy to lose one's way. The soil was a hard clay which appeared to have shrunk with the heat, making it full of huge cracks, the happy hunting ground of scorpions, centipedes, and evil smelling black "blind worms." The heat was stifling.

Dumbell Hill was a peaceful enough spot and enemy shelling was nothing to speak of, movement in the open in small groups attracted no undue attention, and work was carried out by day.

The enemy could be seen entrenching 5,000 yards away at the Attawineh Redoubt on the Beersheba Road. On our left front, in front of the apex at Sheikh Abbas was Tank Redoubt, so called from the derelict tank, perched high on the ridge, which parties of the 8th Hampshires had actually reached on April 19th, supported by the tank, only to meet a common fate, whilst in front were two minor features which marked the limit of the advance of the Northamptonshires and the Norfolks, whose dead lay very thick on the slopes, as if they had been washed up on a shelving beach by a high tide and left there by the ebb. Between us and Attawineh ran the broad and fertile valley of the Wadi Sihan; dotted with small homesteads. The Imperial Camel Corps and the cavalry had fought a great fight in this valley wide on the flank of the infantry attack. A large number of dead camels polluted the plain and when the wind lay from the east,

Dumbell Hill was anything but salubrious. Still further to the right was a branch valley running east, which was dubbed with grim humour the "Vale of Dead Horse." We threw out a line of outposts in front by day and night, but beyond getting a chance shot at the enemy cavalry patrols in the dusk of the morning they had little excitement. The Turkish cavalry were always out before daylight and it was interesting to watch their patrols at work. Our own mounted patrols usually started later and covered the same ground, pushing well forward and frequently coming under rifle fire from the enemy's outposts. In comparison they appeared to me more enterprising than the Turks, but, perhaps, not quite so "canny" in their methods.

One day we saw a whole battalion of Turks harvesting barley beyond Attawineh. A tempting target, but too distant for our guns, apparently, for they were not molested.

On May 3rd Horton, with an outpost patrol, captured two Turkish infantry men at daybreak. They had apparently lost their way and didn't appear to lament the fact that the war was over as far as they were concerned. They belonged to the 167th Regiment of the 53rd Division. The same day Lieut.-General Sir Philip Chetwode, commanding Eastern Force, inspected the position held by the Battalion.

On May 6th we were ordered to move by night to take over the centre of the new 161st Brigade line on the Sheikh Abbas Ridge. It was very bright moonlight and the enemy aeroplanes were indulging in some night flying. Several units happened to be on the move and one plane swooped low over the Royal West Kents and dropped a bomb among them, inflicting 40 casualties. We managed to escape attention by keeping on the dark ground, off the beaten tracks. Our camel transport, with their metal water "Fantassis," which flashed in the moonlight in a most annoying manner, moved separately. We were relieved on Dumbell Hill by the dismounted Fife and Forfarshire Yeomanry, now called the 14th Battalion Black Watch, and took over the new line from the 5th Bedfords. The new line was in the plain, well in front of the escarpment, with which it was connected by three long communication trenches. By day all except a thin line for observation purposes were withdrawn behind the steep escarpment and made themselves fairly comfortable. Two small officer's patrols were sent out in front nightly, frequently bringing back articles of equipment, pay-books, maps and identity discs from the dead, who, in nearly every case, were found stripped of all their outer clothing and their boots. The Turks appeared to do little patrolling but fire was frequently drawn from their outposts, which were generally found a little in front of their wire.

On the night of May 11th a patrol under C.S.M. Coote, located an enemy patrol with a machine gun, advancing on "Essex Hill," which was held by a picquet of the 6th Essex. After a sharp

BATTALION HEADQUARTERS AT SHEIKH ABBAS.

*To face page 84.*

little engagement, in which the 6th Essex picquet took part, the enemy patrol withdrew to the east.

On the 13th the enemy tried to raid Essex Hill with what appeared to be a Company. They found both 5th and 6th Essex posts wide awake, however, and did not reach their objective. A few prisoners were taken, who stated that the raiding party were volunteers who had been promised £10 for every prisoner they took back to their lines. They did not make any money that night.

On the night of May 17th, D. Company effected the capture of 2 men of an enemy patrol. On the 18th we were relieved by the Ayr and Lanark Yeomanry and Devonshire Yeomanry Battalions and moved into support in what was called a "rest" gully. "Rest," as our men were by this time fully aware, meant digging trenches for other people instead of digging them for themselves; and the move out of the front line, which we had been occupying for the last four weeks, excited little enthusiasm.

On May 20th I had a letter from our Honorary Colonel, Field Marshall Sir Evelyn Wood, to whom I had, of course, communicated an account of the great part his Battalion had played in the first battle of Gaza. He said he had obtained the sanction of the Adjutant-General to publish my letter in the County papers, and it duly appeared, without any names or identifications, of course. The Field Marshal went on to say that he had suffered during the past hunting season from a diminished stud, but more still from bad health. In fact, that he had thought in March that he was a 'gone-er," but he was better and "hoping to live to see our Battalion again." "Please, when you get back tell them I am proud of them."

On the 25th the 54th Division moved into general reserve and the Battalion marched at 8.15 p.m. eight miles to a sandy spot not far from the mouth of the Wadi Ghuzzi, called Regents Park. Who it was who perpetrated this atrocious libel on London's green and well-watered health spot, I cannot say. Its only redeeming feature was its contiguity to the sea. We took over this area from the 5th Battalion, the Welch Regiment, and lived in it until June 12th. During this period some useful training was carried out, which, however, was somewhat interfered with by reason of having to send parties of 100 nightly, to dig in the front line trenches three miles away, which were manned by the 52nd (Lowland) Division. This proceeding afforded another definition of "rest," viz.: "Further to go to your work." Of course, nobody minded it, really, but officers and men were getting just a little bored with digging—and it was very hot. Bathing was very dangerous, owing to a very strong back-wash, and had to be confined to bobbing up and down in waist-deep water. However, a *warm* sea-bath at five in the morning was a luxury we should have raved about in England, and it deserved more appreciation that it got.

On June 12th the 54th Division relieved the 52nd in the Coastal Sector, which stretched from the sea at Skeikh Ajlin, on the left to Lees Hill inclusive on the right, a frontage of about 7,000 yards. The 161st Brigade relieved the 157th of the 52nd Division in the right sub-sector, the 5th Essex taking over from the 5th Argyle and Sutherland Highlanders, who held the salient of Lees Hill and Blazed Hill and a considerable length of the line across the Kurd Valley. The position was well organised in two lines of trenches connected by frequent communication trenches (which stood well in the hard ground) and there were some good dug-outs. There was also a most convenient dry wadi bed running laterally in rear of the whole length of the Battalion Section, in which ration, water and R.E. dumps were established, easily accessible by pack transport. Observation and field of fire were alike excellent, but the trenches on the forward slope of Blazed Hill looked very conspicuous from the front and a really heavy bombardment could easily have demolished them. They were a little over 500 yards from the enemy's front line on Outpost Hill, which was part of the same ridge, but separated by a saddle, from which started two wadis, one running to the right round our flank and down the Happy Valley, and the other round the left of Blazed Hill, breaking through the line on our left and following the Kurd Valley. The Battalion moved in lines of platoons in fours straight up the broad Kurd Valley and was met by guides from the outgoing Battalion, who led Companies straight to their posts, making the relief an easy and pleasant one. Advance parties from Companies and Battalion Headquarters had, of course, made themselves acquainted with the line. Brigade Headquarters were behind the crest of Queen's Hill, another feature of the same ridge, about a thousand yards to the rear. It had the rather rare advantage of a good view of a great part of the enemy's front line.

A very deep gully led from Brigade Headquarters to the Battalion Section and this made an excellent covered communication, whilst the lateral wadi-bed before-mentioned afforded excellent ground for inspections of reliefs, movement of ration and working parties, etc., very different from the same thing carried out in cramped and narrow trenches. Battalion Headquarters were comfortably ensconsed in the proverbial "deep dug-out" (where, according to the popular song, the Colonel could always be found) dug into the side of the gully, with orderly room and signal office close by. Sections of Brigade Machine Gun Company and Trench Mortar Battery were attached. Considerable new drafts soon began to arrive and were a welcome addition to the working and fighting strength of the Battalion, which was responsible for a line nearly a mile long as the trenches ran.

The ground in front was regularly patrolled and listening posts were established at night outside the wire. There were excellent snipers' posts and the enemy were not allowed to take any liberties.

A very unfortunate accident occurred on June 20th, when Sergt. Chapman, one of the best non-commissioned officers in the Battalion, was shot dead by one of our own sentries while accompanying Carlyon Hughes on a tour of the posts. A similar thing had happened two nights previously, when Pte. Smith, of "C" Company, was the victim. In both cases the sentries were men of new drafts and were probably a bit "jumpy"; but it was cruel luck that shots fired in the pitch dark should on each occasion have proved fatal.

The weather in July was intensely hot and the men suffered from it severely. Flies were, however, well kept down by strict attention to sanitation and the use of sprayers in

"If thine enemy hunger . . . "

TURKISH PRISONERS.

the trenches. The Turkish artillery was frequently active, varying his targets in a rather perplexing way; one never knew where he was going to start next, and a few casualties occurred. He also used some indirect machine gun fire at night —a more annoying thing even than artillery fire, as it silently swept our slopes of the hill, searching, I believe, principally for the ration convoys who had revealed themselves coming over a saddle in rear by their dust, which shewed up plainly in the extraordinarily bright moonlight. Their time table had to be altered in consequence, much to the annoyance of the Quartermaster's and transport departments. The moon was so bright that enemy working parties were more than once dispersed by well-aimed rifle fire at over 500 yards range.

During our tour on Blazed Hill we had several parties of Indian native officers, each under a British Special Service Officer, attached to us for an insight into the methods of trench warfare and routine. Each party stayed for a week. They belonged to the Hyderabad and Mysore Lancers. They were very keen and always wanting to go on patrol, at which class of work they were very good. We were at this time distributing propaganda by means of aeroplanes and night infantry patrols, for the enlightenment of the Turk, who, we had reason to believe, had a rather perverted idea of the world situation and the rights and wrongs of the war generally. All patrols were furnished with leaflets for leaving in conspicuous places close to the enemy lines. Whether as a result of our propaganda or not, I cannot say, but desertions from the enemy to our lines began to be quite frequent. One explained that he was one of a double sentry and that he walked across while his fellow sentry was asleep. Another, on being questioned as to the apparently undue number of their troops on outpost duty, explained that one of their duties was to prevent their own people from walking into our lines. Some complained of brutal treatment by non-commissioned officers, particularly towards Christians and Armenians, of whom they appeared to have considerable numbers. Another complaint was that men were allowed to purchase their discharge and immediately afterwards pressed into service again. Two Bulgarians gave valuable information about the enemy, pointing out positions of "mitrailleuses," etc. They came in early one morning and were seen in the light of the dawn by the Turks, who opened a brisk fire at them. The enemy's army was a queer mixture of real stout fighters, "pukkah" Turks—soldiers by nature and by choice, as their fathers had been before them—and every type of scallywag under the sun who had been forced into their service. They tried a little pamphleteering on their own account and one leaflet was blown into our wire which read, "Why don't you come out of your holes and fight us?" The Turk must have a poor sense of humour to indulge in such a taunt after the first two battles of Gaza. However, a few nights afterwards the 8th Hampshires raided two of their posts near the sea and claimed to have accounted for 60 of them with the bayonet alone.

Other efforts were directed by the enemy towards shaking the loyalty of the Indian Mohammedan troops—"Why do you fight against your own faith," they said. The Indians' answer was, "We and the Indian Moslems have been fighting for the Emperor of India and his predecessors for a hundred years; how long have you owed allegiance to the Emperor of Germany?"

On July 20th and again on the 27th, the 5th Bedfords, on our left, successfully raided the enemy's post on "Umbrella Hill," a pronounced salient in the enemy's line on the sand dunes. On each occasion the Turks shelled our area vigorously and we had an uncomfortable half-hour without, however, suffering more than a few casualites.

Our airmen, with new and improved machines, were rapidly gaining ascendancy in the air. They shewed extraordinary persistence and courage while spotting for our guns. After we had seen a single plane circling over the enemy for a considerable time, during which over 300 shells were fired at him and it seemed every moment that he must be brought down, a message was sent to the R.F.C., enquiring the name of the pilot. They wired back, "Lieut. F. E. Arnot" ("Fearnot").

After the successful raids on Umbrella Hill the enemy's artillery became much more active, and fired an enormous number of shells into the Battalion area, without, however, doing much damage. One long range 4.2, from the direction of Attawineh, fired an armour-piercing shell of a pattern we had not seen before. From the front they fired 77 m.m. "whiz-bangs," which frequently found the front line, but we were well dug in and the casualties were not heavy. Minenwerfer were also used from Outpost Hill—huge canisters on the end of poles, which could be distinctly seen by daylight hurtling through the air. One man from the Thaxted country remarked, "Dalled if they ain't hurling *trees* at us now!" The range was evidently a little too long for these weapons, for they seldom reached the front line—which was just as well.

On July 9th Gray was obliged to go to hospital. He had hung on longer than he should have done, but we were short of officers, and his sense of duty was always strong. It was a great grief to all ranks to hear about a month afterwards, that he had succumbed to enteric at Alexandria. Modest to a fault, without the slightest assumption of virtue or trace of "goody-goody," no man ever came nearer to my ideal of a Christian and a gentleman than Leonard Gray.

On the night of August 3rd-4th, we were relieved by the 4th Welch Regiment. Evans, our scout officer, had reconnoitred a route on the previous night and we moved in lines of platoons with all our pack transport straight back over the open up the Kurd Valley. It was bright moonlight and the enemy's trenches could be plainly seen. But there was no dust in the green-stubbled plain and we were not observed. We should have made a good target if the enemy had had a searchlight. We arrived back at Regents Park at three o'clock, moving over the saddle between "Softly" and "Heart" Hills, and skirting "Tel el Ajjul," a prominent mound near the Wadi Ghuzzi. The name means "The hill of the calf," so-called from a legend of a phantom calf, said to have been seen there by a peasant. It was a spot of some importance in ancient times and it was Saladin's camp on two occasions. A fine statue of Jupiter, 15 feet high was found here and is now at Constantinople. The Jupiter of

Gaza was known as Marnas, and the Marneion, or Temple of Gaza, stood on the site of the present Great Mosque, probably the site also of the Temple of Dagon, the scene of Samson's exploit nearly two thousand years before, and certainly the site of the Church which the Christians erected after destroying the Marneion under the energetic Bishop Porphyry, of Gaza, in 402, and which in its turn met with a similar fate at the hands of the Moslem conquerors in 634.

But to return to Regents Park. The Battalion had a couple of days *real* rest after nearly eight weeks in the front line, and on August 6th started platoon and company training. Parties also attended a very useful "consolidation" course under the R.E., and musketry was carried out on a range on the shore, firing out to sea. Owing to the specialist nature of so much of the modern infantryman's training the experiment was tried of forming the Battalion into a School of Instruction on the lines of the Army Schools, whereby all benefited by the services of the best instructors in each subject, companies and platoons being broken up for the purpose. For this class of training the experiment was certainly a success. An hour in the afternoon was, however, always given to the application, by the platoon as the fighting unit, of the methods learnt in the classes.

On the 18th the Battalion moved still further back, to the serenity of "St. James Park," there to continue its training under less comfortable conditions, but beyond the range of the Turkish guns, which occasionally lobbed a shell at Regents Park, generally into the mule lines, which were difficult to conceal from the air. I remember one shell going clean through a mule and into the sand without exploding, which was lucky for the transport men engaged in "stables," but rough on the poor mule. On the 24th we returned to Regents Park, and on the following day the Division relieved the 52nd in the coastal sector. The 5th Essex relieved the 2/4th Royal West Kent Regiment in Divisional Reserve at Marine View, on the side of a sand dune, about a thousand yards from the sea and about two miles from the front line. On the 27th we made room for the Fife and Forfar Yeomanry (229th Infantry Brigade) on the same ground. The Yeomanry were engaged in digging in the front line and on the night of August 29-30th it was decided to advance the line about 500 yards to straighten out the re-entrant between "Jones's Post" and "Fusilier Ridge," which was rather too distant from the enemy's line at the "El Arish redoubt," to attack that stronghold from, when the time should come for that operation. The Battalion furnished the wiring and covering parties for the work. The bright moon made it easier for the diggers, but not so convenient for the wiring parties, who had to work on rather prominent ground, and the enemy kept up a continuous machine gun and artillery fire throughout the night. The work was consequently interrupted, and although 1,200 yards of continuous wire entanglement were put up it had to be strengthened on a subsequent night. Four other ranks were killed, including Sergt. Mitson, of "A" Company, and five wounded, including Sergt. F. R. Wilson, who remained on duty with the covering party, after being shot in the ankle, for over an hour, until the working parties withdrew. Large digging parties were employed nightly in the front line, and cables towards the front were buried three feet in the sand. It was the beginning of the preparations for the attack which it was evident would take place before the winter; and it was also evident that this time nothing was to be left to chance.

On September 15th the Battalion relieved the 4th Essex in the front line. The position consisted of three lines, the front being the new trench, now called "Yeomanry Trench," the second being the old front line, and the third a series of strong posts capable of all-round defence. The whole of the trenches were dug in sand—not the fine sand of the Sinai Peninsula, but still sand—and entirely revetted with sand bags. Although the works were really half-breast work and half-trench, the parapet was not conspicuous when sand was banked against it, except with a low sun behind it, making a shadow, which only occurred for a very short time each day. They stood shell-fire very well indeed. Dugouts were made on the same principle, only half-underground, but gave good protection against anything but direct hits.

Work was commenced on deeper dugouts for command posts, signal offices, aid posts, etc., for the coming push, and the R.E. put in some good work. Patrolling went on as usual, but there was little doing—so much so that the higher command rather welcomed the news of a patrol encounter as tending to keep up the "offensive spirit." The Turk was by no means so enterprising as he had been and we had for all practical purposes control of No Man's Land. The enemy generally used large patrols, who did not come far from their front line. One apparently half-hearted attempt at a raid, without artillery preparation, had been crumpled up by the fire of the 4th Essex and their supporting battery long before it reached their lines a few nights before we took over. The lines were a thousand yards apart and both sides worked uninterruptedly on their front lines.

There were two ways of harassing the enemy's working parties; by fire from patrols and by occasional salvoes of shrapnel and H.E. and indirect machine gun fire. The former method left the patrols at a great disadvantage in the open and liable to be cut off; the latter occasioned a good deal of waste of ammunition, through inadequate observation, owing to the distance. An attempt was made on the night of October 5th to direct artillery fire by means of a patrol in close observation, with a telephone run out in front. At the start the plan was effective. Fire was brought to bear on large working and covering parties with success. But the patrol was a large one—two platoons—and the plan was designed to include a fight with any enemy patrols which should be sent out. The latter duly appeared, one in front and one on the right flank. The patrol was too large to manœuvre in the dark and much confused firing was the result. The officers, through no fault of their own, failed to maintain control, and it must be confessed that the platoons lost cohesion. There was nothing to be done but to withdraw and reorganize. L/Sergt. S. J. Fryatt, a most useful Lewis gun non-commissioned officer, and Pte. Woods were killed and brought back with one dead Turk and another severely wounded. Other Turks were known to have been wounded, but the result was disappointing and inconclusive. I confess to feeling very doubtful whether these deliberate invitations to the enemy to attack us on his own side of No Man's Land effected any good purpose. Men who are absolutely steady in an advance with a definite objective become jumpy and unreliable in uncertain and foggy situations in the dark, and the effect on their moral is not good. I hesitate to criticise plans made by higher authority, and do not think I could be charged with any lack of loyalty in carrying them out. But in my humble opinion it was a mistake to send out two whole platoons in the dark nearly half-a-mile from our own line, with a practical certainty of having to manœuvre to meet uncertain enemy action; and I venture to think that the object of the patrol could have been better achieved by an artillery observer and telephonist covered by a few scouts specially selected for the work. But when all is said in extenuation it was a poor show—the only poor show I have to record in this book, which is not written to hide facts, even if they are unpleasant ones, but to record them.

Small officers' patrols did excellent work in a thorough ground reconnaissance of No Man's Land, over which the Battalion might have to attack, and in getting familiar with land marks and points in the enemy's front line. The latter process was supplemented by very careful spotting by daylight, through glasses, from the front line. The Rafa redoubt looked a formidable proposition, looming high above the sandy plain, from which it rose in a steep slope destitute of cover of any kind, while the Zowaid trench could only be seen in flank and the ground behind both was a *terra incognita*, hidden from view by the ridges on which the front line ran. El Arish redoubt was a network of trenches, with a second line which commanded it and the whole of No Man's Land. More than once I caught the glint of the enemy's artillery observer's glasses as they looked into the sun in the afternoon, and our artillery made it very uncomfortable for them, getting several direct hits on their "O.P.s.' The enemy found one of ours too, a slight knoll about 100 yards from Battalion Headquarters, and one day he gave it a regular dusting with his "5.9's." His shooting was very good, fortunately for Battalion Headquarters, which received nothing worse than splinters (one of which decapitated my tooth brush which was drying in the window of my dugout). The knoll was fairly plastered and one shell blocked the exit from the O.P. The observer dug himself out, and, as he had a drink afterwards in the Headquarters mess, confessed that he had had a rather uncomfortable quarter-of-an-hour.

Talking of shell fire, we had a wire-haired fox terrier, named "Cuthbert," who would cock his ears and follow the sound of the shells as they screamed through the air, watch the burst, and immediately rush to the spot in great excitement, apparently to ascertain the cause of the explosion. He was originally very "shell shy," but completely got over it, although he never lost his interest in the proceedings.

On October 7th the Division came out of the line, being relieved by the 52nd Division in the coastal sector and the Battalion resumed its occupation of Regents Park. We moved back by the seashore. The phosphorescence of the surf was remarkable, making a continuous silvery line along the water's edge. As my horse pressed the damp sand with his hoofs he seemed to squeeze out thousands of glittering gems at every step.

It was now known what was to be the objective in the forthcoming offensive, and full-sized models were made of the Rafa redoubt and Zowaid trench, all trenches having been carefully noted by means of aeroplane photographs. To dig actual trenches in the sand was hardly practicable and they were simply marked out in outline with sandbags. Frequent "attacks" were made by day and night to familiarise each section with its own particlar job.

On October 25th a shoal of fish was seen quite close to the shore. They were bombarded by Mills's bombs, with great effect, and several fish of five to six pounds were landed.

On October 27th a successful Battalion sports meeting was held, followed by a concert in the evening by members of the Tank Corps, who had taken up their quarters nearby, their two tanks called "Ole Lukoi" and "Otazel," respectively, being tucked away in gullies near the seashore. The concert came to an abrupt conclusion through a violent storm of rain and wind, the first of the season. The officers' mess and orderly room were completely swamped and the stationery boxes, files, etc., narrowly escaped being washed into the sea. The gullies quickly became raging torrents, and the sea, under the influence of the gale, rose to meet them, so as to make it difficult to decide whether we were going to be drowned out by the sea or by the flood. Most of the Battalion were in dugouts on the higher level of the cliff. The dugouts consisted merely of holes in the gound covered by bivouac sheets, and, of course, were soon nothing more than water-holes, full to the brim. The next day was fine and everything was soon dry again, but it was a most uncomfortable night.

CHAPTER X.

# THE THIRD BATTLE OF GAZA.

HE 27th was also notable as the first day of the systematic bombardment of the defences of Gaza. It was the biggest artillery effort that had been made on this front and proceeded more or less continually for six days. Great damage was done to the enemy's works and wire cutting was thoroughly carried out. I was in the line every day and found the gunners as obliging as usual in dealing with any point desired. By night thorough reconnaissances were made of forming-up places in front of the line, careful night bearings were taken and everything done to ensure that the attack was successfully launched. Ramps were made by which our two tanks were to cross the trenches, and our own wire was cut into gaps to expedite the egress of the attacking Companies and avoid anything like confusion.

It was realised that to advance over these sandy wastes of No Man's Land for a thousand yards or more in broad daylight against such formidable positions was to court disaster. The tactics of April 19th were not be to repeated, and the attack was to be made at night. To give a clear idea to the reader of the general plan I cannot do better than quote the following extracts from the Commander-in-Chief's official despatch :—

" The Turkish Army in Southern Palestine held a strong position extending from the sea at Gaza, roughly along the main Gaza–Beersheba road to Beersheba. Gaza had been made into a strong modern fortress, heavily entrenched and wired, offering every facility for protracted defence. The remainder of the enemy's line consisted of a series of strong localities, viz., the Sihan group of works, the Attawineh group, the Baha group, the Abu Hareira–Arab el Teeaha trench system, and finally, the works covering Beersheba.

" I had decided to strike the main blow against the left flank of the main Turkish position Hareira and Sheria. The capture of Beersheba was a necessary preliminary to this operation. . . .

" This front of attack was chosen for the following reasons :— The enemy's works in this sector were less formidable than elsewhere, and they were easier to approach than other parts of the enemy's defences. . . .

" It was important, in order to keep the enemy in doubt up to the last moment as to the real point of attack, that an attack should also be made on the enemy's right at Gaza in conjunction with the main operations. One of my Commanders was therefore ordered to prepare a scheme for operations against Gaza on as large a scale as the force at his disposal would permit. . . .

"During the period from July to October the enemy's force on the Palestine front had been increased. It was evident that the enemy was determined to make every effort to maintain his position on the Gaza–Beersheba line. He had considerably strengthened his defences on this line. . . ."

It will thus be seen that the attack in which we were to take part was not the main attack. At the same time it was to be a serious attack, the primary object of which was (again quoting from the official despatch), "to prevent any units being drawn from the Gaza defences to meet the threat to the Turkish left flank, and to draw into Gaza as large a proportion as possible of the available Turkish reserves." The attack on Gaza, being subsidiary to the main operations on our right, had therefore to be carried out by a by no means strong force. It could not be done on a larger scale than the force at the disposal of our Corps Commander would permit, and at the same time the enemy was to be constrained to keep all his units there, and even to draw upon his reserves to meet the attack. We had therefore no light task in front of us.

On October 31st the welcome news was received that Beersheba had been taken and the Turkish detachment there almost put out of action. The left flank of the enemy's position now lay open for the decisive blow. The latter was not, however, to take place until the attack on Gaza had been made and hostile reserves drawn thereby into the Gaza sector.

On the morning of November 1st we were informed that it was "Z—1 day." In other words the attack was to take place in the small hours of the following morning.

At three p.m. General Hare saw all officers and spoke a few final words of advice and encouragement. At four p.m. I saw each Company on parade. They were ready "to the last button" and full of confidence. They knew well that they had a tough proposition in front of them but I could see from their faces they were quietly determined to carry it through.

"A" and "D" Companies (Franklin and Deakin) were to attack the Rafa redoubt, Deakin being in command. "B" Company, with two platoons of "C," were to take the Zowaid trench, led by Frank Bacon. "C" Company, less two platoons, were in Battalion reserve under Colvin and were given a point of assembly behind a slight rise about two thirds of the way across and almost equi-distant from the two works to be assaulted. The 1/6th Essex were to attack Beach Post and Sea Post. The 1/7th Essex were then to carry the operations a stage further by attacking Cricket redoubt and the Rafa-Belah trench. The tanks were to support the 1/5th in the attacks on both their objectives, afterwards concentrating to the north of Rafa redoubt ready to take part in the second stage in support of the 1/7th. They carried a good load of material for consolidation. The 1/4th Essex were in Divisional reserve. The third stage was to be an attack on Sheikh Hassan and Tortoise Hill by the 162nd Brigade, moving by the sea coast.

At 4.30 p.m. a short service was held, which was well attended. At five p.m. the Battalion went to sleep. Rest was essential, as we knew we had some disturbed nights in front of us.

At 11 p.m. a good square hot meal was served with a pint of beer to wash it down. At the same hour Umbrella Hill was attacked and captured by a Brigade of the 52nd Division. This was a necessary preliminary to our own attack, as the Umbrella Hill position completely flanked the line of our advance, which was timed for 3 a.m. The enemy opened a heavy bombardment in reply, both on the captured position and on the front line, but paid no attention to the back areas, and we ate our meal in peace to the accompaniment of the bombardment by both sides.

At half-an-hour after midnight we left the bivouac to take our position of assembly just behind the front line. The latter had, of course, been carefully selected beforehand and routes arranged to prevent units crossing, etc. The bombardment continued until about one a.m., when it practically ceased altogether. The Turk was evidently taking a pause to decide what was to be done next—or to let us decide for him, which we did.

At 2.30 we reported all ready at the position of deployment in front of the wire and it seemed a long wait until 2.55, when we were timed to start. Silence reigned supreme and we stood unscathed on ground, which an hour before had been a veritable inferno. It was a good start. The tanks had been got over safely and at 2.55 the Companies moved off. At three precisely, the artillery commenced. The moon had just disappeared and the light got very bad. The smoke and dust of the fire made a thick fog and the compass had to be relied upon for direction. Battalion Headquarters was in the front line trench, an advanced Headquarters, under Evans, followed "A" and "D" Companies to establish as soon as possible the new Headquarters in "Rafa Junior," an off-shoot of the redoubt. They laid a wire forward as they went. This was soon cut, and for some time I was without any information. Worse still, the carefully-buried line to Brigade Headquarters also refused to work and remained on strike to the end of the proceedings. After about half-an-hour a runner got back to say that the enemy's front line was in our hands, Lancaster, who had been told off to check the direction, had been killed, also Evans our invaluable scout officer, who was shot dead just outside the enemy's parapet. The Turks had put up a wonderful fight, many of them lying in forward positions in the open to avoid the bombardment, and meeting our men with the bayonet.

Still the reports were very confusing, as both attacking parties claimed to be in the Rafa redoubt. No word was received as to the Zowaid trench. Runners lost their way in the thick haze and it was impossible to tell exactly what the situation was. The air seemed filled with fine sand and smoke, which hung about like a thick ground fog and made it very difficult. Reports came in from the right that the attacks on El Arish Redoubt and El Burj trench had been repulsed. I was very anxious about Zowaid, which joined El Burj. The reports, however, proved incorrect. It was now broad daylight and the enemy was firing furiously from his second line. The 6th had taken Beach and Sea Posts with little trouble. The 7th had taken Cricket redoubt, but had not succeeded in their attack on that very important trench the Rafa-Belah. The tanks had broken down and neither had reached even its first objective. The loss of their support was a serious blow to the 7th.

The morning wore on and still no more definite news of Zowaid. But a wounded man said he saw some of advanced Headquarters personnel in Rafa Junior and it was decided to move Battalion Headquarters to its new position. The enemy kept up a brisk fire from his second line (which it will be remembered commanded the first and was in full view) and we were held up half-way across by a very persistent machine gun, which afforded a convincing argument, to my discreet mind, for altering our course by way of Beach Post, to which there was a more covered approach. This route also took us away from the direction of Zowaid trench, of which I was still doubtful as to the occupiers, as a good deal of fire came from that direction. I am afraid these peregrinations of our little band of Headquarters may appear to the reader as rather affected by undue caution ; but I confess I had no mind to walk across the front of a possible enemy trench at a distance of 300 yards. Zowaid trench was occasionally visible through the haze, but shewed no sign of life, and was not at that time being shelled, though it got a terrible dusting later. To cut a long story short we eventually reached our new position via Beach Post, and made our home in a shell hole. I had found poor Lancaster about half-way across, quite dead, with a smile on his handsome face. I took off his signet ring and sent it afterwards to his wife.

As I entered Rafa redoubt I was surprised to meet Frank Bacon being carried out, his foot badly shattered by a bomb. He was too much knocked about to stop and question as to how he got there, but the situation was gradually cleared up by further enquiry. An extraordinary thing had happened.

The two attacking parties, going to divergent points, necessarily moved independently. Deakin, making straight for his objective—Rafa redoubt—suddenly saw a swarm of men clambering up the steep sandy slope which led up to the work. It was "B" Company, whose objective was Zowaid trench, and who had lost direction in the darkness and struck Rafa instead. How it happened will probably never be known; Lancaster alone could, perhaps, have told. But it can be safely conjectured that compasses proved unreliable with so many steel rifle barrels and steel helmets in the vicinity. Deakin did not take long to make up his mind. He quickly realized that whoever the attacking party were and whichever position it was he was needed elsewhere. He told me afterwards that he thought he himself might have lost his direction and that it was the 6th Essex storming Beach Post in front of him. Acting on this supposition he changed his direction and felt for the next work on his right, which proved to be Zowaid trench. All the works were very much alike in that light; all were sited high, and had low ground behind them. Once you are in the trenches it is very difficult to tell the plan of the position you are in. Hence it is not so surprising that I received, *from Zowaid*, a sketch of *Rafa*, shewing the parts of that trench which had been taken. It should be explained that officers of each party had been supplied with sketches of their objectives on which to make their reports.

Deakin's presence of mind saved the situation, but the change of direction had taken time, and the barrage had lifted some minutes before he arrived. The Turk was manning his parapets and it was only really good leadership and resolution that enabled the assaulting column to fight their way in. The casualties were heavy. Deakin's leg was broken by a bullet and he dropped outside the work. But Franklin carried on, and Wray, who was also wounded, and other officers and non-commissioned officers. Sergt. Watsham, Corpl. Jarrold and Pte. Long greatly distinguished themselves. Sergt. Cooper, D.C.M., fell gallantly leading his platoon after they had swept over the front line. The second line lay on the low ground and those detailed for its capture—what was left of them—gallantly carried on and occupied it; but none of them ever got back. Support was not forthcoming from the right as expected and the position was untenable. However, the main trench on the high ground was won and held, though subjected to a murderous bombardment from howitzers and minenwerfer. The Turks had held on to it with the utmost tenacity and had to be bombed out by working along the trench. It was splendid work, and the way successive difficulties were overcome reflected the greatest credit on "A" and "D" Companies and their leaders. Meanwhile, Bacon had made good the redoubt with his Company and a half, although it was considered a big enough job for two Companies. They got in close up to the barrage, but the Turks stuck to their machine guns, two of which were captured, as well as a British Lewis gun, taken in one of the first two battles. At the bottom of the rear slope two minenwerfer were silenced and deserted, but here again the low ground was untenable, completely commanded by the second line trenches, and without support which was expected from the left. It is to be feared that the unfortunate mistake above referred to was partly responsible for this. Part of the 7th Essex were to pass by the right of Rafa redoubt and attack the Rafa-Belah trench in flank whilst another part attacked it from the direction of Cricket redoubt. When the right half of the 7th arrived they shouted—to make sure—" Is this Rafa ? " The answer, in all good faith, was, " No, Zowaid ! " The result was that the Rafa-Belah trench was not attacked in the way intended by the Brigade scheme. The enemy held it, and from it played havoc in the ranks of the 7th and of the 10th Londons, who were making for a further objective in conformity with the rest of their Brigade, who were moving by the seashore. The result was that although the front line works were captured and held and the 162nd Brigade had also captured the Sheikh Hassan position far to the north, the Rafa-Belah trench still held out. It was effectually blocked from the Rafa redoubt end, where Archer did great work with his Lewis gun, fighting it himself almost single-handed after Sergt. C. T. Alloway, his most efficient Lewis gun non-commissioned officer, had been killed and most of the team knocked out. C.-S.-M. Wilson did splendid work in helping to organize and consolidate the position. Richmond and Lockwood, I remember, were conspicuous too, in Rafa redoubt; but it is hardly fair to mention names, there were so many others.

The Turks still shelled us very heavily, especially with minenwerfer, from the direction of " Island Wood," behind Zowaid, but our guns could not locate them. I had repeated messages from Franklin in the latter place and they were evidently suffering severely. It seemed likely that the enemy might counter-attack Zowaid, which proved, perhaps, a more difficult place than Rafa to hold. Its capture would have made Rafa more or less of a trap, particularly as the enemy held the Rafa-Belah trench. I therefore reinforced Zowaid with Colvin and the remainder of his Company. I had little fear for Rafa as it had a good field of fire to the north, which could be improved by digging another trench during the night. The enemy contented himself with bombarding it, and occasionally opening heavy rifle and machine gun fire upon it, without following it up, and it appeared to be more "wind" that anything else. The pioneers connected up two or three holes and made Battalion Headquarters a little more commodious. The work became rather crowded with men from other units who had apparently lost their way. They were organized into working parties as there was plenty of work for everybody. During the night a complete new trench was dug on the northern slope, the dead were buried, and the trenches cleared of debris and strengthened with materials brought up by carrying parties from Brigade Headquarters. The enemy made one counter-attack during the night, but only a few determined men reached the work and these were disposed of. Soon after dawn both works were subjected to a furious bombardment, but if the enemy thought we were to be shelled out after a night's consolidation he reckoned without his host. Zowaid got it perhaps worse that we did, and our gunners were still unable to silence those elusive minenwerfer. During the day I was obliged to leave, owing to wounds in the hands which I had received the previous morning. Avery, my M.O. (who had been doing splendid work under heavy fire) insisted on my having further treatment and a tetanus injection, and I very reluctantly handed over the command to Franklin, who was fetched from Zowaid, Colvin taking command of that place. I had every confidence in my successor, but it was galling to have to leave the Battalion once more when they were "going through it." However, it was the fortune of war. The Brigadier subsequently sent for Wilson, who was in waiting, and he took over the Battalion at midnight. My sad trudge back to the Field Ambulance was relieved by one amusing remark which I heard from a carrying party going up to the line. I was dressed in "Tommy's" uniform with no prominent badges of rank, and, I fear, did not look my best. "Poor old ——," one of them remarked to the other. "I call it a shame to send old blokes like him up there."

The capture of the Rafa redoubt and Zowaid trench was a feat of which the Battalion may well be proud. That the enemy offered a determined resistance was shewn by the fact that our casualties in the action were two officers and 73 other ranks killed, seven officers and 172 other ranks wounded and nine other ranks missing. The killed included, besides those already mentioned, such good non-commissioned officers as Sergts. H. Byles, N. Bruce and D. Ambrose, Corpl. P. Anderson, and L./Corpls. H. Quilter and Tasker.

It afterwards transpired that the enemy had drawn a whole Division into Gaza to reinforce the defence. Thus, the attack not only succeeded in capturing its objectives but also achieved completely its primary object, which was to keep the enemy's forces tied to Gaza, and to draw his reserves into that place.

The main attack on the enemy's left at Sheria took place at dawn on November 6th and was completely successful.

The account of the capture of the town of Gaza on November 7th and the subsequent advance through Philistia, I must leave Wilson to tell, as I was *hors de combat* until December 22nd. Before closing the chapter, however, I must refer to a few instances of gallant conduct which came to notice.

Wray was particularly conspicuous. He took command of his Company in the assault, on Deakin being hit. After seeing them firmly established in the positions they had won he went back and found Deakin lying in a position of great danger. Although wounded himself in the leg, he then carried his Company Commander under a very heavy fire to a place of comparative safety, made a report on the situation through the reserve Company, and returned to Zowaid trench, where he again shewed conspicuous gallantry. He refused to leave to have his wound seen to, and remained at duty until four days later, when the enemy evacuated Gaza.

In any other war he would have got the V.C. for which he was recommended by the Brigadier and the Divisional Commander. Instead, he received an immediate D.S.O.

The great fight which Archer put up with his Lewis gun in Rafa redoubt has already been mentioned. In this encounter he was wounded in the head, but continued to set a great example to his men, and after organising the consolidation of the work, went out and helped to bring his Company Commander, Bacon, into safety, being again hit.

Finn was as cool and business-like as usual ; no amount of fire could upset his equanimity, which made him an ideal Adjutant in action.

During the attack on the Zowaid trench, the column having become a little " loose," owing to the change of direction, and some of the new-comers being a little inclined to hug the shelter afforded by friendly shell holes, Pte. F. Long, grasping the situation, rushed forward and stood on the parapet, cheering on his comrades to the attack. Later, though hit in the thigh, he went back and found Deakin (whose batman he was) lying in the open. He carried his officer for some distance back, but becoming weak from loss of blood, he was obliged to leave him in a shell hole. He managed to reach the dressing station and sent back some stretcher-bearers, not being allowed to leave the station himself. It may be added that owing to Deakin having been moved by Wray to another place the stretcher-bearers failed to find him. Deakin, however, managed to crawl back the whole remaining distance, about 600 yards, with his broken leg.

Corpl. A. R. Jarrold was conspicuous for his coolness and bravery, making frequent journeys over the open, from trench to trench, organizing and leading storming parties to clear various portions still head by the enemy. During the minenwerfer bombardment he took his Lewis gun into the open and succeeded in silencing one of those weapons, until his Lewis gun was knocked out by machine gun fire.

Sergt. Harold Watsham took charge of the first wave of his Company when his officer was wounded. He led the assault and afterwards cleared a communication trench single handed with bombs. He had started to clear another when he was wounded in several places.

Pte. Harold Andrews, when his section leader was killed, took command and cleared the trench allotted to them with bombs. Later in the day he brought in seven wounded men who were lying in the open, three of them under direct machine gun fire.

Sergt. G. J. Kemp, when a group he had posted at a block in the trench was rushed by an enemy counter-attack, covered by artillery fire, immediately organized a party and broke up the attack, accounting for most of the raiders.

Pte. J. Clayton rushed in and bombed some enemy dug-outs, killing several of the enemy, receiving a severe wound, which resulted in the loss of a leg.

A word must be said for the stretcher-bearers, who one and all worked like heroes. Ptes. Charles Broyd and F. J. Harrington were particularly noticed for their devotion in attending wounded and carrying them back under heavy fire.

The above cases are only typical of many others, and the value of such examples can hardly be over-estimated.

CHAPTER XI.

# THE FALL OF GAZA AND THE ADVANCE THROUGH PHILISTIA.

By Major W. E. Wilson, D.S.O.

DURING the afternoon of November 3rd, I received a wire from 54th Division, ordering me to take command of the Battalion, Colonel Gibbons having been wounded. I left the nucleus camp at Belah a little later, being ordered to report at Divisional Headquarters on my way. I saw the G.S.O. (1), Colonel Garsia, who informed me of the situation and impressed upon me the importance of the Battalion holding on to their positions, particularly Rafa redoubt, which he explained was practically the key position of the whole line. He added that counter-attacks and heavy bombardment must be expected. On arrival at Ajlin Mosque I reported myself at Brigade Headquarters and proceeded to Rafa redoubt where I arrived at midnight. The night was still, not a sound to be heard; the moon almost at the full, lighting up the sand like day. I found that both Rafa and Zowaid had suffered severely from our previous bombardment. Rafa especially looked like an old clothes shop, the burst Turkish sandbags, many of them made of shirts and other clothing, being strewn everywhere. In both works the men were busy with the consolidation of the position. Nothing of interest occurred during the night, in fact the stillness of the whole front was almost uncanny. This peaceful state of affairs continued, as far as we were concerned, until about 10 o'clock on November 4th, when, without warning, the Turks opened a heavy fire with 5.9 H.E. on Rafa redoubt. As hour after hour went by no cessation of the hostile fire took place, in fact it rather increased in intensity during the afternoon. Considering the great amount of shell fired at us it was extraordinary that the casualties were so light; this may probably be accounted for by the fact that a great percentage of the shells buried themselves in the sand before exploding.

The men worked with a will on the work of consolidation during the day, but the new work was quickly spotted by the Turkish observers, and more often than not demolished.

As darkness came on the Turkish fire changed to 77 m.m. and 4.2 shrapnel. This was aimed principally at the rear of both Rafa and Zowaid to hinder movement. In this it was effective, and some difficulty was experienced in bringing up water and supplies. The Camel Transport not being able to reach the Post it became necessary to detail fatigue parties for this work.

The Turkish fire continued with varying intensity all through the night, changing again to 5.9 H.E. as morning broke.

On the following day, November. 5, the bombardment was heavier than ever, and I felt that if something were not done to check the Turkish gunners we stood the chance of serious casualties. About 10 o'clock I spoke to the Brigadier and explained the position to him, and he promised to do his best to arrange for artillery support.

During the morning a message was received to the effect that the 8th Hants would relieve us at Rafa and Zowaid.

About 4 o'clock, as the Turkish fire again increased in intensity, I again spoke to the Brigadier, and asked for artillery support, and some half-hour or so later we heard our heavies strafing the batteries which had paid us such attention, and after that, except for the 77 shrapnel, the Turkish fire diminished appreciably.

At about 8 o'clock the 8th Hants took over Rafa and Zowaid, and the Battalion moved back to Sheikh Ajlin. By this time the Turks had again started a strafe with their 77's, on the communications, and it was a relief on arrival at Ajlin to find that no casualties had occurred.

I reported arrival at Brigade Headquarters, fully expecting to be told that the Battalion would be given a day or two's respite. However, the General informed me that we had been withdrawn to take part in the attack, the next night, on the Rafa-Belah trench, a position which up to then had defied capture, and was causing a great amount of inconvenience.

Orders were received during the morning of November 6th for the attack on the Rafa-Belah trench. The attacking troops consisted of the 1/11th London Regiment, 1/5th Bedfordshires, 1/6th Essex and 1/5th Essex (less two companies), the 1/5th working on the right of the 1/6th Essex.

I detailed "C" and "D" Companies (Colvin and Franklin), and arrangements were at once put in hand for the forthcoming attack.

During the afternoon rumours were current to the effect that the Turks were withdrawing from Gaza. At 11 p.m. we moved from Ajlin along the beach, to the place of assembly, Battalion Headquarters being established in Cricket redoubt by midnight.

At 12.45 a.m. on November 7th our gunners opened an intense bombardment on the Rafa-Belah trench and surrounding works, and at 1 o'clock, when the attack started, the machine guns joined in, giving a most efficient barrage.

We waited minute after minute for the Turkish reply to this hurricane of fire, but none came. Some 20 to 30 minutes later the Battalion reached the objective without opposition. Consolidation was at once started. It appeared that the strength

VIEW OF GAZA FROM THE ENEMY'S FRONT LINE.

*To face page* 105.

of the Rafa-Belah trench lay in its strong points, situated at intervals along it.

At dawn, in conjunction with the 1/6th Essex, I sent out patrols. These returned about an hour later, having penetrated to the outskirts of Gaza, and reported " All Clear." The Turks had withdrawn during the night.

The morning was taken up with the work of salvage and the burying of the dead. Among the latter were many of our comrades of the 1/7th Essex and 1/10th London, who had fallen in the gallant but fruitless effort to capture the Rafa-Belah trench early in the battle. At 11.30 we rejoined the Brigade on the beach and bivouacked near Sheikh Ajlin. At 4 p.m. the Brigade marched to the " Anchor Inn," a hut standing on a track leading into Gaza from the N.E., and there stayed the night.

The following morning we marched in Brigade to take up an outpost position S.E. of Jebalieh, a village two or three miles N. of Gaza. This march took us through the northern outskirts of the town and gave us some idea of the terrific fire to which the Turk had been subjected by our gunners. The quantity of material left behind was enormous, and it required quite careful manœuvring to avoid the shells, bombs, etc., which lay along the tracks.

The area now occupied by us had evidently been the position of some important Turkish command (I understood afterwards that it had been the headquarters of the Army Corps) and the chairs, tables and other joys left behind proved of service to all ranks.

After two days on outpost duty we moved back again to the Anchor Inn, where it was expected that we should spend some days. On November 11th the whole Brigade was busy with salvage work. A fatigue party, under Colvin, was sent, with the sanction of the Brigadier, to the Green Hill, to do their best to trace those of our comrades who fell on March 26th. Although time for the work was short a good many bodies were recovered, amongst others, that of Capron. The work was resumed on the following day—November 12th.

Having been informed that it was more than probable that we should stay in our present bivouac for some days, I despatched three or four limbers to the Canteen at Belah to get some provisions for the men. Within a short time of their departure, however, orders were received that the Brigade would move to El Mejdel that day, the starting point to be passed at noon. The salvage parties were quickly recalled and the men had hardly returned to bivouac before the march started. The recalling of the transport was out of the question.

El Mejdel is the old Canaanite town of Migdal Gad (Tower of Gad, the Canaanite god of Fortune), a city given to the tribe of Judah ; one of the principal cities of the Philistines, and later, a fortress of the Crusaders. The village lay some 16 miles north of Gaza, and the road to it was of the roughest description.

Even in the most favourable circumstances the march would have been a severe one, but our men went splendidly, and we arrived in our bivouac ground just S.W. of El Mejdel at 9 p.m., very tired and quite ready for a night's sleep.

MEMORIAL CROSS ON THE GREEN HILL.
(Note the wild flowers.)

We were early astir next morning—November 13th—and started on the march again at 6.15, our destination being Julis, some five miles N.E. of Mejdel, where we arrived at 8 o'clock. I understood that the Brigade was to be in reserve to the 75th Division, which was a few miles ahead, pressing hard upon the retreating Turks. We spent some hours resting in a delightful hollow, wondering what our part in the day's work was likely to be. It was evident that a brisk action was in progress, and from a vantage point above our hollow the Turkish shrapnel could be seen bursting in white puffs high above what were evidently the attacking troops of the 75th Division. I understood the objective to be "Junction Station," the junction with the Jerusalem railway at the foot of the hills about 15 miles away. Some miles to the west the 52nd Division was also seen to be engaged.

At noon orders were received to resume the march. After marching some three miles we halted just south of the village of Es Suafir Gharbiyeh. Here we stayed by the side of the road for some hours, expecting every minute to be under way again. However, at about 3 o'clock, we had orders to bivouac, and soon made ourselves as comfortable as possible for the night.

The next day's march brought us to El Kustineh, a village of mud huts, which we reached early in the afternoon, halting for the night N.E. of the village. A start was made the following day at 8.30, our destination being Yebnah, some twelve miles distant, where we arrived at 2 p.m., pitching our bivouac just south of the village.

Yebnah presented a most picturesque appearance, its dwellings clustering round about a knoll. It was once the Canaanite town of Jabnael and was taken by the Philistines from the tribe of Dan. One of the mosques now occupies the site of an early Christian church.

The march was resumed at 9 o'clock on November 19, our destination being El Ramleh, a town of considerable importance, situated on the Jaffa-Jerusalem Road. It was for some time an important station of the Turkish Flying Corps.

Our progress was quite normal until about midday, when within a few miles of Ramleh a halt was necessitated by the fact that our road was blocked by a broken-down tractor.

It was then found necessary for us to make a wide detour, which greatly delayed us, for the country in that neighbourhood was extremely close, consisting of vineyards, intersected by very high and thick hedges.

An amusing incident occurred during our halt. A car having threaded its way through the narrow lane, arrived at the head of the column to find its road barred also. Its occupants turned out to be General Allenby, our Chief, and General Wingate, High Commissioner for Egypt. Some difficulty was experienced in turning the car in the soft earth, and both these famous generals lent their weight with the rest on the wheels of the car. A few kind words from the Chief pleased us all mightily.

Some little time after we had resumed our march I received orders that the Battalion, in conjunction with the 1/7th Essex Regiment, was to find outposts that night covering Ramleh from the east. The outpost line was some three miles east of Ramleh, along the rocky ground of the foothills.

It was nearly 4 o'clock when we reached the line, and we could hardly enthuse at the sight of the wild and rugged country, unvaried in any direction. To make matters more complex the light was failing fast; luckily the Jaffa-Jerusalem—practically the only metalled road in this part of Palestine—gave us the necessary direction.

It was almost dark when we arrived, but Portway and Bateman, commanding the outpost companies, handled their men splendidly, and about an hour later reported themselves in position.

During the afternoon signs were not wanting that we might expect rain, and at about 5 p.m. the rain started, soon becoming a downpour, which lasted throughout the night.

This first heavy rain of the season gave us an idea of what we might expect during the following months. Without our blankets we spent an unhappy night, every minute expecting the transport which carried them. It was not, however, until past midnight that they turned up, their delay due to the flooded state of the ground, great difficulty having been experienced in moving the camels over the "cotton" ground.

Towards dawn the weather cleared and we were thankful for the drying sun and stiff breeze which sprang up. The morning was spent in settling down on our outpost line, and we had our first experience of building sangars.

Early in the afternoon orders were received to rejoin the Brigade at Ramleh, and at 2.30 we concentrated and marched to the Brigade bivouac.

This was close to the railway station: the ground was deep in mud after the preceding night's rain—a condition of things which was not improved by another downpour which started soon after our arrival, and lasted the best part of the night. Luckily, large stacks of wood, used by the Turks for their locomotives, were utilised to make huge bonfires, and around these we sat in an endeavour to keep one side, at least, of one's person warm and dry. The Turkish airmen missed a good target that night.

The next morning broke dull, but cleared early; the bivouac ground had however become by this time such a morass that it was found necessary to move to high and drier ground close by.

The day was principally spent in drying ourselves and procuring fresh eatables, which at the time were parted with quite willingly by the natives.

To our temporary second-in-command and Mess President, Willmott, a lasting debt of gratitude must be accorded for his endeavour to supply all ranks of the Battalion with vegetables, bread, etc., the first we had tasted since November 2nd. Although supplies were limited, they came as "rare and refreshing fruit," after three weeks of bully and biscuit.

Archer, with an eye to the local pigeons, became a benefactor to those who partook of his bag.

By the evening we had forgotten our troubles of previous days, and to make our content complete, our lost limbers arrived from Belah full to the brim with canteen joys—fags, drinks, and many things dear to the 5th Essex heart.

Brigade Headquarters with the 1/4th and 1/6th Battalions left us the following day. The reason of their leaving us did not then transpire, except that I understood that Jaffa or thereabouts was their destination.

On November 25th, with the 1/7th Battalion, we moved from bivouac at 8 o'clock, en route to join the Brigade at Selmeh, a village some five miles east of Jaffa.

On passing 54th Division Headquarters, which were just west of Ramleh, I met Tubby Horton, who cheered us up by informing us that we were bound for comfortable billets in Jaffa—winter quarters in fact; however, that supreme optimist was for once at fault—very much so, as later events proved.

It must have been almost half way, while the two Battalions were starting the usual long halt, that a message was sent me from Colonel Wilmer (1/7th Essex) who was in command of the column, informing me that word had been received from the Brigade to the effect that the 1/4th and 1/6th Essex were in action; and that we were required to move at all speed to Sarona. Sarona, a charming village five miles N.E. of Jaffa, and just S. of the Auja, is situated in the midst of the orange district, and was one of the many German colonies which were founded some years ago in Palestine.

Sarona reminded one of an English village, and in its cleanliness was like nothing we had as yet seen. We arrived at 2 o'clock, and found the place in a hubbub of excitement, what with the German inhabitants and our own troops—a number of wounded men of the 1/4th and 1/6th Batts., and a sprinkling of Anzacs, telling us that some fighting had taken place.

The situation had been unpleasant, and was still fraught with possible difficulties. It appeared that both the 1/4th and 1/6th had pushed two companies each across the Auja the evening before, but early that morning had been attacked heavily by quite a fresh Turkish Division, and after gallantly withstanding this attack, had been obliged at last to withdraw these companies to the south bank—thereby suffering some loss.

After a brief reconnaissance, we were detailed to relieve the 1/4th Essex, on the right of the Brigade line, south of the River Auja, facing north and north-east.

At 3.30 we moved as far as we could under cover, but as this part of the front was very open and under direct Turkish observation, it was deemed that to attempt relief by daylight would be a mistake.

As soon as dusk fell we reached the 1/4th and the relief was carried out without any untoward incident, companies reporting all correct by 8 p.m.

Portway's company held the right sector, which included a commanding hill, known later as "Portway Hill," from which the whole valley of the Auja was under our observation—a fact which did not escape the notice of the Turkish gunners. Colvin's company was well forward, in the centre, covering the approaches to the mill and bridge. Franklin held the left sector with his company, in touch with 1/7th Essex on our left. The remaining company, under Bateman, was in reserve at Battalion Headquarters.

The terrain in the vicinity was a curious mixture of hill and flat, thickly wooded in places with orange groves, but for the most part open. The River Auja, wide and exceptionally deep for a river of Palestine, was impossible to cross, except by bridge or boat, a bridge by a broken water mill being the only crossing on our immediate front.

North of the river the ground rose sharply from the bank, giving the Turk a dominating position along it, and blocking out observation to their rear (northwards).

On the south side the ground was swampy and flat, for a varying distance of 300 to 500 yards, then rising gradually in the centre and sharply on each side of our sector. The centre was thickly wooded with orange groves, while the hills were quite bare.

To the east the ground fell steeply to an undulating plain beyond which were the thick almond groves round Mulebbis.

The situation was, briefly, as follows:

The Turks having made good the N. bank of the Auja, were, it seemed, satisfied for the moment, to stay there, and appeared to have no desire to push home their advantage of the morning.

To the east, and south of Auja, the Australian Light Horse patrolled Mulebbis, a Jewish colony of considerable size, some three miles from our line. These supplied a screen for our flank.

From Portway Hill our line comprised posts held by Light Horse and Camel Corps, bent back in a S.E. direction to Rantieh and Wilhelma. At nightfall on November 26 a patrol from "C" Company reconnoitred as far as a ford some three miles up the river, with the intention of getting into touch with a standing patrol of Australian Light Horse, which we understood to be there. The patrol on its return, however, reported the ford unwatched. I reported this to Brigade Headquarters, who assured me that the report must be incorrect, but a further patrol on the following night confirmed the original information.

As dawn broke it was observed that the Turk was showing more activity than usual; numbers of his troops were to be seen moving on the north bank of the river. The gunners turned their attention on these movements; intermittent fire was returned from Turkish batteries.

As far as we were concerned, there was nothing of interest to report till about 9 o'clock, when suddenly a motley crowd of panic-stricken refugees came over Portway Hill towards our Headquarters. From their broken French we gathered that the Turks had entered Mulebbis in force, and were moving both west and south along the railway. The refugees were sent under escort to Sarona, and as they left our Headquarters came under considerable fire from the Turkish gunners; but although the shells seemed to fall right amongst them they managed to get clear without casualties.

Events now assumed a more warlike aspect. The Turks started a systematic shelling of our positions, which, however, did little damage, except in the case of "C" Company, where an ill-timed shell, falling in Company Headquarters caused some casualties.

It was evident that hot fighting was in progress to our right rear, and at about midday we understood that the Turks had occupied Hill 265.

This menace to our right rear was rather disquieting, bearing in mind the possibility that at any moment the enemy might try to force a crossing over the river on our left; but the Brigadier, in order to forestall possible eventualities, moved up the 1/6th Essex from Sarona to a position some half mile to our rear. A little later the situation was greatly relieved by the news that Hill 265 had been retaken.

During the evening our Bridge Head Post was heavily shelled, but luckily sustained no damage, and the rest of the night was passed quietly.

The morning gave us confirmation of a report that the Turks had established themselves on the south bank of the river. Their strength was estimated at about 200, and they had entrenched themselves along the river bank, covering the mill and the bridge.

In order to dislodge them, it was decided that they should be raided that evening. Lieut. Keeling, an officer who had recently joined us, was chosen to lead the raiding party, with 40 N.C.O.'s and men picked from "A" and "C" Companies.

In the afternoon a reconnaissance was carried out, and it was decided that the raiding party should move across the open marshy ground, well to the right, in order to take the Turks on their left flank and sweep them along the river bank.

It was arranged that no artillery fire should be used till three minutes after our men had attacked, the guns were then to barrage the bridge crossing in order to stop possible reinforcements, or to catch any of the retreating enemy.

When darkness fell Keeling moved his men, under cover, to a suitable jumping off place, and for the next hour or so we possessed our souls in patience.

At 8 o'clock Keeling's party attacked, and for the next few minutes pandemonium raged around the Bridge Head, the sound of machine guns, rifles and bombs being intermingled with the cries and yells of the Turks.

As arranged, three minutes after the attack started, Major Laurence, commanding the supporting battery, opened shrapnel fire with his 18 pounders, every round bursting low over the bridge, which was the only Turkish line of retreat. Then a little later, in order to cover the raiders' withdrawal, lifting to the Turkish positions upon the higher ground of the north bank.

Grateful thanks must be accorded to Major Laurence and his gunners for their valuable advice and help. Their firing undoubtedly stopped any reinforcing movement, and in the later stages made it possible for our men to withdraw without serious casualties.

The raid was completely successful. Of actual trench-work there was little, the Turks were under the steep river bank, and were estimated at about 150 men with three machine guns.

Except for the sentries, the Turks were mostly asleep, many of them in their blankets. They were completely surprised, and were given no time to make any organised resistance. Our men worked with bomb and bayonet, and in a very short space of time a number of Turks, estimated at quite 50, were killed. Those that were luckier escaped across the river, many only to be caught by our barrage.

Eight prisoners were captured and brought in, with one machine gun ; the two remaining machine guns were left, owing to the difficulty of carrying them, but rendered useless before the party left.

Our casualties were seven other ranks killed, including Sergt. B. Upchurch of "A" Company, and L/Corpls. B. G. Newman and L. Richardson. Two other men were wounded, but were brought back safely to our lines.

As the raiding party withdrew, the Turks opened a heavy fire with machine guns from their positions along the north bank. However, as previously stated, thanks to the co-operation of our gunners the party returned safely.

For this brilliant little affair Keeling was awarded the Military Cross next day by the Australian G.O.C., under whose command we were at the time.

Sergt. Piper, of "C" Company, and Pte. A. Cook, of "A" Company, were awarded the Military Medal. All three decorations were splendidly earned.

Evidently by way of reprisal for the shock of the night before, the Turks heavily shelled the posts held by "B" and "C" Companies for the best part of the next day—but the casualties were trifling. On November 30 our positions were heavily shelled all day, the attentions of the Turks being directed upon our right and centre sections especially. Unfortunately we had to report several casualties, " A " Company, who had relieved " C " Company the night before, suffering the most.

On December 2 " A " Company of the 1/6th Essex raided the Turks, who had again crossed the river, and established themselves in their former positions on our side of the stream The raid took place soon after dark. At 9 p.m. " A " Company, in the centre section, were heavily shelled by the Turks from the direction of Mulebbis. The fire was pretty continuous throughout the night, and although doing little damage, caused considerable inconvenience.

The Battalion (less " D " Company) was relieved the next evening by the 1/4th Essex; " D " Company kept their position in the line, and came under the orders of the relieving Battalion.

The relief was carried out without incident, being completed by 8 o'clock, and the Battalion moved to Sarona.

For the next few days the Battalion found guards in Jaffa. The weather again became execrable, with torrents of rain. Luckily the houses and cottages afforded excellent shelter.

On December 8th orders were received during the morning that the Reserve Battalion of the 156th Brigade (52nd Division) would relieve us that day, and that we were to move to Yasur, en route for Ludd. The Scotchmen arrived during the afternoon, and by 4.30 the relief was completed.

At 5 o'clock we started our march to Yasur, in pouring rain, the roads resembling rivers more than anything. Owing to the bad state of the ground it was found impossible to make the short cut which we had previously used on our march up; a long detour was therefore necessary to reach the main Jaffa–Jerusalem road. Yasur was reached at 9 p.m., and we bivouacked with the remainder of the Brigade among the olive groves just S.W. of the village.

The next day was spent in bivouac, and the rain was unceasing.

On December 10th we started our march to Ludd at 2 o'clock in the morning, using the main Jaffa–Jerusalem road. The rain had ceased, but the road was in a very bad condition. We arrived at 9 o'clock, and once more our bivouac, which was close to the station, was among the olives.

On December 13th we relieved the 1/5th Norfolks, who were detailed for an offensive. On the 15th their Brigade (163rd) made their attack on the Tireh-Cistern Hill line early in the morning, and successfully reached all their objectives. The enemy shelled our post on the railway, about 600 yards south of Wilhelma station, during the day. After dark we handed over our line again to the 1/5th Norfolks and marched direct to Safirieh, via Ludd, reaching the Brigade bivouac at 6 a.m. At 3 o'clock the next morning the whole Brigade marched to Selmeh, arriving at 7 o'clock. The going was very heavy, and the weather did not improve, the rain being almost incessant every day.

An attack was ordered for the Brigade to take place on December 22nd, the objective being Mulebbis and the high ground beyond, overlooking the Plain of Sharon.

Dec. 21st was spent in making the final arrangements for the next morning's attack. During the evening Colonel Gibbons rejoined us, and was heartily welcomed by all ranks.

Dec. 22. We moved at 3.30 a.m. in Brigade to our position of assembly. The ground was in a bad condition, making the going very heavy. The Battalion reported in position at 5.50.

The 1/6th and 1/7th Essex were to attack, with the 5th Essex in support, echeloned 200 yards in the rear.

At 8 o'clock the attack started. No opposition was met with across the open, and the Battalion reached the almond groves at 8.45.

Mulebbis was entered at 10 o'clock, after very slight opposition and the inhabitants, who greeted us warmly, informed us that the bulk of the Turkish forces had been withdrawn some hours previously. An officer and 13 other ranks were captured by the Battalion. Colonel Gibbons arrived about noon, and by 3 p.m. all companies were billeted in the town.

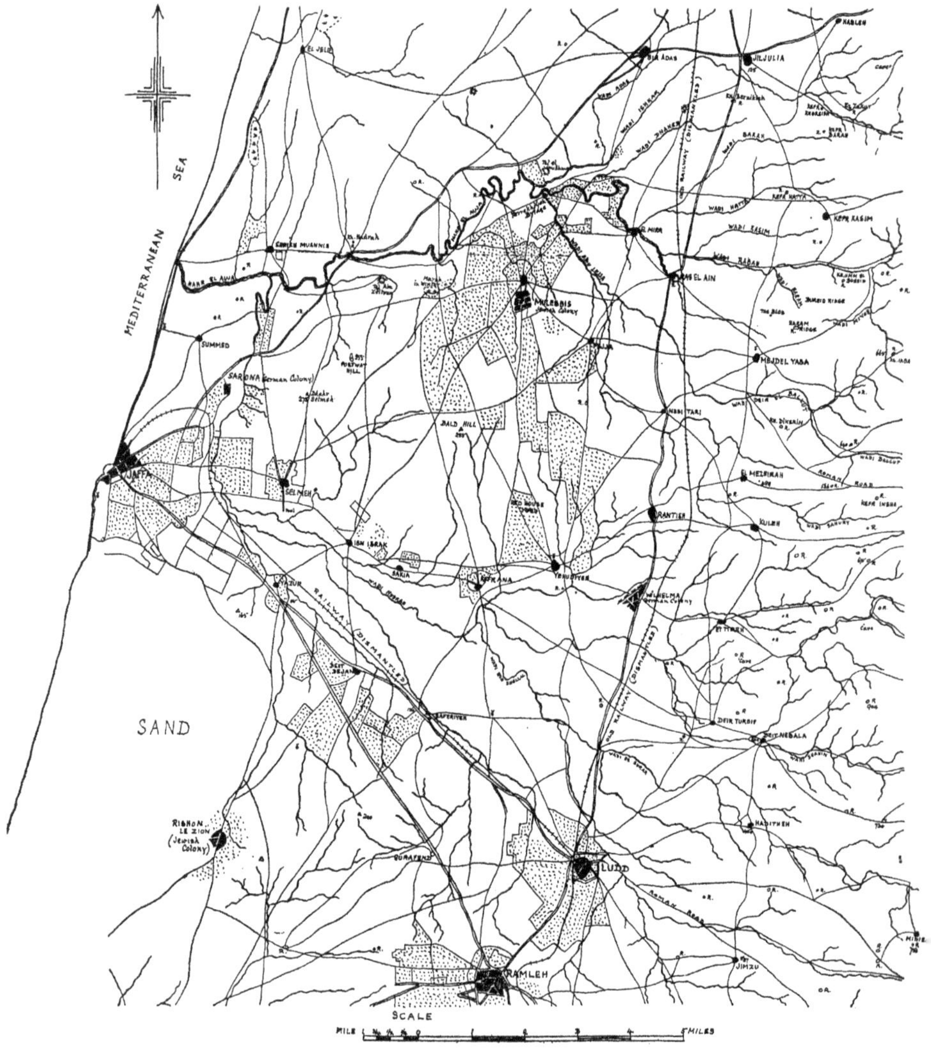


THE COASTAL PLAIN—JAFFA DISTRICT.

*To face Chapter XII.*

## CHAPTER XII.

# "GENERAL MUD" CHECKS THE ADVANCE.

URING my time in hospital I heard little about the Battalion or the campaign generally, except what was published in the *Egyptian Gazette.* The latter, however, included an account of the raid referred to in the previous chapter, although it didn't say which Battalion it was, and I could only hope it was the 5th. On the same day in the Alexandria Museum I came across an old map of the campaign of 1801 under Sir Ralph Abercrombie. One spot was marked "Here the 44th Regiment charged a large force of the enemy and drove them from the bridge." It was good to think that the Essex "Terriers" were upholding the traditions of the 44th (now the 1st Battalion The Essex Regiment).

On the same day I had a delightful letter from Sir Evelyn Wood who always kept his Essex Territorial Battalion in mind. He said "Having lived as far as this I do want to live to see our Battalion come home, so I hope you won't have to stop out until Jerusalem has quite settled down into happiness." After telling some hunting yarns, which his letters were never without, he concluded "If you ever get a chance of knowing when you are coming home tell me and I will try especially to live on to greet you all." I had already told our Honorary Colonel all I could about the last Gaza Battle and in a later letter in reply he said, "I am greatly interested in your account of the doings of our Battalion. I am indeed proud of it, and one of my wishes to live to the end of the war is connected with my desire to see you and it again."

The Field Marshal gave me an interesting account of some good hunts in the Essex country, which included a ducking he had in the Chelmer not far from Dunmow, and all about a heavy toss he took in the Roothings, which necessitated his riding home early, in the sympathetic company of a certain pretty girl. (They all loved the gallant F.M. who, with his 80 years, would still go with the best of them over a country). The letter went on "Now I will go back to soldiering, which interests me even more than hunting. You did not mention the name of the officer who had the pleasure of leading the front companies in the attack. If ever you get time to write to me again I wish you would tell me, for then, if I live to see the Battalion again, I shall have more pleasure in greeting them."

On December 19th, after a struggle at the Infantry Base Depôt at Kantara, where they made a point of detaining everybody for several days, if they could, I made my escape from that place of sandy boredom, and the next morning my train drew up at Gaza station. I should have liked to stop and look over that historic ground, but had to content myself with what could be seen from the carriage window. It was a curious sensation to be travelling by rail up the "Border Valley" across the old front line near "Heart Hill," flanking "Umbrella Hill," over No Man's Land and the Turkish trenches among the orchards, and drawing up in Gaza itself to see the Ali Muntar ridge from the "other side." The town was in a terribly ruinous and filthy condition. Well might one say, in the words of Jeremiah, "Baldness is come upon Gaza." Hardly a roof remained intact. Not only had our bombardment done much damage but the Turks had stripped the town of timber for dugouts. The great mosque was a heap of ruins, buried in which had been found a huge ammunition dump. The inhabitants were already returning and cultivating their gardens and fields. Railhead was at Deir Seneid, and there I duly found Mavor, who gave me some lunch. A Turkish railway ran from here to Ramleh, all the bridges having been repaired, so I boarded a munition train and got on another 30 miles, tightly wedged in a carriage full of picks and shovels, to Junction Station, where the train stopped. It was 10 p.m. and pouring with rain, but I got into a railway shed and spent a good night. I had no idea where the Battalion was and was rather surprised to see a 5th Essex limbered wagon at the station the next morning. The driver said the Battalion was at Ludd, so I put my kit on the wagon, with some cigarettes for the canteen and other little things, and took a ration train for Ramleh in the afternoon, walking on to Ludd by moonlight—to find that the Battalion had been suddenly moved, none knew whither. As luck would have it the Field Ambulances were still there and I spent a night in clover.

Ludd, the ancient Lod—afterwards Lydda—is a picturesque village surrounded by groves of olives, almonds, and oranges, and containing a fine well. It was the most westerly of the Jewish settlements after the exile, and was the frequent scene of battle and treaty between the Jews and the Syrians and Romans. But its chief claim to notice is its connection with our patron saint St. George, whose supposed relics it contains. The Crusaders built a cathedral over his tomb and made it strong enough to be used also as a fortress. Therefore Saladin destroyed it, but, according to Dr. G. Adam Smith, the present church contains much of the original. The Greek priest who shewed me over it said some of it dated from the 4th century, and it is probable that the tomb itself, under the church, may be as old as that. It is a square chamber, lighted by a dim lamp, with the sarcophagus in the centre. The walls of the chamber are covered with paintings representing the saint going through every imaginable form of martyrdom, from St. Catharine's wheel to boiling oil—as though one martyrdom were not sufficient for such a distinguished saint. The priest, after some pressing, shewed me the relics, two or three small bones mounted in silver and contained in a beautiful silver casket, which was kept behind the altar.

Ramleh is a larger town, with a fine Crusader's church, now a mosque, and some extensive and interesting ruins of another mosque, with a high tower called the "Tower of the Forty Martyrs," a prominent landmark, from which I obtained a magnificent view of the plain of Sharon and the Judæan hills. The top was reached by a flight of over 100 steps, and was used as a watch tower in time of war. It was now occupied by the Divisional Signallers.

I borrowed a horse at the Field Ambulance and rode to Divisional Headquarters at Ramleh, where the General gave me some lunch and sent me on in his car. The route lay by the Jaffa–Jerusalem road—the only road fit for wheeled traffic during the wet season—through Jaffa to the German colony of Sarona, where a flourishing trade had been done in Palestine wines, chiefly by German firms. The name, of course, echoes the name of the plain—Sharon—near the southern extremity of which it is situated. The old name is Lasharon, whose king Joshua smote (Joshua xii., 18). Baker, my trusty groom, was at the village to meet me and we reached the Battalion in the early evening at Selmeh. The tracks were in a terrible state, hock-deep in mud of the "pea-soup" variety.

I only saw Jaffa going through in the car. A few details of its history may, however, possibly interest my readers, particularly those who had a hand in driving the Turks from its precincts.

The ancient rabbis would make Jaffa as old almost as the world itself, for they attribute its foundation to Japhet the son of Noah. But Josephus, with greater reason, says it was founded by the Phœnicians. It was here, according to the same writer, that Perseus rescued Andromeda from the sea monster. Josephus is sure of it, for he says he saw the remains of the chains that bound the fair damsel to the rocks. The name Joppa appears in the great Temple of Karnak as one of the cities taken by Tholmes III. about 1600 B.C. Hither the Phœnicians brought the timber from Lebanon for the building of Solomon's temple. Here Jonah embarked on his eventful voyage. Hezekiah took the city from the Philistines, and it afterwards fell to Sennacherib. Judas Maccabeus in 165 B.C. attacked it in the night and burnt all the ships in the harbour. Antony gave it to Cleopatra, who kept it until Antony's defeat by Augustus at Actium. In early Christian times Joppa was the scene of the raising of Tabitha by St. Peter. The house of Simon the Tanner is still shewn to visitors.

During the Jewish insurrection Cestius Gallus set fire to the place and put 8,400 men to the sword. It played an important part in the Crusades. Godfrey de Bouillon and Baldwin held it in turn. Taken by Melek el Adel, Saladin's brother, after the battle of Hattin, it was restored to the Christians by a truce concluded between Richard and Saladin after the latter's defeat at Arsuf (1191). Melek seized it a second time in 1197 and massacred 20,000 Christians there. Gauthier de Brienne made himself master of it in 1204, and St. Louis of France landed there in 1251.

Napoleon laid siege to it and took it in 1799, and Ibrahim included it in his conquests in 1831. It abounds with oranges, figs, and almonds. As early as the fourteenth century B.C., an officer of Rameses II. boasted of the delicious fruit to be found in its gardens—and the soldiers of General Allenby have cause to remember them too.

I arrived at Selmeh just in time to attend a conference at Brigade Headquarters, at which I learnt that there was to be a battle the next morning. Knowing nothing of the situation I was naturally not called upon to take charge of the Battalion for the operations, of which I was invited to be a spectator from Brigade battle Headquarters. The 162nd Brigade were to attack the enemy's rear guard on "Bald Hill" in the early hours, and the 161st was to work round the left of that position and take Mulebbis.

Next morning, after seeing the Battalion start for the attack (Bald Hill having been taken earlier by the 162nd in a spirited and brilliant attack) I galloped off to battle Headquarters, a magnificent position, which had formerly been held as an outpost by Portway's company and was known as "Portway Hill," and from which a good view of the whole show could be seen. Things went well, so well that, as Paris the Brigade Major remarked, it was a "rotten battle." The fact was that the occupation of Bald Hill had made Mulebbis untenable and the Turk was already making the best of his way northwards. The artillery barrage thoroughly searched the woods which surrounded the village, and the Brigade followed closely in its wake, meeting with practically no opposition. The Turkish columns could be plainly seen streaming northwards along the plain, and only the long range guns could reach even the fringes of them. Although they had put up a good fight on Bald Hill the enemy had clearly anticipated us, and, as I was afterwards told in Mulebbis, had all preparations made for the retreat. Pursuit was out of the question. The plain was getting very soft, in a few days the wadis would be running in flood, and there were no roads.

Receiving the orders for holding the new line personally from the Brigadier, I rode on to Mulebbis. Our men were right through it and had killed and captured a few stragglers on the outer edge. The enemy was shelling the outskirts from Mejdel Yaba but nothing to speak of. The inhabitants were delighted to see us and there was much bowing, doffing of hats and cheering. A good many could speak English, of a sort, and all said "Good morning, sir," and shewed me which way the Turks had gone, which, of course, I knew only too well. I sat down on a log of wood to write some orders for the companies, and immediately they brought out a table and chair. They put a white cloth on the table and a plateful of oranges and nuts; a nice attention, I thought, for the Englishman come to spend Christmas with them.

Outposts were soon in position and the next thing was to find quarters. The Mayor was soon forthcoming, and with the help of an English-speaking guide we soon had things fixed up. The men were all billeted in houses by three o'clock, and were made a great fuss of by everybody. Dry billets were very welcome after the soakings they had recently had in bivouacs.

Among the street names in Mulebbis I noticed a "rue Rothschild," a "rue Montefiore" and a "rue Baron Hirsch." We selected a very respectable looking house in a central position for Battalion Headquarters. I regret to say it turned out to be not so clean as it might have been, but otherwise satisfactory.

The whole population were apparently Jews; every kind of Jew under the sun, except the rich fat ones one sees in London and Brighton. The Turks had treated the people badly, they said, and robbed them of almost all they had, including money. Our landlord got through a trap-door into the roof of his house and produced his candlesticks, spoons, and other treasures, chuckling at having saved them from his late tenants.

We asked for beef for dinner and were promised it by eight o'clock. It was a little late, but duly arrived. It was so tough as to be almost uneatable, and no wonder. It was the Sabbath, and the butcher didn't kill it until 6 o'clock, at which hour the Sabbath ends.

The next day was Sunday, and we had a Battalion service in a large public hall, which the amiable Jews had profusely adorned with Christmas decorations in the form of huge wreaths of evergreens. They even offered a Christmas tree!

In the orchards and woods to the south of the town the Turks had made some wonderful dugouts, revetting them with poles from the eucalyptus trees which abounded in the neighbourhood. Very little was found in them, clearly shewing that the enemy had not been surprised.

We occupied the native village of Fejja on the edge of the plain and began to prepare a line there, but the 5th were soon placed in Brigade reserve, in billets in the town.

Tuesday was Christmas day and was duly celebrated. Shops were opened and did a roaring trade in all kinds of provisions.

In the afternoon there was a torrential rain which flooded the roads and cut them up into deep ruts. We were lucky to be under cover.

The capture of Mulebbis, and the line left and right from the coast near Arsuf to Et Tire, had increased the distance between the enemy and Jaffa from three to eight miles, thus rendering Jaffa and its harbour secure, and covering the movements of troops, etc., along the main Jerusalem–Jaffa road. Jerusalem itself had fallen on December 9th, and the enemy had been pushed for some miles to the north and east of it.

In the middle of the plain on a slight elevation lay the fine ruins of the castle of Ras-el-Ain where the River Auja rises in several very strong springs. It is the ancient Antipatris, a palace, and possibly fortress, of Herod's where Paul was taken under cover of the night (Acts xxiii., 31) on his way to Cæsarea and Rome. Further to the right, on the foothills, stood the fine tower and village of Mejdel Yaba, a fortress of Saladin, to which he retired after his defeat by King Richard at Arsuf in 1191. To the left of Ras-el-Ain, on the Auja, was the village of El Mirr—the Mirabel of the Crusaders.

On December 28th we relieved the 1/4th Northamptonshires in the line. On the 30th a patrol visited Ras-el-Ain and found it unoccupied, returning along the old railway line by way of Nebi Tari. A few nights after a good quantity of shells were brought in from there, and on another night a derelict ammunition wagon, which had struck in the mud loaded with shells. If only the heavy rains had come a week earlier the enemy could never have withdrawn his guns across the plain, which was a veritable quagmire.

The enemy shewed little activity beyond shelling us occasionally from Mejdel Yaba. He was, however, busy digging a line further north in front of Jiljulia. The latter place is the ancient Gilgal, one of the cities of the plain taken by Joshua (Joshua xii., 23).

The weather was horribly wet, the men suffering extreme discomfort with nothing but their " bivvy sheets " to cover them. The ground was dryest in the eucalyptus woods, where the trees seem to absorb the wet from the ground, which was very light and sandy. There were a few scattered houses, which accommodated Battalion and Company Headquarters.

There was large marsh about three miles off, near the river Auja, which abounded with duck and snipe, and I have pleasant recollections of a day's shooting with Archer and one or two of his prize company poachers (using the word, of course, in its Army sense and with no derogatory intention). The guns were of rather primitive type, as used by the inhabitants, and the cartridges were loaded (by Archer personally) with huge charges of black powder and fragments of shrapnel and any old bits of metal. Having been refilled several times they were rather tight in the chamber and had to be ejected after each shot by a stick from the muzzle end. But what are such trifles to the true sportsman? The few misfires were amply compensated for by the thoroughness of those that did go off. The recoil was tremendous and the report terrific; the enemy must have thought we were experimenting with a new type of minenwerfer. As a result of a more than usually violent explosion the stock of my gun broke in two early in the afternoon, but the effect on the bag was probably not felt—I was not shooting my best—and Archer and his men went merrily on and knocked up quite a respectable bag. And so home on horseback, the men following on mules, hung about with the trophies of the chase, to the great admiration of the inhabitants of Mulebbis.

Some excellent trenches were made in front of Fejja through the almond groves. We found several men who became expert at making hurdles from eucalyptus branches, and these made first rate revetments. Some of the bivouac areas were exposed to view from Mejdel Yaba, but rows of the young trees, transplanted whole, made excellent "blinds."

The view of the Judæan hills across the plain was very picturesque. There was hardly a hill top which was not capped by a building or a ruin of some kind—some fortress, tomb, or city of ancient times—giving an impression of age and decay which is the dominant feature of any landscape in Palestine, and appears always to have been so, even in ancient times, judging from the Hebrew writers. The Land of Promise! The thoroughfare of armies, the contention of empires, it now lies desolate, ruin upon ruin. . . "forsaken and not a man to dwell therein." Such, almost, has it become, through its successive conquests and destructions, culminating in 400 years of Turkish rule.

An enemy 'plane bombed us on January 9th, and considering how low he flew he made very poor practice at our little houses.

Candles were very short at this period but olive oil was obtainable in small quantities, and when we couldn't get that we used dubbin with success, though the light was not brilliant.

On January 14th we moved back into our billets in Mulebbis. On the following day the enemy suddenly began to shell the town, causing a few casualties, chiefly among the civilian population. The latter became very alarmed and a large number trekked off to Jaffa. On the same day I received orders for my home leave, and as I rode into Jaffa I passed a continuous stream of refugees, many of whom must have started well before the shelling commenced. How they got notice of it is another matter, into which I confess I did not stop to enquire. Our artillery quickly located the enemy's guns and Mulebbis was not shelled again.

## CHAPTER XIII.

# IN SHARON AND EPHRAIM.

URING my absence in England the Battalion spent a fairly quiet time. A Divisional concert party was started which gave frequent entertainments. The weather gradually improved. H.R.H. the Duke of Connaught held an investiture at Divisional Headquarters at Yasur, at which Wilson, Finn, Colvin, Wray and Keeling received their decorations. Brigadier-General Dodington left for England, to the great regret of all ranks he had led so well. He, above all others, had *made* the Brigade, and its greatest achievements will always be associated with his name. He was succeeded by Brigadier-General H. E. Orpen-Palmer, D.S.O. The new Brigadier was very keen on transport matters and a Brigade show was held on March 23rd, at which the Battalion won the Lewis gun turn-out. The 5th Transport men were always very good, being country men who had been used to horses all their lives, and the way the transport was turned out was always a credit to the Brigade.

On March 12th there was a considerable advance on the right, the village and strong position of Mejdel Yaba falling to the 162nd Brigade. El Mirr and Ras-el-Ain were occupied without opposition and became part of the new line. The Castle at the latter place made a good observation post from which a closer view could be obtained of the Jiljulia and Kefr Kasim defences, on which the enemy was continuously at work.

I arrived back on Good Friday and found that the Battalion was out practising night operations, not returning until two in the morning. The strength had been increased by drafts up to 32 officers and 828 other ranks. They were in quite a nice bivouac in the olive groves near Kefr Ana, the ancient city of Ono, which figures in so many campaigns, lying as it did right in the path of the conquering armies which so frequently swept up the maritime plain. In scriptural history it is generally grouped with Lod (Ludd) and Hadid (Haditheh) and it is related in Ezra ii. 33, how 725 souls returned to these three cities after the captivity in Babylon. Nehemiah speaks of Lod and Ona as " the valley of craftsmen " occupied by the children of Benjamin. Near by was the village of Yehudieh, the " Jehud " which was given by lot to the children of Dan (Joshua xix. 45) with Bene-berak (now Ibn-Ibrak) another village about two miles to the north-west towards Jaffa. Jehud was one of the cities which fell to Shishak, King of Egypt, in his conquest of the country.

Kefr Ana provided a good and pleasant training ground (though a good deal of it was rapidly coming under the plough) and training was carried out in earnest. A Divisional school was started at Red House Wood and was a great success under the able direction of that keen soldier and tireless worker, Lieut.-Colonel Garsia, G.S.O. (1) 54th Division. Divisional Headquarters were now at Mulebbis, Brigade Headquarters at Wilhelma, a German colony on the plain. The colonists had been transported to Jaffa. They left a fine herd of cows, which, after allowing a ration for their owners, provided some excellent dairy produce for the Division, under the efficient management of Archer, of the 5th Essex, and some of the men who knew all about cows.

On April 16th the Brigade went into the line, the Battalion being in support to the left section, and pitching its bivouac amongst the rocks of the Mejdel Yaba ridge to the east of the village. One company did a route march every day, the remainder being employed on road making and the construction of defences in the new front line. The latter consisted of trenches where it was possible to dig them but for the most part of stone sangars, as the ground was nearly all bare rock.

Behind us lay the deep and winding valley of the Wadi Ballut, cutting right through Mount Ephraim, and in the old days forming the natural boundary, first between Northern Israel and Judah, and later between Samaria and Judæa, "sustaining" says Dr. G. Adam Smith "the arch schism of history." The floor of the valley was flat, and wide enough for some cultivation on each side of the bed of the stream, which was now practically dry. The sides were very steep and rocky, and covered with coarse grass and shrub. They contained some very capacious caves.

The Battalion area was rather too cramped for a position so close to the front line and companies were dispersed about 400 yards apart, connected of course by telephone. On April 22nd we were moved to a more central position in rear of the line held by the Brigade, on each side of a tributary of the Wadi Ballut. The ground had not been previously occupied, and swarmed with scorpions, which lay under every rock. Clearing the ground for the bivouacs brought them to light. "A" Company claimed to have killed 180 before they settled down for the night.

The wild flowers were wonderful, and the whole country looked like a big rock garden. Daisies, "Stars of Bethlehem," lilies, scarlet anemones, wild tulips, and poppies abounded, and every kind of brilliant blossom from tiny "forget-me-not"-looking flowers to great holly-hocks, eight feet high. The rocky ground was covered with thin grass and aromatic shrubs, among which flew myriads of winged insects. A small locust-like creature with brilliant red under wings which only shewed during its short flight, was very common. The "Lily of the Field" was not seen here, but was common in the Sharon plain and all down the sandy belt by the sea, to Gaza and beyond. It flourished in the most arid places, a beautiful white lily on a tall slender stem.

Our working parties went nightly to the front line, and their efforts were much appreciated by its occupants, who were loud in their praises of the good work done by the 5th. We reaped the benefit of our labours when we relieved the 1/7th Essex in the line in front of Mejdel Yaba on May 2nd. The defences consisted of small works giving mutual support, and were designed for a mobile defence, two companies being in reserve. Battalion Headquarters was in a large disused lime kiln on the edge of the wadi just in rear of the village of Mejdel Yaba which stood on a high rocky hill. The village itself was not occupied, except by observation posts on the forward slope of the hill. The country was so rough that the siting of the works was a matter of much difficulty and one in particular—of which more hereafter—was in my opinion badly placed; but the line had been carefully selected and had to be made the best of. The enemy shelled

MEJDEL YABA. CAPTURED MARCH 12, 1918.

Mejdel Yaba pretty regularly and made much dust in that venerable stronghold, but the company areas were well camouflaged and the works very lightly held by day, so that casualties were small.

The human inhabitants of Mejdel Yaba had of course departed, but the fleas were multitudinous—and aggressive. They came out of the houses in thousands to meet you as you approached, hopping over the stones and wagging their tails (metaphorically speaking), in anticipation of the visitor's blood. Consequently I did not explore the place as thoroughly as I should have liked.

The house of the Sheikh is built against the wall of an old church now used as a stable. A side door has as a lintel a stone with a Greek inscription in memory of St. Kerikos, whoever that saint may have been. It affords a wonderful view of the plain. I think there is little doubt that on this spot stood the "Tower of Aphek" mentioned by Josephus in his account of the invasion of the country by Cestius Gallus, the Roman General.

The historian tells us how Cestius, marching from Cæsarea, reached Antipatris, and sent a party to drive the Jews out of this tower of Aphek before resuming his march to Ludd.

"Mejdel" means a tower. The hill on which the village stands commands the whole plain from Antipatris to Ludd, and Cestius could hardly have proceeded from the former place without first making good Mejdel Yaba. This identification of Mejdel Yaba with Aphek agrees with the list of Thotmes, which places a city called "Apukn" in this vicinity, and at least makes it possible that the place was the "Aphek" at which the Philistines assembled their forces before attacking the Israelites (1 Sam. iv. 1). The Philistines, it will be remembered, in the battle that followed at Shiloh captured the Ark and took it to Ashdod (now Esdud) and afterwards to Dagon (Beit Dejan) with what result we know.

During the month of April the serious position on the Western front had necessitated the transfer of a large number of troops from Palestine to France. The 52nd and 74th Divisions had gone intact, while in addition nine Yeomanry Regiments, five and a half siege batteries, ten British battalions, and five machine gun companies had been withdrawn from the line, preparatory to embarkation. To some small extent the gaps had been filled by Indian troops, which, however, had not seen service in the present war. During May the depletion continued, a further fourteen British battalions being withdrawn.

As a result of these changes the enemy became much more active both in artillery and patrol work, the latter no doubt having for its chief object the identification of the troops holding the line and the shaking of the moral of the new units.

Patrol work on our side therefore became heavier. Enemy patrols assumed the character of raiding parties and the strength of our patrols had to be increased to deal with them. Small reconnoitring patrols also had to be constantly out to give warning of enemy activity.

There were two prominent hill features in No Man's Land, "Haram Ridge" and "The Blob," which were occupied by observation posts by day and standing patrols by night, in direct communication with Battalion Headquarters by telephone.

On the evening of May 13th I was visiting one of our works on the spur to the left of the village when the enemy put down a heavy barrage on the whole of the front line posts, at the same time bombarding the wadi and the vicinity of Battalion Headquarters with 5.9's. This was followed by heavy rifle fire from the front and it was evident that something in the nature of a raid was in progress. I did a rather undignified scramble over the rocks, dodging the "overs," back to Headquarters and learnt from Colvin on the 'phone that his "C.11" post was being heavily attacked. This post was badly sited, being on a reverse slope with dead ground up to within 50 yards of the front. The Lewis gun position was in advance of the main part of the work, to command this ground, and contained little room for the employment of rifle fire. The enemy had crept up to within bombing distance on the flank while the gun was firing to the front and knocked out the N.C.O., Corporal A. V. Call, and the gun itself, two other members of the team being wounded. Lucas, the platoon commander, was also wounded in an attempt to reach the forward post. The Stokes' Mortars dropped some bombs into the hollows in front and the enemy's fire soon died down. On investigation it was found that the wounded Corporal and the Lewis gun had both disappeared. Battalion Headquarters came in for a good deal of enemy attention during this little affair. One of my best runners, Pte. Wheeldon, was killed and R.Q.M.S. Read was wounded in the head. He died a few days afterwards, a real loss to the Battalion. The Lewis gun Corporal recovered while in Turkish hands and was eventually repatriated.

A Court of Inquiry into the loss of the gun rightly criticised the position in which it was placed. Had I had my own way the whole work would have been sited on the forward slope where the gun was, and I believe this was afterwards done, making the post defensible and enabling it not only to command the ground in its immediate front, but to support the posts on its right and left. Battalion commanders did not get the latitude they would have liked in the manner of holding their front. The laying out of a rigid line and the strict adherence to it, is a necessity in close trench warfare, but the posts we were holding were more of the nature of outpost picquets in open warfare, and I think it would have been better if I had been allowed to change the site.

We had one officer and 12 other ranks wounded, in addition to the casualties already mentioned. Communication with Brigade Headquarters was hampered by the line being twice broken by shell fire, but the linesmen carried out the repairs with their usual promptitude and disregard of danger. The artillery gave ready support, firing on their night lines, which, however, covered comparatively little of the extensive space of No Man's Land, and they probably did more moral than material damage. The Stokes' Mortars were more suited to the situation and Hunter, their officer, worked them well.

During the night of May 19-20 our standing patrol of one N.C.O. and six men was driven off the Haram ridge. They said they were attacked on three sides, and returned to our lines. I was not quite satisfied, and sent them out again, adding six more rifles, to regain touch with the enemy, which they ought not to have lost. The enemy was found to have gone, leaving traces of having visited our little observation post, but had not apparently found the wire, which was intact.

I reported exactly what took place, attaching very little importance to the matter, but the Divisional Staff replied by letter, pointing out that according to my report it appeared that the enemy's patrols were left in undisputed possession of the ridge until they chose to withdraw. This seemed to indicate that my action was not approved. But it really was not my fault that the enemy had chosen to withdraw instead of waiting to be driven off by the patrol, which I had reinforced for that purpose. The letter went on to say that my reasons for strengthening the patrol were not clear. I confess I was a little discouraged by this detailed criticism. I felt that it cramped my style. I also felt how easy it would have been to have avoided criticism by reporting the matter in a different light. It is so easy to trim the narrative of a little affair of this kind to make it appear quite a creditable performance. Everyone knows that this sort of thing is done, not only in patrol reports, but in important despatches. "Eyewash" has its value, and is by no means to be despised, but reports of operations should be studiously free from it. The object of a report should be to convey exactly what took place, and not to impress higher commanders with the energy and ability of the writer, or the superiority of his unit.

Another thing which tended to embellish the reports of some units was the fact that the gist of them appeared in an intelligence summary, issued by the Intelligence Staff. The latter always appeared to me—I will not say too credulous, but too ready to accept "news" of any kind which made "copy" for their reports and the latter were by no means always reliable.

The increased activity of the enemy at this time was clearly due to his knowledge of the changes and depletions which had taken place in our order of battle. It began to appear to me that it was attributed to want of vigilance or enterprise on the part of units holding the line. I do not think, however, that this could be fairly said of the 5th Essex.

On the following nights I posted strong fighting patrols on the "Blob" to our immediate front to break up or harass any further raiding parties the enemy might send over. On the night of the 21st the enemy tried another raid on "C 11," employing on this occasion, according to prisoners' statements, a whole battalion for the purpose. (It should be stated that enemy battalions at this period were not more than about 200 strong.) Eden was the officer in command of the patrol, which consisted of a platoon 32 strong. While disposing his platoon in a waiting position on the "Blob" he came in contact with the raiders. Nine of his men became detached and being under fire, not only from the enemy but from our own front line, which was by this time being attacked by a storming party which the enemy had sent on in front, they made their way back to our lines. With his remaining 23 men Eden kept up the fight with the main body of the enemy, being to some extent sheltered by our own fire by the dead ground before referred to. The result was completely to disorganise the enemy's attack. When all his ammunition was exhausted Eden turned about and was last seen giving the order to charge through a portion of the enemy's storming party which was making its way to a flank. This party made off in the darkness and the patrol regained our lines with nine men wounded. Eden himself was never seen again. His action was beyond praise. Placed in a most difficult situation, he displayed courage and initiative of a high order and by his death the Battalion lost a gallant and devoted officer.

Meanwhile the garrison of the little post had put up a most spirited defence. I could not give them artillery support until I knew the fate of the patrol. C.S.M. James, of "C" Company, was in command of the post at the time of the attack, and it was largely by his excellent example and disregard of his personal safety that the enemy were driven off, only two of them reaching the wire. The old Lewis gun post had been enlarged to accommodate six rifles under Corpl. A. G. Drury. This N.C.O. displayed great coolness and courage in disposing his men among the rocks and foiling an attempt to outflank his position.

The gunners gave the enemy a bad journey back to their lines and they were seen to be carrying casualties back in stretchers after daybreak. Search parties failed to find any trace of Eden. Prisoners said the enemy paid a high price for an officer brought back, dead or alive, and there is doubt his body was got away. Our hope that he was a prisoner was not destined to be realised. The party found three dead Turks and brought in two prisoners, one badly wounded. These evidently belonged to the storming party. The main body's casualties were doubtless removed in the darkness. Corpl. A. Coates, a most promising and cheery N.C.O. who had served with credit in the Battalion since it left England, was also killed. The wounded numbered 15. C.S.M. James received the D.C.M. and Corpl. Drury and Corpl. Dann (of the patrol) got Military Medals.

The following wire was received from XXI. Corps, "The Corps Commander wishes to congratulate 'T.G.' (*i.e.* 1/5th Essex) on their spirited patrol action last night. He greatly deplores the loss of the gallant patrol leader." The Brigadier added his own concurrence.

The enemy did not attempt any more attacks on Mejdel Yaba. On the 23rd, having completed our three weeks in the line, we were relieved by the 1/5th Norfolk Regiment and went into bivouac in the orange groves near Mulebbis. It was a pleasant enough spot and a shady one, but the insects which infested the trees were rather a nuisance. The Battalion was now employed in the war against mosquitoes, the chief measures of which were clearing and "canalising" the Wadi Ishkar (Issachar ?) which ran in front of the line. Reeds and other

RAS-EL-AIN (ANTIPATRIS).

*To face page 129.*

growths were cleared and banks cut straight to allow a free flow of water and any stagnant pools were covered with oil to stop breeding. This procedure was carried out for nearly a thousand yards to the front of the line in the plain, and was done by daylight, the banks and long grass giving good cover from view. During our stay in the orange groves I occasionally visited Ras-el-Ain, now occupied by our troops. It provided a good view of the enemy's positions on the foothills in front of Mejdel Yaba. The River Auja which rises there in several very strong springs, becomes a considerable stream almost at once, and its course is fringed with the most luxuriant growth of small trees, shrubs, grasses and flowers. Ras-el-Ain, seen from a distance, looks merely the gaunt shell of a castle, set bare in the plain, but a close approach reveals many hidden beauties. It is a favourite resort of the Mulebbis people in the summer, and altogether a delightful spot after the burning rocks of the hills. Alexander Jannæus fortified the place against the Syrians under Antiochus (B.C. 105–78) and constructed lines, probably along the course of the Auja, consisting, according to Josephus, of a wall with wooden towers and intermediate redoubts, but no trace of these remains. Herod built a town here, calling it Antipatris, in honour of his father Antipater, son of Antipas.

A large Christian community was massacred here in 744 A.D. after which it is not mentioned until 1064, when an empty castle existed on the site. It was probably restored and fortified again by the Crusaders but after standing a siege during the brief civil war between Baldwin III., King of Jerusalem, and his mother in 1149 it fell into the hands of Saladin in 1187 and he dismantled it after his defeat by Richard at Arsuf in 1191.

It is now a mere shell, but a noble one, covering 280 feet north and south and 260 feet east and west with a massive tower at each corner.

The whole of the plain hereabouts resounds with the exploits of the Crusaders. It was at Mirabel close by, in 1192, that Richard Lion-Heart, having outpaced his retainers, came up with about 80 Turks and lay about him with such effect that the survivors fled before the arrival of the rest of the English. In the same year Godfrey de Lusignan, Count of Jaffa, raided a Turkish post at the same place, killing 30 and taking back 50 prisoners. He kept 25 of them and ransomed the remainder for 8,000 besants, representing £300 a head in modern currency. There has been a slump in Turks since those days.

On June 6th the Battalion relieved the 1/5th Bedfordshire Regiment in the front line in front of the River Auja. It was a delightful place, the trenches for the most part being in orange groves laden with fruit, and there were good bathing facilities. There were also good fish in the river. The most effective method of getting them was by firing at them with a rifle. The bullet seldom hit them but they were stunned by the impact for several seconds, during which they turned on their sides and floated on the surface, to be taken by a sandbag on the end of a pole. All ranks slept at night under mosquito-net "bivvies" and sentries had their faces and hands and knees anointed with anti-mosquito grease. The result of these precautions, and of the cleanliness of body and clothing made possible by the abundance of fresh water, was a good record of health, in contrast to the conditions at Mejdel Yaba where sand-fly fever and other complaints were rife and malaria fairly common. The whole of this district is of course very unhealthy in summer, a fact frequently noted in historical records, and it speaks well for the efforts of the Medical Services that the health of the Army was maintained in the way it was.

Battalion Headquarters had a mess and a signal office in a small house which contained the pumps for watering the groves. The latter were very well managed and yielded enormous crops. During our stay in the groves we had a working party of 20 men engaged daily in picking oranges, which were carted away in limbered wagons for the garrisons of less favoured parts of the line. They averaged about 20,000 oranges a day, and a fortnight's picking did not seem materially to alter the appearance of the groves.

We were separated from the enemy by an enormous tract of the plain, the distance varying from two to three miles. The plain was absolutely flat and the coarse reeds and grasses rose in places to a height of five or six feet. The only features were the course of the Wadi Ishkar and one or two other dry and shallow watercourses very difficult to define, and the disused railway tract from Ras-el-Ain to Jiljulia. Patrolling this large area was a big business. The patrols were out nearly all night and came back wet to the skin with the heavy dew which hung on the long coarse rushes. Direction had to be kept mainly by the stars. Nevertheless, excellent work was done. The enemy's outposts were all located and hardly a night passed without drawing fire from them. His patrols were seldom met with, and there is no doubt that we had complete command of the plain. The 1/5th Bedfords had scuppered a post which the enemy had on a slight elevation, marked by a single tree, near the railway, and he never put a post there again. On June 21st the following appeared in Divisional Orders—"The G.O.C. 54th Division wishes to place on record that between the 7th and 14th June, 1918, good patrol work has been carried out on the front of the Division as below. . . . The following are specially deserving of praise for their bold and skilful leading and for the results obtained." Patrols led by Lockwood and Watts were included under the above heading and others led by Eames, Keeling, and Richmond were mentioned as having been "well led" and as having "done good work." A similar Order appeared later in which patrols led by Lucas and Baird were singled out for praise. I believe names of other officers were mentioned, but I regret I have not a copy of the later Order. The credit was of course fully shared by the N.C.O.'s and men, particularly the Battalion scouts, trained by Keeling. Some of them went out with each patrol, and got to know the ground very well.

Allusion has already been made to the despatch of large numbers of troops from the Palestine front to France. On the 24th orders were received from Divisional Headquarters to be in readiness for embarkation at short notice, and on the 27th we were relieved by the 2/7th Gurkha Rifles. Handing over was a matter of some difficulty as the incoming unit was very short of white officers and none of the Gurkhas could speak English. They were very smart and intelligent and we were much struck with their keenness. We marched the same night to Red House Wood where we stayed the next day, marching again at dusk to Surafend which is about three miles from Ramleh, on the Jaffa-Jerusalem road. The Battalion equipment was thoroughly gone into and completed in every detail. Some units of the Division had already entrained, when the order came cancelling those for embarkation. We were not for France after all. Much disappointment was felt and expressed, but for my part I consider we were fortunate in being allowed to take part in the grand finale of the Palestine campaign, which throughout must have been much more interesting for all ranks from a military point of view than close trench warfare, which formed such a large part of the operations on the Western front. Many things were missed by us no doubt—comfortable "spells" in billets among a civilized population, little holidays in Paris, and above all more frequent leave to England. But the East had its advantages, not least of which was the dry climate, making it an ideal one for soldiering for most of the year round.

On July 1st the G.O.C. 54th Division issued an Order directing that "his appreciation be conveyed to all ranks of the Division for the extremely efficient manner in which the move out of the line for entrainment was carried out" and his opinion that "the expedition shewn in carrying out the orders reflected great credit on all those responsible for the necessary arrangements and on the discipline of the troops concerned."

Surafend was a large camp and our bivouac, close to a very dusty road, was not a comfortable one. But there was plenty of water and some good training ground, and we went in for some close order and ceremonial drill, which provided a change, and was useful in smartening up generally and in correcting a certain slackness which is bound to creep in during a protracted stay in the front line. There was good opportunity for games and a successful Brigade race-meeting was held. Deakin won the Brigade Company Commander's race on "Wild Rose." My fast Arab pony was unfortunately lame and I could only finish fourth on Bacon's "Flying Fanny" in the six furlong race, won by Paris the Brigade-Major. Willmott was responsible for the running of the Totalisator which considerably augmented the race fund. A good start was made with Polo, but the ground crumbled rather badly.

On July 9th we again crossed the plain, moving via Ludd to Beit Nebala, where we stayed during the night in the olive groves. Beit Nebala is a picturesque and typical Palestine village at the entrance to a pass through the hills. It is the ancient Neballat, mentioned by Nehemiah as one of the cities of the tribe of Benjamin to which they returned after the captivity. The next day we marched through the foothills to Kefr Insha for work on one of the roads which was being made in preparation for the autumn advance. We were still close to the Wadi Ballut but on the south side. We pitched our bivouac close to some very interesting ruins, apparently of some old monastery, on the old Roman road from Jerusalem to Antipatris. It was a rocky spot and we made ourselves fairly comfortable, although it was very hot. The chief drawback was absence of water which had to be brought four miles, either from the wells at Kuleh on the edge of the plain or El Lubban in the hills. The mules had therefore to walk 16 miles a day to get two waterings, which was practically a day's work. Provisions had to be carted from Ludd, about 12 miles distant.

A detachment of R.E. were in bivouac close by. They marked out the road and superintended its making. The infantry did the work—it is, as Mr. Birrell would say, "the badge of their tribe." And be it said, it was good work the infantry put into those roads. Six a day were the working hours, beginning very early in the morning and finishing in the forenoon. Task work was tried. The men did it in five hours. The task was then increased by the R.E. on the ground that the men were "getting used to it" and could do more. This was hardly good enough, and we went back to working by time. Fourteen inches of solid metal was put into these roads, and they will last longer than the Roman ones. The bottom layer consisted of great stones about eight inches in diameter, not thrown in anyhow, but fitted in to each other. The second layer was of four to five inch stones, the remainder finished with macadam of smaller stones. Where the road was above the surrounding surface it was retained on both sides by a well-built wall two feet thick at the top and thicker at the bottom. The whole of the material had to be carried by hand in baskets from the ground near by. A football ground of sorts had been cleared of rocks by the R.E. and was continuously used. A Field Ambulance near our camp had cleared another. The ground was very small, but a competition for platoon "sixes" was arranged and excited much interest. We also had some good matches with the R.E.

The old Roman road could be distinctly traced, though it was overgrown with grass, and the wear of the wheeled traffic could be seen in many places on the stones. Another Roman road joined it at El Lubban.

It was a nice country to ride about in. The Wadi Ballut was very picturesque higher up, and some of its tributary valleys were beautiful, with terrace upon terrace of olive trees, watered by delicious springs of water. One of them, the Wadi Reiya, had a sparkling rivulet along its whole length, running through grottoes of rocks and small plantations, a very paradise in that arid country. The stream started up in the hills near Beit Rima, a picturesque village perched up high on Mount Ephraim. It was the birth place of Samuel—Ramathaim it is called in 1 Samuel i. 1, and Ramah in the same chapter. It was one of the cities ratified by Demetrius to the Jews in B.C. 145 under the Maccabees, being then transferred from Samaria to Judea. It afterwards became famous as Arimathea, the home of Joseph, the friend of our Lord.

Work on the roads continued until July 31st when we moved back to the vicinity of Beit Nebala. The bivouac was a pleasant one, in an olive grove, but it was a very sultry spot, shut in by the hills on three sides. Just to the south the Wadi Surar broke through on to the plain. The water of one of its tributaries had been held up in ancient times by a massive dam which must have formed a large reservoir. It was probably Roman work. The dam was so good and thick that it made an excellent gallery rifle range, and some useful musketry was carried out. On the south side of the entrance of the Wadi into the plain stood the village of Haditheh, the Hadid of the Bible, in a fine situation on a natural bastion of rock overlooking the plain. It, like Neballat, was a city of Benjamin. It played an important part in the campaigns of those great warriors the Maccabees. Simon Maccabeus "set up Adida in Sephela" (the foothill country) and made it strong with gates and bars." (1 Maccabees xii. 38). After his brother Jonathan had been imprisoned by treachery in Ptolemais (Acre) by Tryphon, who "gathered together a great host to invade Judea," Simon "pitched his tents at Adida over against the plain." Tryphon, approaching, sent messengers to Simon saying he would ransom Jonathan for a hundred talents of silver and the prisoner's two sons for hostages. The children and the money were duly sent, but Tryphon, the rascal, "dissembled, neither would he let Jonathan go" but murdered him instead. The whole story is told in 1 Maccabees xiii.

About three miles further in the hills stands the village of Midieh, formerly Modin, the home of the Maccabees, whither Simon took the bones of Jonathan and buried them, setting up "pillars over his tomb to be seen by those who sail the sea."

We did a good deal of training on this historic ground, over which ebbed and flowed the struggles against the Syrians (B.C. 166) and the Romans (66 A.D.). Sometimes the tide flowed westward, as when Jonathan swept right down to Jaffa and took it; sometimes eastward, as when the Syrians rolled up to the walls of Jerusalem itself. The same thing repeated itself thirteen centuries later, with Saladin and Richard in the leading parts.

We were able to form a Battalion Officers' mess at Beit Nebala, making quite a comfortable mess room with spare bivouac sheets fastened together, with wagon poles for uprights and captured angle-iron pickets to hold up the sides, which were left open to let in the air. It is a good thing for all the officers of a Battalion to get together, even if only at feeding times. Companies and Battalion Headquarters are too much "on their own" when distributed in the line, and officers are apt to get "cliquey," a condition which is not conducive to the best Battalion spirit.

Particular attention was given to training the platoon as a fighting unit. On August 12th Watts's platoon of "C" Company did a little scheme which was attended by the Divisional Commander and a large number of officers from other formations, and provided the occasion for a useful discussion on the platoon in the attack in hill country. The performers played their parts well. On the 18th a successful Battalion sports meeting was held and on other days turn-out and driving competitions for the transport, cookhouse turn-out, etc.

We left Beit Nebala on August 21st and relieved the 1/4th Northamptonshires in the left-central sub-section on a front of 1,500 yards. It joined our former Mejdel Yaba line, continuing it to the eastward. In front of us lay the Bureid Ridge, which was at first occupied by our troops after the capture of Mejdel Yaba. The line was afterwards withdrawn to the one now held, as there were no covered communications with the ridge. The enemy had not occupied it, though he had a deep wadi—the Wadi Rabah—in rear of it and could have done so if he had chosen. It was patrolled by both sides at night. Enemy picquets were located in the hollows to the east of it, protected by barbed wire, also on Umm el Bureid, a spur of it running north, which was held by day and night. The latter had, as we discovered afterwards, an almost sheer face of rock just behind it, dropping to the Wadi Rabah, to which the picquet retired when the place was shelled, as it frequently was. The enemy appeared jumpy and often threw bombs a long distance from our patrols, also firing at the slightest sound and putting up Very lights. It was very difficult for patrols to avoid being heard, going over the slippery rocks and treading in the dry rough grass. Propaganda leaflets were left in our old sangars on the ridge, and those were found, on subsequent nights, to have been duly collected. Small brushes with enemy patrols were frequent on the ridge, the latter generally retiring north into the Wadi Rabah. Some very good work was done by patrols led by Lucas, Lockwood, Foley-Whaling, Barnard, Archer, Wray, and Sergeants Rolph and French. Two deserters came in on September 1st and two more on the 4th, including a warrant officer, who said that the enemy kept a reserve company north of the ridge, who had orders to occupy it in case of an attack at night. The information gained by the patrols, added to reconnaissance by day with field glasses and telescopes, gave us a very good idea of the ground over which we were destined to attack, and proved of great value.

On the night of September 8th we were relieved by the 1/5th Bedfords and again recrossed the plain to Red House Wood, to rest and refit for the attack.

The Commander-in-Chief had decided to make his main attack "on the coastal plain, rather than through the hills, where the ground afforded the enemy positions of great natural strength and taxed the physical energy of the attackers to the utmost" (official despatch). The hills round Kefr Kasim, in front of Mejdel Yaba, overlooked the plain and had to be included in the frontage of the main attack. The latter was entrusted to Lieut.-General Sir Edward Bulfin, K.C.B., who, we were proud to remember, had once commanded the Essex Territorial Infantry Brigade. The groves around us were full of troops. Every night the plain was alive with columns of all arms moving westward. There was little movement by day, and even if there had been the enemy had little chance of seeing it, for our ascendancy in the air was well nigh complete. During the last week in August the total number of enemy planes which crossed our lines was eighteen. During one week in June there had been over 100. I saw one brought down quite close to Divisional Headquarters with a bullet through its petrol tank. The pilot made a good landing and was entertained at one of the Divisional messes. I was told—I don't know how true it was—that the staff "did" him very well, in the hope of loosening his tongue, but that he turned out more than a match for them at the table. He talked freely about everything but the enemy, kept them up half the night, and got up in the morning with the only head of the party which didn't ache!

A few nights after we left the line the 1/5th Bedfords had an officer shot dead on patrol on the Bureid Ridge. On the following night we saw and heard a regular battle going on on the same ground. The report of this engagement was read at a Brigade conference a day or two after. Our successors in the line stated that they were given to understand that they could walk about freely on the Bureid Ridge, but that when their patrol visited it they found it strongly held by the enemy.

It is true that our patrols had walked about freely on the ridge, but, as the log book could have shewn, they were frequently fired upon by enemy patrols, though it was never strongly held.

The following night the 1/5th Bedfords, after a short artillery bombardment, attacked the ridge in considerable force and met with strong resistance from enemy infantry. Presumably, on the strength of the report on this action, the Bureid Ridge was now stated to form part of the Turkish main system, wire was said to be known at one point and suspected at others, and a considerable length of enemy sangars appeared on the official maps. All this was directly contrary to the information supplied by our patrols who regularly reported the ridge clear of any enemy works ; and it is only fair to these patrols to say that when the 1/4th Essex and ourselves advanced over the whole ridge in the attack which afterwards took place, there was no sign of wire, nor were there any prepared positions except our own old sangars on the northern slope. What, I think, happened when the Bedfords attacked, was that the enemy, thinking their main positions were being attacked, sent out the reserve company of which the warrant officer prisoner had told us.

However, it must be said that the action, in which the Bedfords took part with so much credit to themselves, had the important result of bringing down the enemy's barrage, the location of which led to certain alterations in the plan of attack which probably saved the Essex Brigade many casualties in the following battle. Another valuable result was that the enemy's bombardment enabled the "sound rangers" to locate the batteries themselves. Consequently, when the real attack came off every enemy battery had one of our "heavies" turned on to it, with excellent results, as we afterwards saw with our own eyes.

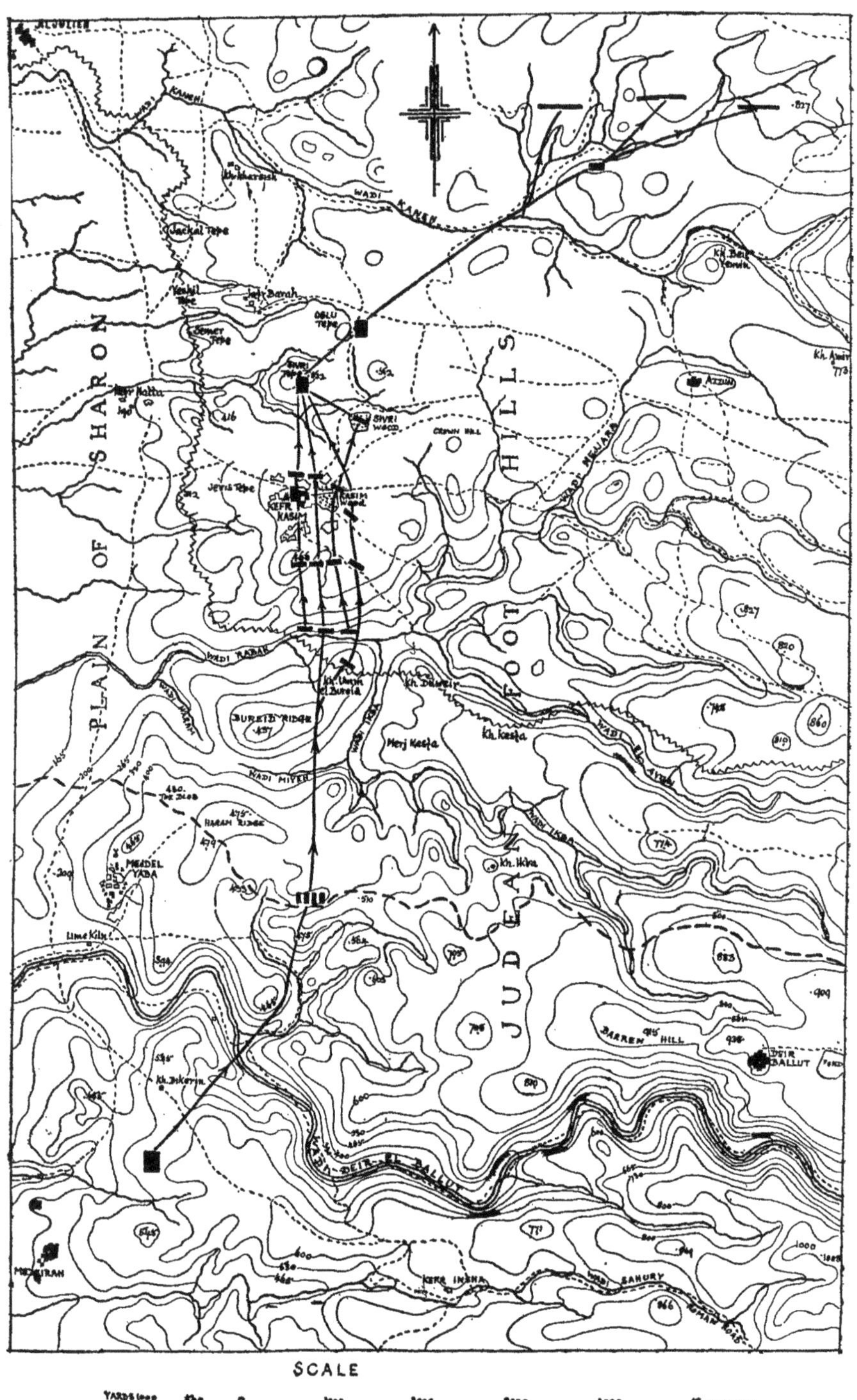


SCALE

YARDS 1000 500 0 1000 2000 3000 4000 5000 YARDS

APPROXIMATE BRITISH FRONT LINE
" ENEMY " "

**THE BATTLE IN THE FOOTHILLS, SEPT. 19, 1918, SHOWING THE MOVEMENTS OF THE BATTALION.**

CHAPTER XIV.

# THE BATTLE IN THE FOOTHILLS.

N September 14th we moved across to the hills again and bivouacked in a valley near Mezeireh, the next four days being occupied in studying the details of the attack, in bayonet fighting, and in practising the attack over the rocky country, which was a counterpart of the country in front.

I do not propose to go into details of the grand plan of operations. They are stated with wonderful clearness in the official despatch. But the root idea was as follows :—The enemy's line was to be attacked on a line running from the sea, along the whole width of the plain of Sharon and for some distance into the foothills. A gap was thus to be made for the cavalry to break through on the plain and make straight for El Afule on the plain of Esdraelon, and Beisan, two important points on the enemy's lines of communication forty-five and sixty miles distant respectively, before the enemy could make his escape. When the foothills north of Kefr Kasim were taken the XXI. Corps was to swing to the right and advance in a north-easterly direction through the hills, so as to drive the enemy into the arms of the cavalry.

It will thus be seen that rapidity was the keynote of all the operations. Once the attack commenced the enemy were to be given no time to organise a retreat or to get away his guns.

The frontage of the attack for the 161st Brigade was from the edge of the plain to Oglu Tepe. This line made good, we were to advance to the hills to the north of the Wadi Kanah, and another Division was to carry on the pursuit. On our right was the 163rd Brigade and a detachment of French troops. On our left was the 3rd (Lahore) Division. The 162nd Brigade was in 54th Divisional reserve. It should be mentioned that owing to the great changes made in our order of battle by the despatch of British troops to France, the 54th Division was now the only complete white division on this front. All the others were Indian, with a sprinkling of British units forming part of their composition.

The attack of the 161st Brigade was divided into six phases. The first was to take us over the Bureid Ridge to the line of the Wadi Rabah. The second to the crest of the hills to the north of it. The third to Jevis Tepe, to the west of Kefr Kasim, the village itself, and the cactus gardens to the east of it, called by us Kasim Wood. The fourth to Semer Tepe, north-west of Kefr Kasim, Sivri Tepe, a commanding position strongly fortified about a mile north of the village, and Sivri Wood, to the north-west of it on lower ground. The fifth to Jackal Tepe still further north, Kefr Barah, and Oglu Tepe. The sixth a further advance on the left, pivoted on the Oglu Tepe.

The first three phases were entrusted to the 1/4th and 1/5th Essex, the last three to the 1/6th and 1/7th Essex.

It was thus once more the good fortune of the 1/5th Essex to be in the leading line. In the advance over the plain at Suvla we were accompanied by the 1/7th. At the first battle of Gaza we were side by side with the 1/4th. At the third battle of Gaza the 1/6th were up with us. And now the 1/4th and ourselves were once more to be shoulder to shoulder to kick off for the Essex Brigade.

On September 18th we were told the secret of "zero" day. It was to be on the morrow—the 19th. The Divisional Commander saw all officers in the afternoon. General Hare was not given to much talking. In a few words he impressed upon us the importance of our task, and the necessity of rapidity in the advance, in order that the high ground to the north of Wadi Kanah might be captured as soon as possible to support the advance of the 3rd (Lahore) Division on our left, and to roll up the Turkish flank and secure the advance of the 10th Division through the difficult hill country on our right. We could all see that the General was quietly confident, and as he shook hands and wished us luck we felt his confidence was infectious.

All the details of the scheme—infantry, artillery, machine guns, trench mortars, communications, &c., were issued from Brigade Headquarters in a series of "Instructions" over the signature of Paris, the Brigade Major, and no instructions could have been clearer or more complete. Not only were they a model of lucidity and form, but the way they worked in practice shewed a complete grasp of the needs of every possible situation.

Although arranged in "phases," after the manner of trench warfare, the scheme was sufficiently elastic to allow of the best means being taken, by units already launched to the attack, to carry out the intentions of the Commander, whatever emergencies should arise. In one important matter they differed from the ordinary trench to trench scheme of attack. After the initial phases the infantry were no longer tied to an artillery barrage, and the supporting artillery worked by the infantry and not vice versa.

The zero hour was fixed to coincide with the very first peep of dawn. This made it possible after the first enemy resistance was broken to "see what he was up to" and to act accordingly.

A few words as to equipment may be of interest. Shorts and khaki jackets were worn by all ranks. I voted for trousers but was overruled. Shorts give greater freedom of movement and are cooler, but the nature of the rocks and wiry grass we were to attack over was very rough on bare knees, as we found to our cost. Haversacks were left behind and everything was carried in the pack. This was sound, as haversacks carried at the side are very uncomfortable, and it made more room for two water bottles, which were considered a necessity and proved a great boon. In the pack were 50 rounds of extra S.A.A., cardigan, cap comforter, washing and shaving kit, two iron rations and a pair of socks. Each man had a triangular tin disc sewn on the back of his pack, which, flashing in the sun, let the artillery know where we were. Each company carried five Very pistols and a proportion of flares for signalling to the aeroplanes. Each platoon carried two yellow flags to mark the position of the front line. Signallers were provided with "flappers" for visual signalling to the rear. Each company carried 30 rifle grenades and a few dischargers for firing them from, also a few hand grenades, in case of necessity, convertible to rifle grenades, if required, by screwing sticks into them and firing them from the old cup attachment.

The men had their evening meal at 5.30 and after a good sleep were served out with a light meal of hot cocoa at midnight. At 1.10 a.m. we left our bivouac and arrived at the front line at 2.30 where a halt was made. Lewis guns and ammunition were off loaded here and carried by hand. It was impossible country for mules and these were placed in charge of R.S.M. James with orders to move to Kefr Kasim by the best available route as soon as circumstances permitted.

The R.E. had laid a tape earlier in the evening for us to form up on, to ensure a true direction at the start. It was rather in front of the line originally selected and was on a forward slope of the ground. The R.E. were seen or heard by the enemy while laying the tape and were interrupted a good deal by artillery fire. The enemy was evidently apprehensive and expected *something* was going to take place, but there is no doubt he was deceived as to the point of the main attack. I did not worry about the tape. I knew the ground better than many parts of my own parish, and officers and men who had been on patrol knew it far better. I therefore formed up about 200 yards in rear of the tape, behind the crest. The enemy opened fire with his 77's and a certain amount of wild rifle fire from his outposts on the ridge but the platoons lay down in column of fours and awaited the moment to start. One or two casualties occurred and General Orpen-Palmer and his staff, who were there to see us off, had rather a narrow escape from one shell. It was still very dark and platoons did not open out as much as originally intended owing to the number of men required for connecting files. Companies, however, knew exactly where to go, and there was no need for wide extensions at this stage, although the frontage of our first objective was a thousand yards. There was not the danger of losing direction that there was at the last Gaza battle over the sand. The hills were all known and their outlines familiar to most of us.

The advance commenced at 3.50 a.m. in absolute silence. The guns were not due to open fire until 4.30 which was zero hour.

Slowly we moved forward up the gentle rise and over the high ground. The enemy put over a good deal of H.E., which, however, did little damage, although there was a very "devil among the tailors" on the rocky ground sloping down to the Wadi Miyeh. The Wadi Ikba on our right was receiving considerable attention and was avoided as an avenue of approach, the right platoon moving on the slope to the left of it and overlooking it. The Wadi Miyeh itself, in front of us, was well plastered. Just before we reached the bottom the gunners struck the zero hour in no uncertain fashion along the whole front from the sea. It must have been a fine display of fireworks for those who had the luck to see it. We could only see immediately in front of us, but the noise was terrific, and the reflections of the flashes lit up the sky to our left like summer lightning.

It would be twenty minutes before we could pass over Bureid Ridge owing to our bombardment of it, which proved to be quite unnecessary. We passed quickly over the Wadi Miyeh and stayed on the slope until we could get on. The enemy's outposts had retired after firing a few shots, and white Very lights began to go up, also green ones in pairs; the latter were signal lights to their artillery, who must have had a busy time responding to the many frantic calls for support. Our guns were now taking on Umm el Bureid, which was held, and "A" Company deployed for the attack. The enemy, however, did not wait for the bayonet and was evidently thinking about the best way back. There was no wire.

"A" Company reorganised at this point and came into Battalion reserve. Battalion Headquarters also stopped here until the next position was made good. The remaining three companies deployed going down the hill and corrected their line on the more or less straight Wadi Rabah on a front of a thousand yards.

Rather more resistance was met with on Hill 479 and the spur to the left of it. The sangars contained machine guns and were protected by barbed wire. The Lewis guns did good work, pushing well forward, using the rocks for cover and bringing oblique fire on the sangars. It was now daylight. The mobility of the Lewis guns proved of great value. On three occasions enemy machine guns were silenced by Lewis guns acting alone, two of them were captured and the whole of the teams taken or killed by the bayonet men. Hardly a rifle had been fired; it was unnecessary, as the advance had never been checked. The reserve company ("A") crossed in rear of "B" Company who were attacking Hill 479 and watched the right flank, where it was difficult to see what was going on. "B," "C," and "D" pushed straight on over the next ridge and advanced on Kefr Kasim Village and Wood, which was being given a severe dusting by the artillery. They got in immediately after the barrage lifted, under fire from a position in rear, shewing that again the enemy had not waited for the assault. The enemy's artillery kept up rapid fire, including 5.9's, but could not keep pace with our advance. Their fire always came down after we left each successive ridge. The 1/7th were close up behind us. Then the enemy turned his attention to the village. The Lewis guns pushed on with groups of rifle men in support to the front of the village, where they had some excellent shooting at the enemy retiring on Sivri Tepe and Wood. But cover was scarce and there was several casualties, among them Sergt. Jarrold, who had already been mentioned in despatches for gallantry, and was killed while commanding his Lewis gun section with his usual bravery and dash.

We should have preferred to go straight on while the enemy were on the run, but had to stop where we were, at the disposal of the Brigade Commander, while the 1/7th Essex went through us. The latter Battalion were well up to time, but the enemy had been able to make a stand in Sivri Wood, and on debouching from the village the 1/7th were met with a steady fire from artillery and machine guns. From the village to the wood was nearly flat ground for about 800 yards, and it was a bad bit of ground to get over. Eventually Colonel de Lancy Forth, their C.O., came back to my Headquarters with the news that his Battalion had not been able to get on. I at once offered him a Company in support—the most I was allowed to do by my instructions, but he generously refused to commit it to the second attempt, and walked across to Brigade advanced headquarters, now up in line with us, under Franklin of the 1/5th, to wire for instructions.

There was not much likelihood of a counter-attack, but "A" Company lined a small ridge to the south-east of the village ready for any eventuality. The attack on our right was now up in line with us, though there was a considerable gap. We were in communication with the 1/8th Hampshires by visual, to which means of signalling the country was well suited. We lost touch with our supporting field battery through their cable mule being killed, but the 8th Mountain Artillery Brigade had a line up and did good work with their noisy little 2.75 guns. I shared an observation post in a house at the north-west corner of the village with the Battery Commander. At 10.35 Finn transmitted me a wire ordering the 1/5th to attack Sivri Wood and Hill 512, which commanded it from about 400 yards in rear. Orders were quickly sent round. "C" Company firing line, followed by "D," with "A" and "B" in local reserve. At the same time the 1/5th Bedfords from Divisional reserve passed through our " A " Company (which was echeloned to the right). The Bedfords thus covered the right flank of our advance and threatened the enemy's left. I soon saw from my O.P. in the village that the enemy were beginning to clear out of Sivri Wood, not soon enough, however, to escape the Bedfords who made a considerable number of them prisoners. The order now came for us to attack Sivri Tepe. " C " Company, who had already started, were allowed to go on and occupy Sivri Wood, from which they would be able to support our advance, and the other three companies were sent straight for the hill, " D " Company, under Deakin, leading the way, followed by " A " and " B " and two companies of the 1/7th Essex. I had had a good view of the bombardment of the hill. Several times the enemy had been shelled out and as many times had returned to his defences. But he had not yet been threatened by bayonets, and I had little fear of the result. The artillery had a good view of the hill from the left and would be able to see our men swarming up it. This enabled them to give covering fire up to the last moment, and soon " D " Company were cheering on the crest of that formidable hill, which had frowned down on us for so many months. " C " Company were called up from Sivri Wood and the Battalion reorganised on the slope. Two Turkish field kitchens were found in the gully to the right of the hill, with fires going and a meal of boiled lentils, all hot. There were some water barrels also, which replenished our water bottles and were highly appreciated ; it was a scorching day. We had advanced already over five miles over a very rough rocky country in battle formation, and were glad of a rest. The enemy kept up a heavy bombardment of Kefr Kasim after we left it, and I saw a 5.9 pitch plump on to our late temporary residence, completely demolishing it, a few minutes after we had vacated it. Sergt.-Major James, thinking we might want the ammunition, had pushed on with the mules regardless of the shelling, and was soon up with us ready for the next move, for which we were now complete.

It was a great honour to us to have been entrusted with additional objectives after completing our allotted task at the third. The Divisional Commander gave us all the credit of the capture of these additional objectives after another unit had failed. But the fact is that our task was a very different one from that of the 1/7th Essex. In our case the resistance was very small, owing to General Hare's own quick grasp of the situation and his handling of his reserves, which he threw in just at the right moment.

Our losses had been surprisingly small. This was chiefly owing to the fact that the advance was so rapid that the enemy's artillery fire was continually behind us, except, of course, at Kefr Kasim, where we were obliged to sit still for some time.

ENEMY GUN-LIMBER IN THE WADI KANAH.

*To face page* 145.

The killed numbered 14 only, but included two officers—Fenn, who had only recently joined, and who fell in the attack on the second objective, and Eames, who was killed by a shell in Kasim Wood. He had seen service in the ranks in France, and had a genuine taste for fighting. There were about 45 wounded. Portway, commanding "B" Company, was among the wounded, only stopping after being hit for the second time.

We enjoyed our picnic meal on Sivri Tepe, tired but happy.

We had a good view of the attack of the Lahore Division on Jiljulia and Kalkilieh from the west. The frontal attack over the flat plain, so well known to our patrols, had been avoided, and they were taking most of the works in flank, but the enemy put up a stubborn resistance.

Everybody's knees were in a shocking state from the sharp rocks and prickly grasses, and I regret to say many cardigans were minus their sleeves, which were used as knee protectors.

At 3.45 p.m. the code word "general chase" was received. This was the order for us to cross the Wadi Kanah and to occupy the hills to the north. The Battalion moved in artillery formation straight across country via Oglu Tepe, and took up an outpost line facing north. Several enemy guns were found deserted, and any amount of discarded material of all kinds. Touch was obtained with the 1/10th London Regiment on our right and with the 1/6th Essex on our left. No enemy remained to contest our advance, and the line was occupied in the dark without incident. Before daylight the Lahore Division and the 7th (Meerut) Division had crossed our front, pressing eastward into the hills, and our task was over. Brigade Headquarters was at Oglu Tepe, and we were in communication with them by lamp during the night.

By eight o'clock next morning water and ration camels had arrived.

At half-past ten orders were received to move to the vicinity of Kefr Kareish on the Wadi Kanah, south of Jiljulia. The wadi was full of deserted guns, and all kinds of material. The shell holes found the battery positions showed how well our artillery had located them. One battery had all its bullocks killed in the traces, in an attempt to get the guns out of action.

It was a wide and deep wadi with a well used road, which had been one of the lateral communications of the Turks. It is known in the Bible as the "Brook Kanah" ("the reedy"), and was the boundary between Ephraim and Manasseh. The bed of the stream was now quite dry.

A few days were spent collecting salvage of all kinds. Battalions were given specified areas to search. The enemy's abandoned observation posts were visited and gave very interesting views of our old line. Some of the regimental headquarters had made themselves very comfortable.

A day or two after the battle I met the Divisional Commander at Brigade Headquarters, and he was good enough to say that he was thoroughly satisfied with the work of the Battalion on the 19th. He fully appreciated the strenuous nature of the operations and said the way they were carried out was "extraordinarily good." The Brigadier also spoke highly of the 1/5th. The operations had been essentially a section leaders' and soldiers' battle—a series of small actions—the broken ground calling for plenty of initiative and good fighting qualities on the part of the rank and file. Officers also had all done very well, particularly in keeping their companies and platoons together on terrain which was conducive to disorganisation and the breaking up of fighting units; and when asked to select an officer for an immediate award of a Military Cross I had some difficulty in making a nomination. I eventually recommended Lockwood, who had done consistently well on previous occasions, as well as the present one. Finn again proved himself an ideal battle Adjutant. He never let me forget anything, and I have a shocking memory. It is a great asset for a Battalion Commander to be able to give his whole attention to the tactical situation without being distracted by the possibility of forgetting half-hourly situation reports, returns of captured weapons, estimated casualties, etc., etc.

Sergt. R. T. French led his platoon with much skill and pluck throughout the action.

Sergt. Christopher Green displayed great dash, particularly in the capture of an enemy machine gun, which he rushed with the bayonet, and captured with a small party of men. Lce./Corpl. P. E. Byford had a similar feat to this credit. Under cover of Lewis gun fire he got in with his section and captured the gun with nine prisoners.

Among the other section commanders, Sergt. Tyler, Corpl. L. W. Newman, and Lce./Corpls. John Gray, W. J. Ranson, and E. A. Lofts, with their Lewis gun sections repeatedly broke up enemy parties opposing the advance, whilst among the "Nos. 1" of the guns the following were conspicuous for cool and skilful handling of their weapons:—Ptes. A. E. Cox, H. H. Smith, and A. Balaam. The latter was a holy terror to the Turkish machine gunners.

The Lewis gunners can be fairly said to have deserved a very large share of the honours of the day. The ground suited them, and they used it well. At the first Gaza battle on the level plain they never had a chance. They could only go on firing until they were knocked out by concealed machine guns, an ordeal which they faced without flinching. At the last Gaza battle, the attack being in the dark, they were only used in defence against counter-attacks, a role in which they proved their value. It was not until the attack over the Judean Hills that their efforts in the attack were rewarded with a full measure of success.

Other section leaders who were noted were Lce./Corpls. John Spaull, F. L. French, and K. T. Harrington.

Pte. R. Lockwood, although twice wounded, continued to advance, and set a fine example of pluck and determination to his comrades.

Pte. Daniel Hockley's work as a company runner was beyond praise. He repeatedly crossed fire-swept zones with messages and exhibited great pluck and endurance.

Pte. A. J. Daveridge volunteered to carry a message to Battalion Headquarters through a heavy H.E. barrage. He was knocked out for nearly half-an-hour by a shell, but succeeded in delivering his message.

Ptes. C. E. Hawkes and Frank Saville upheld the fine reputation of the stretcher bearers in going out and bringing in three wounded men under particularly heavy fire.

The Battalion, whilst in the Wadi Kanah, got some fresh clothes with which we were able to cover the nakedness of some of the worst cases. Hill fighting is very destructive to clothing.

CHAPTER XV.

# ON TREK.

ALL details were arranged for the march northwards, wagon loads made up, etc. Camels were used for carrying the day's water and each Battalion had two G.S. wagons on which it carried officers' kits (35lbs. each), orderly room boxes, mosquito bivouacs, two or three tents for orderly room, medical room, etc., some spare boots, and clothing and equipment, dubbin and oil, two large canvas water tanks, armourers', pioneers' and shoemakers' tools, and a few other indispensable things. The men were heavily loaded; full marching order and a bivouac in addition.

On September 28th the Brigade concentrated on the plain near Jiljulia. An immense amount of digging had been done there by the Turks and it had evidently been designed as a strong point of resistance. It was inhabited, but the inhabitants looked in a wretched state.

On the 29th the Brigade marched to Kakon, headed by the Brigade band (under Sergt. Ross, of the 1/5th) and as we swung past the ancient Gilgal to its martial strains, through the long lines of wondering natives, one could not help feeling the elation of victory, tempered with sorrow for all those brave comrades we had left behind, at Gaza, on the Auja, and in the hills, the fruits of whose sacrifice we were now reaping to the full. After a very hot and dusty march of 14 miles we reached Kakon.

Kakon was an important military point from the earliest times. From it branches the most eastern of the three routes over Carmel to the plain of Esdraelon, viz. that by the plain of Dothan, the one more usually taken both by invaders from the north and from the south. It was by this road that the company of Ishmaelites came from Gilead and brought Joseph from his brethren (Genesis xxxvii.) The route we were taking—round the promontory of Cape Carmel by the seashore, which the Crusaders called Les Destroits, was not so often used. As Napoleon said, it was "passage difficile à forcer s'il etait defendu." But Carmel had already been cleared for us by the cavalry, and Haifa was in our hands, having been taken by the Mysore and Jodhpur Lancers on September 23rd.

Napoleon was attacked at Kakon by a body of Samaritans from Nablus, when on his way to the siege of Acre.

On the following day we resumed our march due north, keeping to the plain. It was terribly hot and dusty but the men stuck it well with their heavy packs. The flies were innumerable, as they always were in the wake of the Turk. The country was strewn with dead animals and there were still a few Turks unburied, staring, black-faced and horrible, into the sun.

Streams of prisoners were met coming in—all returning motor lorries were packed with them, but many had to march, and one pitied the long straggling columns of tired, thirsty, footsore men. The feeding and watering of the enormous number of prisoners was a big strain on the transport, and was in fact delaying the advance.

Soon after midday, after crossing the swampy bed of the Wadi El Khudeirah—the "Dead River" of the Crusaders—we reached our bivouac near Kurkur on a hill where were the remains of an extensive oak forest. This forest formerly spread over a great part of the plain of Sharon, at one time giving it the name of "Drumos" (Isaiah xxxv., xxvii., etc) Strabo calls it "a great Forest," The Crusaders "the Forest of Assur," Tasso "The enchanted Forest." Only a few scattered trees now remained, though a large area was covered with stumps. About three miles away, on the coast, stood all that remained of Cæsarea. We were delayed for a day here, possibly owing to supply difficulties, and advantage was taken of the river for bathing; but the banks were so marshy that the bathers came out covered with mud.

On October 2nd we resumed our march, keeping for some distance to the right of a low rocky ridge, which had been extensively quarried for the building of Cæsarea, which must have been a very fine city, judging by the amount of stone used in the building of it. Herod spent twelve years in building Cæsarea and in making it a haven for his ships. The breakwater was 200 feet wide in twenty fathoms of water—no wonder half the rocky ridge seemed to have been taken away. For miles the rocks were cut into great steps and galleries. The road turned suddenly west, through a narrow defile, containing some wonderful caves, probably originally used by the quarry men and later, doubtless, by the robbers who used to infest this part of the country, taking refuge in the intricate marshes of the Nahr Ez Zerka—the "Crocodile River" of the Crusaders—which we were now approaching. Pliny speaks of the town and river of crocodiles at this spot; and a crocodile was killed here as late as 1902.

Marching for a further four miles between the marshes and the ridge we came to the town and Jewish colony of Zimmarin. It was a stiff climb up to the town, the road enclosed by high hedges and several inches deep in white dust. Our bivouac was a very pleasant one, on the slope towards the sea. Provisions were obtained in the town and the more energetic set out for nearly three miles to the sea for a bathe.

The town seemed very full and was practically *en fête*. Most of the Jewish maidens had put on their best frocks and marched up and down the High Street giving the glad eye to the Essex boys, but the latter were not visibly impressed. There was evidently little fear of the "brutal and licentious soldiery" in these parts. The town boasted a hotel, which supplied very bad liquor but little in the way of food, which had all been snapped up by the two other Brigades which had preceded us. The next day we marched to near Athlit and bivouacked on the edge of the sand about a mile and a half from that place. We passed Tanturah on the way—the ancient port of Dor, the northernmost limit of the tribe of Dan, formerly a settlement of the Canaanites, with its little harbour among the wild rocks of this lonely shore; but we had no time to visit it.

The ruins of Athlit were numerous and massive, with the remains of a strong castle, a church and a sea wall. Twice it was held against all the rest of Palestine, says Dr. G. Adam Smith. In 130 A.D. it was the last stronghold of Jewish independence, and in the thirteenth century it was the last fortress of the Cross. It was then known as the Castle of the Pilgrims. To-day it stands in silent desolation—a desolation common to the whole coast. "A mournful and solitary silence," says Gibbon, in closing his chapter on the Crusaders, "now prevails along the shore which once resounded with the world's debate."

The following day saw us on the outskirts of Haifa. Moving by the coast with a refreshing breeze from the sea, we passed a large well, Bir el Ebdaouiyeh, the "Well of the Bedouins," where we watered the animals. Further on, on our right, El Tireh was passed—the Tyrus of William of Tyre. Skirting the German colony of Neuhardthof, with the interesting ruins of Kefr es Samir, the camp of the Samaritans, at the foot of Carmel, we threaded our way round the promontory at Tell es Semak—the ancient Sycaminos—and bivouacked on the seashore. Above us, high on the cape, was the Carmelite Monastery. About three miles round the cape lay the town of Haifa. Two days were spent on the shore, which was principally interesting for the "murex trunculus," the purple shell which yielded the famous Tyrean dye. There was good bathing in the sea.

On October 7th the Battalion marched through Haifa, and the whole Brigade bivouacked on the plain to the east of the town, under the shadow of Carmel and between it and the Nakr el Mukuttah—the brook Kishon—which meandered through the level plain and emptied itself into the sea about two miles to the north.

As we passed through Haifa we met many German and Turkish officer prisoners, very "beat," being helped along by their kindly Indian escort.

Haifa does not appear to have played an important part in ancient history, and but little is heard of it until Saladin took it in 1187, only to destroy it four years later when Acre was taken by the French. The Crusaders rebuilt it but it was again

THE BROOK KISHON, FROM THE SLOPES OF CARMEL

*To face page 150.*

totally destroyed by the Arabs after the former had given up Palestine. Napoleon took it in 1799 and Ibrahim Pasha in 1837. In 1840 it was badly knocked about by the combined fleets of England and Turkey. There is a considerable German colony, laid out in straight clean streets, with some very nice houses, which the various Headquarters found very useful.

About eight miles to the north, across the beautiful bay, Acre could be seen, shining white in the sunlight.

Carmel is a beautiful range of well wooded and verdant hills, stretching from the cape far to the south-east. The northern slope is very steep, and is deeply groved with many valleys of streams and burrowed by innumerable grottoes and caves, places of refuge in ancient times. The celebrated story of Elijah and the prophets of Baal is too well known to need repeating here. The view from the top of the hill was magnificent—on the one side the long coast line stretching to the south, the plain of Sharon and the hills of Judea—on the other, the bay of Acre and the ladder of Tyre, the plain of Esdraelon with rounded top of Tabor and the hills of Gallilee further to the east, whilst over all hung the snow capped peak of the mighty Hermon.

We stayed on the flats of Haifa nearly three weeks. It was anything but a healthy spot and sickness was rife. The ground was full of cracks, and the cracks were full of scorpions. They came out at night and the place was alive with them ; one night in our little Headquarters' mess we killed seventy during and after dinner. The padré, Marriott, suggested that they were trekking to the hills in anticipation of the rains, which would soon turn the plain into a morass. This seemed probable as they were always moving in one direction—towards the hills.

On October 12th General Hare presented the ribands of decorations won by officers and other ranks of the 161st Brigade in the last battle. On the following day a Brigade Church Parade was held.

Training was carried out every day on the "school of instruction" principle, except when we did a short route march, taking water and "dixies" with us and having the midday meal by the roadside or by the seashore—the meal being preceded in the latter case by a universal bathe.

On October 23rd we moved to the seashore just east of Haifa and stayed there on the 24th ; the last named date being, I think, the most uncomfortable day we had spent since the Gallipoli blizzard. There was a gale of wind blowing and the sand was the finest imaginable. No bivouacs would stand up in it and cooking was practically an impossibility. We were not sorry when we marched the next day to Acre, along the edge of the sea, the only existing road, very deep in places. We passed a large camp of French troops on the shore and crossed the Kishon near its mouth by a wooden bridge. The coast was devoid of interest until the Nahr Namein was reached. This was probably the Sihor Labanath, the White river of the Bible, and certainly the River Belus of the old historians. On its banks the Phœnicians first made the discovery of transparent glass. According to Pliny a ship full of nitre ran ashore here, and in order to cook their food the merchants stood their saucepans on some pieces of that substance. The nitre, melting with the sand, made a transparent liquid—the first glass ever made. The shells giving the Tyrean purple dye are also found at this place, amongst others along this coast.

We pitched our bivouac between the town of Acre and the hill called Tell el Fokhar—the hill of the Franks—where stood the Toron, a fort of the Crusaders. From this hill Napoleon bombarded the town in 1799 when he was foiled in his attempt to take it by the genius of Sir Sydney Smith, an event which, according to Napoleon, vitally affected the history of the world.

The town of St. John of Acre is first mentioned in the Tablets of Tell Amarna in Egypt under the name of Aka. It is mentioned in Judges (i. 31) as a town of the tribe of Aser and is called Accho. The Arabs called it Akka, Ptolemy re-named it Ptolemais, by which name it is known in the Acts (xxi. 7). It has had an eventful history, having been taken in turn by the ancient Egyptians, the Babylonians, the Assyrians, the Persians, the Macedonians, the Greeks, the Syrians, the Romans, the Crusaders, the Saracens, the mediæval Egyptians, the Turks, and lastly by the modern Egyptians, who were compelled by the Powers to give it back to Turkey.

Of the many sieges it has undergone, the best known are that by the Crusaders which lasted for two years (1189–1191), which cost the attackers 60,000 men before they took the city, and that exactly a century later by the Sultan El Malik with an army of 200,000 men. The Christians made a heroic defence with their small garrison, but the city was overwhelmed and the gallant defenders and the whole of the inhabitants were put to the sword. The only gate of the town is on the east side, where also the water is brought in by an enormous aqueduct from some miles away in the hills. The lower part of the aqueduct is sealed over and the water rises to a considerable height by gravitation in several towers which are erected along the route. The town itself is very interesting. It is defended on the land side by a wide and deep moat, and has an inner and outer wall with a small space between. The port was bounded by a pier defended by several towers, the ruins of which still rise above the water. The walls on the sea side are still intact and the heavy guns lie about all over the battlements. In the centre of the town was a huge arsenal, containing old guns of large calibre and hundreds of thousands of solid cannon balls all mixed up in the greatest confusion. Some of the guns had English marks with the monogram "G.R." and were doubtless part of Sir Sydney Smith's ordnance. The principal mosque has a beautiful court with trees and a fountain. The streets were all paved with stone and very slippery. There was a good supply of provisions of all kinds in the markets, particularly vegetables, fruit and eggs. There was a torrential rain during our visit, but there was plenty of shelter for us and our horses under the many old archways.

We marched at 8 o'clock the following morning. The mules had all their work cut out to pull the wagon loads out of the sticky ground. For some distance we moved nearly parallel to the aqueduct—a massive structure with at places two tiers of arches, which still carries water to Acre from the springs at El Kabri in the hills, a distance of ten miles.

After marching for about half an hour we passed under a huge arch of a second aqueduct which runs from the same springs as the first, but by a different route. The reason for this prodigal use of aqueducts was not clear.

The road was a poor one, and the going was heavy in places, but the numerous wadis flowing to the sea were crossed by well built stone bridges. On the right of the road several villages were passed, among them, Khirbet el Amoud, the "Ruins of the Pillars," identified with Amad, a town of the tribe of Asher (Joshua xix. 26). Further on, on the seashore, perched on a hil or artificial mound, stood the village of Ez Zib, the ancient Achzib, among whom the Asherites were constrained to dwell, "for they did not drive them out" (Judges i. 31). We pitched our bivouac for the night at Musheirefeh, where there was an excellent well, also a stream running along the foot of the high ridge in front of us, 1200 feet high, the Jebel el Mushakkah, which falls towards the sea, to about 250 feet, whence it drops almost sheer to the water. Over this headland climbs the road, formerly merely steps in the rock, but now quite a good road, though very steep, made by the R.E. field troops.

Starting again at 9 the next morning the transport were sent forward with a party of men to each wagon to help it up the hill—and to hang on down the slope the other side, which was even steeper. We waited on the plain at the foot of the hill until the last wagon disappeared round the headland, when at a signal from the Brigadier, who was at the top, we started the climb. It was a stiff one, about a mile long as the road ran. Below us on the left we could see the ancient track, following a shorter and much steeper line to the top. The point is called Ras en Nakureh and the ascent the Ladder of Tyre, or Ladder of the Tyrians (Scala Tyriorum). From the top of the headland could be seen Acre, beautifully placed in the sea, with Carmel for its background. To the north, on the point of a narrow tongue of land about 18 miles distant, the venerable city of Es Sur (Tyre). The "Ladder of Tyrus" is also referred to in that most interesting and convincing history, the book of Maccabees, as the northern boundary of the dominions of Simon

Maccabeus (1 Mach. xi. 59). The road ran close to the sea, in some places merely a ledge on the side of the cliff. The country was very picturesque. There was now no coastal plain, the ridges of the rocky hills running right down to the sea.

On crossing the beautiful Wadi Ez Zerka some very extensive ruins were seen on a slight hill to the right, called Khirbet el Amoud, said to be the site of the biblical city of Hamon (Joshua xix. 28), on which site also stood one of the three cities called Loadicea. The ruins are of buildings in the Egypto-Phœnician style, and contain numerous inscriptions. Unfortunately we had no time for exploring. Three miles further on we had to climb another " ladder " over the headland of Ras el Abiad, where the road seemed actually to overhang the sea. It is called by Pliny the promontorium Album—the White Cape. The road had been crumbled by the wheeled traffic into six inches of white dust, which made the descent a very trying one, both to man and horse. The thick dust was full of large loose stones which made it anything but pleasant going ; but the view of the coast was magnificent—if one could only have stopped to admire it. At several places the rocks on the right of the road were perforated with rock dwellings or tombs. Everywhere abounded signs of ancient habitation. The map was covered with names of places, nearly all with the prefix " Khirbet," or ruin. It was more a land of ruins even than Judea. The whole country was studded with them ; the remains of numerous small towns which formed, as Heeren says, " almost an unbroken city, extending along the whole line of the coast," in the palmy days of Phœnician prosperity. After a very hard march we came to rest at Ras-el-Ain about five miles south of Tyre. Near the place were several immense reservoirs, which store the water of the springs which supplied the city of Tyre with water in the old days. According to Josephus, Salmazar IV. had already destroyed the aqueducts in the year B.C. 726. In the middle ages Ras-el-Ain was called the Pools of Solomon.

Marching at 7.30 the next morning we left Tyre on our left. It was hard to believe that the small town on the small peninsula was really all that was left of the mighty city of King Hiram, the parent city of Carthage and Cadiz, the wonder of the East for luxury and magnificence, and the centre of the commerce of the world.

A narrow neck of sand connected the town with the mainland. At the time Alexander the Great besieged the city in B.C. 332 it was on an island. He filled up the Straits and made the island into the peninsula it is now. But it was easy to realize why the Prophet Ezekiel likened the city to a beautiful ship with her " masts of cedar," her " sails of fine linen, blue and purple," " very glorious in the midst of the seas " (Ezek. xxvii. 3-26). And easy also to feel in imagination the force of the prophecy of the stern old seer—" I will bring thee to ashes upon the earth in the sight of all them that behold thee (xxviii. 18). Not that Tyre is at present a heap of ruins, though it has been that more than once. It is now a town of about 6,000 inhabitants (of whom nearly half are Christians), but its greatness is no more than a memory.

A little over three hours marching brought us to the River Kasimiyeh, or Litani, the largest stream we had yet crossed—deep and placid, running between green banks, it might have been an English river. It was full of fish. Its ancient name was the Leontes. It rises near Baalbek, close to the other celebrated river, the Orontes, the latter flowing north via Antioch. The Leontes flows south, forcing its way through the narrow passes of the anti-Lebanon chain, and narrowly escaping the unhappy fate of its sister stream the Jordan by breaking through the mountains hemming it in on the west, in what has been called its "difficult and romantic contest with the everlasting pillars of the Lebanon for a free passage to the Mediterranean." We pitched our bivouac a little to the north of the river to escape mosquitoes, and resumed our march at 8 o'clock the next morning (Oct. 29). Crossing the Abou el Asuad by the side of a ruined bridge we passed close by Adlun, the ancient Ornithopolis. The rocks contained many caves, and along by the sea the ground was strewn with the ruins of old buildings. After crossing another wadi—the El Khaiseran—we passed the village of Surafend, the ancient Zarephath or Sarepta, where the prophet Elijah lodged with the widow whose "barrel of meal wasted not, neither did the cruse of oil fail," and whose son he raised (1 Kings xvii. 16–22). Sarepta is also reputed to be the place where our Lord healed the Syro-Phœnician woman (Mark vii. 24–30). Judging by the extent of the ruins it must have been quite a large city. The present village, which was situated on a hill, was conspicuous by the white domes of many tombs.

About a mile further on was a village called el-Khudr, after the Mohammedan representative of Elijah. The peasants have a sepulchral chapel there, dedicated to the prophet. It has no tomb, only a recess. For they say "El Khudr is not dead; he flies round and round the world, and these chapels are built wherever he has appeared. Every Friday there is a light so strong in the chapel that none can enter." Another mile brought us to Ain el Burak, where there was a spring, as its name implied, and here we rested for the night.

Next day we trekked at 7:30, and reached Saida (Sidon) in three hours' marching. The town is surrounded on the land side by extensive gardens, and the last mile or two was in delightful shade. We bivouacked in a field to the east of the town. Sidon had so far survived the curse of the Hebrew prophet as to present quite a flourishing appearance. There were several capacious modern houses near our bivouac, in one of which Brigade Headquarters made themselves very comfortable. The camp was soon visited by numbers of hawkers with fruit and vegetables, and a brisk trade was done. Willmott, our P.R.I., ever with an eye to business, visited the town major, who put him on to a store where he obtained sufficient potatoes to feed the whole Battalion—an unusual luxury, which was much appreciated.

In the afternoon I went with Marriott, the padré, who had lived in these parts many years ago, and called on an American doctor friend of his, who lived on the hill overlooking the town, and who gave us a delicious tea. The doctor told us the tea was as great a treat to him as it was to us. It was probably an even greater one, for until our advanced troops had arrived he had had no tea or sugar for two years. The Turks had let him alone, however, as America was not at war with Turkey.

Sidon is one of the oldest cities of the world, and is mentioned in Genesis (x. 19) as the northern border of the Canaanites. Homer mentions its artizans as celebrated, especially in metallurgy. Its history is similar to that of many others towns we had come through. A fierce rivalry between it and Tyre prevailed for many ages, each in turn regaining its supremacy, generally by the complete destruction of its rival by a foreign conqueror.

It was a beautiful morning on Oct 31st when we marched out of Sidon with our bands playing. The Battalion had managed to raise some drums and fifes, and in spite of many difficulties Sergt. Harris had made quite a respectable little band of them. The hot sun by day and the heavy dews at night had played havoc with the drums, and it was a " toss-up " whether the bass drum would hold out for the march, but it was evidently the intention of the Battalion drummers to make the most of them while they lasted ; in fact, to drum them until they would drum no more. Replacement of drum-heads was out of question, and very few were complete on both sides. The reduction of tone occasioned by this circumstance was, however, amply compensated by an increase of vigour on the part of the drummers.

For over two miles the road made a gradual ascent, passing through the delightful gardens which earned for Sidon in olden days the title of the "Flower-crowned." Those on the left lay before us, stretching nearly to the coast—a mass of green with the sparkling sea beyond.

A fairly sharp decline brought us to the bridge spanning the Nahr el Aoli, the River Bostrenus, which supplies the gardens of Sidon with water. It is tapped higher up, where it breaks through the mountain pass, and the water is conveyed to the gardens by an aqueduct.

Another four miles took us round the promontory of Ras Jedra and two more to the village of El Jiyeh, where stood the ancient city of Porphyrion, so named from the fishing for the famous purple dye. Here Ptolemy was defeated by Antiochus the Great in B.C. 218. It is surrounded by beautiful gardens. The Khan on the outskirts of the village was called the Khan en Nebi Younes (the prophet Jonas). According to the Mussulman legend it was here that Jonah was thrown up by the whale. Rounding the Ras el Damour, another four miles brought us to the Nahr ed Damour, a small river spanned by an iron bridge. It is the ancient river Tamyrus. Just beyond is the Maronite village of Ed Damour, near which we pitched our bivouac for the night.

The Maronites are a sect of Eastern Christians who inhabit a great many villages of the Lebanon. They are a sturdy lot, preserving a certain amount of independence, even now resisting the payment of tribute to the Turks. They acknowledge the Pope, but without giving up their own peculiarities. Among other things their priests insist on the right of marrying if they choose, and their laws allow revenge for murder.

CHAPTER XVI.

# TURKEY THROWS UP THE SPONGE.

DURING the day's march on October 31st a message from Brigade Headquarters was passed back along the column. It read "Hostilities with Turkey ceased at 12 noon to-day." It was not entirely unexpected, but it was welcome news for all that. The three Turkish armies opposed to us had been utterly destroyed. On October 1st Damascus had fallen. On the 8th Beyrout had been occupied, on the 11th Baalbek, on the 13th Tripoli, on the 15th Homs, on the 20th Hama, on the 28th Aleppo, and then the Turk threw in his hand. Between September 19th and October 26th 75,000 prisoners had been captured, including 200 officers and 3,500 other ranks German and Austrian, 360 guns had been taken, with the transport and equipment of the three armies. The captures also included over 800 machine guns, 210 motor lorries, 44 motor cars, 3,500 animals, 89 railway engines and 468 carriages and trucks. The Turkish armies had been completely surrounded, and had in fact ceased to exist. "Such a complete victory," said Sir Edmund Allenby in his message to the troops, "has seldom been known in all the history of war."

The cavalry had indeed done wonderful work—Aleppo is 300 miles from our former front line—and the bulk of the prisoners and material fell into their hands. But we of the infantry had the satisfaction of knowing that it was those few hours fighting in the dark hours of the morning of September 19th which made it possible for the cavalry to accomplish its mission and to reap to the full the fruits of victory.

The men took the news of the Armistice as they took everything else that came along, and allowed themselves to show no signs of excitement, whatever they felt. But after slipping off their heavy packs and taking a short rest they were soon busy with their writing pads, giving the glad news to the folks at home—though there was little chance of getting a mail off until we got to Beyrout. Although there was no demonstration, however, there is no doubt about the satisfaction which everybody felt that the end had come. Not many people were left who attempted to keep up the fiction of being anxious for more fighting.

The next morning—November 1st—we marched at 7.30 and continued our way close to the seashore for several miles, after which the road took a sweep inland and we had a very hot dusty

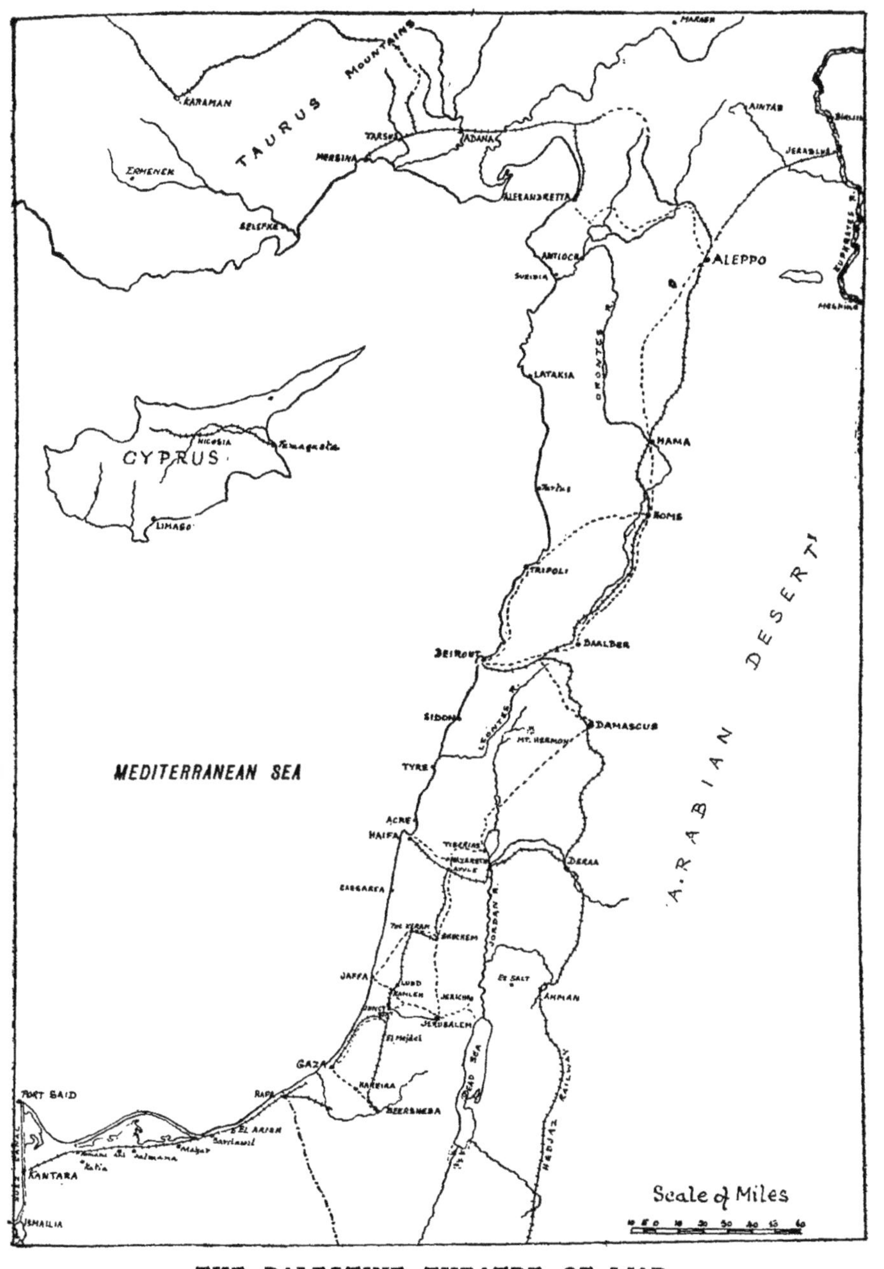


THE PALESTINE THEATRE OF WAR.

hill to climb, making 820 feet in two miles, to the Druse village of Shuweifat. The Druses are an interesting people with a political constitution and religion of their own. Sharply divided politically among themselves they have always combined when anything has threatened their rights, and they have frequently engaged in warfare with their neighbours the Maronites. Their religion is a strange mixture of Judaism, Christianity, and Mohammedanism. They believe in one God, but deprecate any attempt to attribute to Him any human quality, and have no prayers, fasts, or festivals, and practically no worship, except that practised by a privileged class called the Akals, or initiated. They have a high moral code which enjoins truthfulness, contentment, and patience. Like the Maronites they preserve a good deal of independence, and own only a limited measure of allegiance to the Turks.

Another two miles through delightful olive groves brought us to our bivouac at El Hadeth, six miles from Beyrout. A very rough stony bivouac, and all sorts of rumours about Austria giving in, and a British fleet through the Dardanelles.

The following day was the anniversary of the last battle of Gaza, and was marked by the triumphal march of the Brigade through Beyrout. The Corps Commander, Sir Edward Bulfin, took the salute in the main square at 11 o'clock. He told us afterwards that we were the best Brigade on the march through, and said it was a really good show. The 5th Essex was in front that day. We were in a rather ragged condition but the men went with a fine swing, led by the Battalion drums. Luckily the big drum stood the strain. It was my chief anxiety. We had three side drums left—and even if we had had more we had not the drummers to play them.

The inhabitants appeared to be very pleased to see us; there was much cheering and clapping of hands and throwing of flowers in the road. The 6th Essex stole a march on us by playing the "Marseillaise" past the French consulate, and got a tremendous reception from the balcony.

Beyrout is not an imposing town; the roads were in a shocking state and there were no striking buildings. The famous pine woods, where we halted before the march past, were very beautiful and delightfully cool. The Turkish police were still doing duty in the streets and were well disciplined, smart, and most correct in their behaviour towards their conquerors. Large numbers of men in tattered Turkish uniforms walked about the streets, and nobody seemed to bother about them. We marched right through the town and bivouacked on a rocky hill near the village of Mar Rukos about four miles away. The scenery was grand in the extreme. The Lebanon mountains ran nearly up to the town, and hills, 3,000 feet high, had villages on their summits, enveloped in cloud—the favourite summer resort of the wealthier Beyroutites

—whilst beyond rose the majestic table-like top of Jebel Sannin, 8,500 feet high, glowing red in the sunset. All the hills seemed covered with dwellings and were terraced and cultivated with olives, mulberries, grape-vines, and other fruit trees, except where forests covered the slopes. The country presented a great contrast to the sterile hills of Palestine.

The inhabitants of the Lebanon seemed much cleaner and more civilized than the Palestinians and unaffectedly delighted to see us. Poor things, the Turks had made them suffer for being pro-English, and had taken effective means of preventing them from giving us any assistance in case of a landing at Beyrout, which was evidently expected, as the hills were heavily entrenched. The Turkish method was simple. The country cannot produce more than about a quarter of the food necessary to sustain its population, as the latter live by village industries, such as silk manufacture, &c. Their masters therefore put a cordon round the whole district and let none pass, one way or the other. One poor woman told me she had lost over thirty relatives by starvation. The men died off more quickly than the women, and several villages had hardly a man left alive. Altogether a third of the population perished during the war. The distress in Beyrout itself was just as noticeable. It was pitiful to see the women and children hanging round our refuse heaps and incinerators and licking out old bully beef tins and jam pots. Little children walked in the streets of Beyrout absolutely naked, like skeletons, thighs no bigger round than my wrists. I saw more than one lying dead on the pavement. One gets used to horrors in war, but there is nothing quite so sad as this. Measures of relief were quickly taken in hand but it was evident that many more would perish before these could be made effective. Over 50,000 people had died of starvation in Beyrout alone.

There was a good deal of work to be done in clearing our camping ground and everybody was kept busy preparing for the rains which were now due. Drainage was the all important thing, and a whole system of water trenches was dug through the camp. Tents arrived after a few days and when the rain came—and it *did* rain—we were fairly well prepared for it, the trenches working admirably.

The whole Battalion was inoculated again against cholera and every effort made to combat disease. Our march had been through a pestilential country, as many armies before us had found to their cost, and the casualties from sickness had been very heavy. But it speaks volumes for the way companies were looked after by their commanders, and for the excellent march discipline of all ranks that during the whole of the hot and tiring march from the Kanah not a single man had gone to hospital through feet trouble. After every day's march feet had been washed in a solution of permanganate of potash, foot inspections were held, and blisters dressed. Even so, many a man marched in sore pain, but they stuck it like Britons.

We had become very weak in officers. Finn, Wray, Ryan, Womersley, Lockwood, and Frew (M.O.) had gone to hospital from Haifa. On the march up we lost Horton, and after our arrival Deakin and Richmond were stricken down.

On November 11th the news of the Armistice with Germany was received. There was much firing of rifles and lighting of flares in the town. Our Very lights had been handed into store; but this was perhaps an unnecessary precaution, as the news was received by the 5th Essex with its customary dignity. The band turned out and played "God save the King" and popular airs, a sing-song was held, and every one had a pint of beer.

On the Sunday following there was a Brigade Church Parade with a thanksgiving service for peace.

We spent a pleasant enough time at Mar Rukos, though the rain was very heavy at times. Jebel Sannin put on its winter coat of snow, and was a magnificent sight. Excursions were made to the villages on the hills. At Beit Mari there was a German long range gun in a concrete emplacement on the crest, evidently designed to fire over the town far out to sea. The hills were covered with trenches, excellently designed and sited among the trees. Many were protected by wire entanglements. The heights would have been a stiff proposition for a frontal attack.

I called on the Head of the Municipality, H. E. Omar Bey Daouk, who was also President General of the "Defense Nationale" of Beyrout and President of the Chamber of Commerce. He said how pleased they all were to see the English and hoped we should stop. I said I was afraid Syria was not "our pigeon" (or words to that effect). He asked me to a reception (with music) which he was giving at the Municipal Buildings in honour of the Emir Feisal, who was on a visit to the town—an invitation which I was unfortunately unable to accept, owing to military duties. Prince Feisal stayed with the Corps Commander for some time and we frequently had to furnish the guard at Headquarters. His Highness had a large retinue, all of whom drove about in motor cars in gorgeous uniforms. The commander of the guard had considerable difficulty in distinguishing between the Prince and his brilliantly uniformed, personal, and household staff. After the guard had turned out several times to the private secretary, the chief butler, and other retainers, a request was made that His Highness should fly a distinctive flag from his motor car, a request which was complied with, much to the relief of the guard commander.

I also visited, in company with the Padré, the American College at Beyrout, whose principal, Dr. Bliss, kindly shewed us round their very interesting museum. Dr. Bliss is one of the best known of the Palestine explorers, who had been practically a prisoner in Beyrout since he voluntarily undertook to stay there when diplomatic relations between U.S.A. and the Porte were broken off.

The rain was frequently very heavy, and our tents were most of them leaky, but the drainage system prevented the camp from being flooded, and during the considerable bright intervals everything got dry very quickly.

Beyrout was not an attractive place to stay at in winter, and the men found it slow. The ground which was cleared for football, &c., was nearly always unplayable owing to its wet state, and no tents or huts were available for recreation purposes. The news that we were ordered back to Egypt was received with satisfaction. There was some talk of us marching back as far as railhead (which must still have been some distance short of Haifa), but to my relief the idea was abandoned, and the sea route was decided upon. On December 2nd we embarked on H.M.S. "Tagus," the Transport proceeding by another boat. The latter was named the "Ekaterinoslav"—and the Transport personnel said it served her right too! She was not a floating palace.

THE HEAD OF THE BATTALION IN THE OPERA SQUARE, CAIRO, DECEMBER 20. 1918.

*To face page 165.*

CHAPTER XVII.

# BACK IN EGYPT.

N December 4th we disembarked at Kantara and were accommodated at the Transit Camp on the west bank of the canal for the night, proceeding the next day by train to Helmieh, about nine miles from Cairo.

Helmieh was on the sand, and was quite a good site for a camp. There were a few huts, but not nearly enough to go round, and tents were also very short, but we soon made ourselves very comfortable. A sergeants' mess, canteen, and recreation room were started, a large cinema was erected, and several football grounds laid out. Heliopolis, close by, had its pleasure park with scenic railway and other delights, and there was a well arranged racecourse.

On December 20th the Division marched through Cairo. The city was gaily decorated with allied flags, stands for spectators were erected, and the streets kept clear. After marching through a good part of the native quarter we passed the Commander-in-Chief, Sir Edmund Allenby, G.C.B., who took the salute in the Opera Square. The Division got a great reception and everybody said it made a really good show. The only thing we missed was our Regimental Band. We were played past by a very good Royal Welsh Fusilier Band, but owing to an unfortunate misunderstanding it played a tune which was quite strange to our ears. It was a great disappointment that our moment of triumph was not graced by the strains of the march of the 44th Regiment, which we had always used, and which was so dear to us for its glorious associations. But the shock was only momentary and the men pulled themselves together and went past in grand style.

During the month of December the Battalion more than doubled its strength and by the last day of the year numbered 39 officers and 1,070 other ranks. The training consisted principally of physical drill, route marching and ceremonial.

Christmas was spent in the army way, officers waiting on the men at dinner and visiting the Sergeants' and Corporals' messes and the greatest goodwill prevailed among all ranks. Unfortunately we had no tables or forms for the mess huts, but trenches were dug in the floor forming the latter into "tables" covered with ground sheets, etc., and the cooks put up a good show. There was football in the afternoon, and the usual "rag" in the officers' mess after dinner. The 1/6th raided us in force, and there was a good deal of breaking of crockery and good natured chaff. The only way of putting an end to the "raid" was to suggest a combined attack on the mess of the 1/4th, which was duly carried out, after which the 1/7th received due attention and the raiders, having expended all their energy, broke up and went to bed.

The scheme for demobilisation was a disappointment to many, who hoped that we might return to England as a unit, after our long sojourn in the East. It was evident that it was going to be a slow business, and during January only four officers and 88 other ranks were demobilised.

A Battalion education scheme was started with a view to using the time of waiting to the best advantage, and Colvin was appointed Battalion Education Officer. Classes were held every day and the curriculum included English, French, Spanish, Arabic, bookkeeping, shorthand, arithmetic, building construction, poultry farming, petrol engine, and lectures on history, civics, etc. In all cases the instructors were officers, N.C.O.'s or men of the Battalion. Division ran a higher education scheme for more advanced subjects, taught by selected officers and other ranks. There were art classes, classes in Hindustani, mathematics, engineering, agriculture, business methods, etc., etc., and the amount of teaching talent was really surprising. For technical instruction the education department placed their model workshops at our disposal, and even the cinemas provided instruction in film operating. There was something for every taste, and many must have benefited considerably by the opportunities given for equipping themselves for civil life.

Deakin was appointed Divisional Education Officer, organizing and supervising all the divisional classes, and proved himself as good a man in that line of business as he had already shewn himself on so many occasions in the field.

A regular system of sports was instituted, including athletics, boxing, cross-country, football, and hockey. There were company sports meetings, followed by Battalion sports, then a Brigade meeting, followed by a Divisional ditto, and finally by a big meeting in Cairo open to the whole of the E.E.F. The Battalion won the most events (five) in the Brigade meeting, and the 161st Brigade was easily first in the Divisional sports, winning the 100 yards (Sergt. Brady, 6th Essex), putting the weight (Capt. Portway, 5th Essex), veterans' race (C.S.M. Furby, 6th Essex), 220 yards (Sergt. Brady), tug-of-war, and relay race. In the latter the Battalion was represented by Portway (220 yards), and Womersley (half a mile). The latter pulled this race literally out of the fire by a magnificent effort at the last distance, winning by a yard.

There were no money prizes, the only awards being cups and medals. The Brigade Sports Committee gave a Cup for the championship in all sports, and this the Battalion deserved, and ought to have won, having the five events in the sports, the football, hockey and cross-country to their credit. The points given in the sports events were five for a 1st, four for a 2nd, and three for a third. This marking gave too much value to seconds and thirds. Had the marking been three, two, one, as it should have been, we should have won handsomely. As it was the 4th won the cup by a narrow margin—and we were the first to congratulate them. In the Divisional competition we won the hockey cup after a great match with the 4th Northamptonshires and were only beaten in the football competition by the winners (7th Essex) 1—0.

An excellent Brigade concert party was started under the able management of Gilmour, and gave good shows, not only in camp, but in the Halls in Cairo, Alexandria and Port Said, under the name of the "Favourites."

During February, one officer and 177 other ranks were demobilised, leaving the strength of the Battalion at 34 officers and 818 other ranks.

The anti-English, or Nationalist Party in Egypt, who had persistently believed in a German and Turkish victory, had been for a long time working quietly all over the country to bring about among the illiterate population a rising against the British occupation. All sorts of lies were spread about, and the industrious but ignorant fellaheen were made to believe that they would benefit by a declaration of Egyptian independence. The prime movers of this agitation were the extreme Moslem fanatics of the University of El Azhar, and the students. The former were opposed to the substitution of a Christian for a Moslem power as suzerains of Egypt, while the latter were out for official jobs. Neither had the slightest intention of doing anything for the fellaheen, for whom "independence" would only have meant a return of the tyranny of the Turco-Egyptian Pasha, from which they had been delivered by a benevolent British rule. But the agitation had been very cleverly worked, and for the first time the fellaheen had been induced to side with their former oppressors. Riots broke out in Cairo, and the worst elements of the population took the opportunity of indulging in their favourite pastime of looting and outrage. The result was that the British soldier, who had always been most friendly and considerate to the "Gyppoes," had his demobilisation delayed, and was called upon to assist the civil power in the preservation of order—an unpleasant task to the soldier at any time, but doubly so when his one idea was to get back to England as soon as he could after nearly four years' exile from home. About March 12th the trouble broke out in the provinces, and Battalion Headquarters and 300 other ranks were ordered to Benha, an important junction on the railway, which crosses the Nile at this point, and the chief town of the Kalioubieh Province. We arrived at Benha in the evening and were met by the Superintendent of Police, who conducted us to a large empty house, the former residence of one of the Princesses of the late reigning house, who had been living at Constantinople. The town was quiet and the crowds in the cafés took no notice of us as we marched through. On the 14th Carlyon-Hughes, three other officers and 100 other ranks reinforced the garrison at Tanta, the third largest town in the Delta, where serious disturbances had taken place. The Mudir (Governor) of the Kalioubieh Mudirieh (Province) H.E. Mahmond Sidky Bey, called at the Palace and assured me that his people were most law abiding and that the presence of troops would not be required. I told His Excellency that we had no quarrel with them, but that we were there to help him maintain order. He promised to let me know at once if help was required. I returned his call the same day and he gave me some excellent coffee. Everything was quiet, but I was not received with much favour by the populace, who looked very sullen. A picquet was sent to the station and guards were posted on the bridges but the town was left alone. The Mudir said the presence of armed troops would excite the people, and I acceded to his wish.

On March 15th he asked me to send troops to Calioub, where a mob had burnt the station and torn up the line. I refused to split up my small garrison, and Headquarters in Cairo told me on the 'phone that they would deal with it. Later in the day Finn had mud thrown at him as he was returning from a visit to the town. Three officers and 50 other ranks were ordered to stand to, and I went and sat in the office of the Irrigation Superintendent, where there was a telephone. The Palace was some distance from the town and had no 'phone. The Irrigation Superintendent looked apprehensive, but said nothing. Presently the Mudir arrived in haste and said there was " very much trouble " in the town and that rioting and looting of shops was going on. I immediately sent orders for the picquet to go down and break up the mob. Portway was in command, and orders were given that fire was not to be opened unless absolutely necessary for the safety of the picquet, most of whom were armed with pick helves only. They found a mob of several thousands looting the shops of the Greeks and Jews. The action was sharp and decisive. Not a shot was fired but Portway and his men lay about them with their pick helves to such effect that the mob was quickly dispersed. The Egyptian Police apparently did little to stop the looting. By 3 o'clock quietness was restored, but several of the cafés and shops had been completely cleared before the picquet had arrived. It was clear that it was no use relying on the civil authorities to maintain order, and a strong picquet took up its quarters at the Police Station and patrolled the streets. A search was made of native houses and nearly a hundred arrests were made of men who had loot in their houses. They were conducted to the Palace and locked up in a large room.

THE FOOTBALL TEAM, EGYPT 1919.

To face page 169.

A party of about 50 Greek inhabitants came as a deputation and asked for protection. I told them we would see that they were not molested, and sentries were posted at various houses and factories. The Greek colony openly accused the Sub-Mudir of encouraging the rioters.

At 6.30 I walked into the Irrigation Office and interrupted a meeting of the chief men of Benha and the surrounding villages. There was much excited conversation going on which stopped as I entered. The Mudir and Sub-Mudir were there. I asked what it was all about, and was told that the Mudir was trying to collect the names of the ring-leaders and cautioning the chief men to keep order. I told His Excellency and the Sub-Mudir that I held them responsible for the disturbances as I had withheld the troops at their request, but that henceforth, the town would be protected by the military. With that I left the assembly.

All was quiet during the night. The next morning I found the Police galloping about hitting at everybody with long sticks, without any apparent reason, except to show how energetic they really were. The shops were closed and everybody seemed very frightened. During the day several stations on the line above and below Benha were destroyed, and the whole country was evidently in a state of the utmost disorder. I was asked to send troops everywhere, but I refused all requests. Our job was to look after Benha, and we had quite enough to do there. There was a very truculent village just on the other side of the river. The road bridge was swung and all ingress into the town stopped from the north. At night several fires were seen in the distance. The next day three trucks of corn which had been left at a siding on the other side of the river was raided by the inhabitants of the village and the sacks rolled into one of the canals. It was a senseless proceeding. I went over and met the Omdah of the village. I asked him what was the matter with his people. He said they were " magnoon " (mad). I shewed him my revolver and told him if they went " magnoon " again we should shoot. He seemed impressed—and offered me a cigarette.

A threatening crowd assembled near a canal bridge to the south of the station. They were dispersed by the station picquet after throwing some stones. Our men kept their tempers admirably throughout.

All communication by rail was now cut off, as the line was torn up at several points. During the morning an aeroplane dropped a message that Brigadier-General McNeill expected to arrive at dusk with a mounted column by road.

In the afternoon the Greek consul from Zagazig arrived and expressed his thanks for the protection we had afforded to his people and their property. He said he had no doubt that but for our presence they would all have been murdered and their houses and their church burnt down. I had no doubt of it either. The

Brigadier duly arrived with the column about 6 o'clock and were found comfortable quarters in the Irrigation house.

With the arrival of more troops things quickly settled down. The prisoners were all tried by a military court and sentenced to various terms of imprisonment, and I dealt with minor offences against Martial Law daily at the Police Station. The Battalion was given a section of the railway line to look after, and it was a time of somewhat dull routine. There were many minor incidents, but nothing worthy of recording in a " War Book."

Our relations with the civil authorities were quite friendly, and the men behaved with admirable restraint. They treated the common people more like children than anything else, and their attitude towards the young patriots in tarbooshes and patent leather boots who waved flags and excitedly discussed the affairs of the nation at street corners, was one of amused, if rather contemptuous, tolerance. These youths, who were the cause of all the trouble, were never in evidence when the pick helves were busy.

The Australians had a camp at Quesna, about eight miles down the line, where Willmott had a detachment at the station. There was also a German prisoners' camp there. General McNeill formed a Race Committee, and three successful meetings were held at Quesna. The prisoners prepared a good course and there were some good fields and splendid finishes. All the countryside attended and special trains were run. One interesting race was for horses, the property of residents in the Menufia and Calionbia Provinces. This produced an enormous field of Arabs, mostly with owners up, in native costume. The winner was quite an old man with a white beard, on a weedy looking little Arab mare. It was a popular win, the owner being nearly pulled from his horse to receive the kisses of his supporters—the latter, it need hardly be said, all of the male sex.

On April 8th the town was in a great state of excitement over General Allenby's proclamation that the four Pashas who had been deported to Malta during his absence in England, for stirring up sedition, were to be permitted to return, and that all restrictions on travel were to be removed. The town was bedecked with flags and a procession was permitted through the streets, which gave an opportunity for much blowing off of steam on the part of the students. The patrols were withdrawn from the streets and no untoward incident occurred.

There was a large Government school near our temporary barracks. They lent us their football ground, and we played matches with the Police. We also gave young Egypt a few lessons in sportsmanship, which they badly needed. The Brigade band played in the public gardens and was much appreciated.

The Brigade concert party also paid us a visit and gave several good shows. At Quesna they played in the open, and a large crowd of natives witnessed the performance with huge delight

THE HOCKEY TEAM, EGYPT 1919.

To face page 171.

During May demobilisation was opened again, and by the end of the month we were back in Cairo, having been relieved in Benha by a Battalion of the Kamaon Rifles. The officials expressed their regret at our departure, and their appreciation of the courtesy and good behaviour of the troops. The men were indeed to be congratulated on their conduct in very trying circumstances. Their imperturbable good humour and their admirable restraint were a great credit to the Battalion—and to the British Army, if I may be allowed to say so.

We came under the command of Brigadier-General E. M. Morris, C.M.G., commanding 31st Infantry Brigade in Cairo, and after one or two temporary billets were quartered in the Nasrieh Schools, forming part of the Cairo garrison. The 4th were at Kasr el Nil barracks. The schools made excellent quarters and everybody was made much more comfortable. Every man eventually got a bed to sleep in. There was a good messing hall, football grounds, recreation rooms, coffee bar, laundry, baths and other conveniences. Leave was freely given into Cairo, and the duties were not heavy. We had a detachment at Helouan, where there was a large aerodrome and a German ladies internment hostel—formerly a large hotel. The guard recognized among the ladies several old acquaintances from Sarona and Wilhelma. The prisoners were very comfortable and well looked after.

We had some motor lorries and light cars at Nasrieh which were used for street patrols. The native quarters in Cairo were still rather turbulent, but nothing serious occurred. Demobilisation went on, and a draft of 54 from the 3rd Battalion Essex Regiment arrived from England.

On June 29th the news of the signing of the Peace Treaty was received, and the following day was observed as a general holiday. Cairo was *en fête* and the festivities were kept up far into the night. The men were practically given a free hand to do as they liked, only a very small picquet remaining in barracks. There was some good natured ragging, and it must be confessed that a few tarbooshes were lost by their owners in the crush, but the "Gyppoes" took it very sensibly, and everything passed off well. The men fully justified the confidence which was place in them, and Thomas Atkins once more proved himself, in peace as in war, a good sportsman and the best behaved soldier in the world. On June 30th our strength was 18 officers and 341 other ranks. These numbers included the regular draft, and a good number of the remainder were volunteers for the Army of Occupation.

On August 1st the Battalion moved into the Citadel, which was already occupied by the remnants of the 5th Norfolks, and Nasrieh Schools were left free once more for the education of young Egypt.

On the following day I left on a month's leave to England, leaving Willmott in command. I never saw the Battalion again. It was reduced to cadré shortly afterwards and the opportunity was taken of demobilising me while in England. The great majority of those who had fought so well had already returned to civil life, and were carrying on in the same quiet way as when they were called up in 1914, just as if nothing had happened.

By November 19th the 1/5th Essex, after a brief but glorious career, had ceased to exist. The cadré, consisting of Willmott, an N.C.O. and six men arrived at Chelmsford on the 9th and were officially welcomed home by the Mayor on behalf of the county town. On the following day they were demobilised.

So I take my leave of my comrades of all ranks of the 1/5th Essex. What words of mine can do justice to them? Engaged as they were in a distant and subsidiary theatre of war, their deeds, moreover, subject to a rigid censorship, it was not to be wondered at that they received little notice in the Press. With regard to publicity they undoubtedly suffered through being English County troops. For some unknown reason the exploits of Scotsmen, Irishmen, Welshmen, Australians, and New Zealanders were invariably given greater prominence in the English papers than those of Englishmen. And when I look back on the record of these men of Essex—their splendid devotion to duty, their patience in adversity, their cheerfulness under every conceivable hardship and discomfort, their steadiness and bravery in action, and their exemplary conduct at all times, I am in despair at the feebleness of my pen, and wish they could have produced a historian better able to do them justice. But if these few notes of mine have helped, in however small a measure, towards a just appreciation of the part played by an Essex Territorial Battalion in the Great War, of the sacrifices they made, and of the debt which their Country and their County owe to them, I shall not have written in vain.

*Those interested in the bibliography of the 54th Division are reminded that a book of the War Services of the 1/5th Suffolk Regt. is in preparation and it is hoped will be published shortly. The author is Captain E. D. Wolton, The Hall, Lavenham, Suffolk.*

# APPENDIX I.

## CASUALTIES.

1. Killed, Died of Wounds or Died in Hospital.

(Total, all ranks, 311).

(*a*) *Officers.*

| | Date. | | Remarks. |
|---|---|---|---|
| Captain F. W. Bacon .. | 4/12/18 | .. | Died in England |
| 2/Lieut. F. W. Bartley .. | 26/3/17 | .. | |
| Lieut. E. C. Beard .. | 26/3/17 | .. | |
| Lieut. H. M. Browne .. | 26/3/17 | .. | |
| Lieut. T. H. O. Capron .. | 26/3/17 | .. | |
| Capt. H. K. Chester .. | 28/3/17 | .. | |
| Captain A. Denton .. | 16/8/15 | .. | |
| 2/Lieut. F. Eames .. | 19/9/18 | .. | |
| 2/Lieut. C. V. Edmunds.. | 26/3/17 | .. | |
| Lieut. W. H. Evans .. | 2/11/17 | .. | |
| 2/Lieut. A. G. Eden .. | 21/5/18 | .. | |
| 2/Lieut. E. G. P. Fenn .. | 19/9/18 | .. | |
| Lieut. L. Gray .. .. | 31/7/17 | .. | Died of Enteric |
| Captain C. A. Gould .. | 26/3/17 | .. | |
| Major J. Heron .. .. | 26/3/17 | .. | |
| 2/Lieut. H. R. Lancaster | 2/11/17 | .. | |
| 2/Lieut. A. E. Sheldon .. | 23/8/15 | .. | |
| 2/Lieut. R. Turner .. | 15/8/15 | .. | |
| Lieut.. C. O. Wilson .. | 26/3/17 | .. | |

(*b*.) *Warrant Officers, N.C.O.'s and Men.*

| | | Date. | | Remarks. |
|---|---|---|---|---|
| 250075 | Sergt. D. Ambrose .. | 2/11/17 | .. | |
| 250102 | Corpl. P. Anderson .. | 2/11/17 | .. | |
| 250299 | Pte. W. Arnold .. .. | 15/5/17 | .. | Died as Prisoner |
| 250127 | Pte. L. Alliston .. .. | 27/3/17 | .. | |
| 250675 | Pte. P. Adams .. .. | 26/3/17 | .. | |
| 250327 | Pte. W. Ainger .. .. | 26/3/17 | .. | |
| 250376 | Sergt. C. T. Alloway .. | 2/11/17 | .. | |
| 37264 | Pte. P. D. Allen .. .. | 28/11/17 | .. | |
| 36605 | Pte. J. E. Abbott .. | 2/11/17 | .. | |
| 36746 | Pte. W. Appleton .. | 3/11/17 | .. | |
| 36767 | Pte. J. Anderson .. .. | 2/11/17 | .. | |
| 2707 | Pte. A. J. Beard .. .. | 17/8/15 | .. | |
| 1796 | L/Corpl. A. A. Baker .. | 18/8/15 | .. | |
| 2 | Sergt. S. Bartholomew .. | 19/9/15 | .. | |
| 3101 | Pte. A. Brand .. .. | 8/10/15 | .. | Died of Dysentery |
| 250580 | Pte. P. Buckingham .. | 26/3/17 | .. | |
| 250927 | Pte. W. Banks .. .. | 26/10/18 | .. | Died of Disease |

| | | Date. | Remarks. |
|---|---|---|---|
| 250928 | Pte. H. W. Banks .. | 27/3/17 .. | |
| 251399 | Pte. C. Beeton .. .. | 26/3/17 .. | |
| 251344 | Corpl. H. Bezant .. .. | 12/6/17 .. | Died of Disease |
| 251343 | Pte. G. Bruton .. .. | 27/3/17 .. | |
| 251375 | Pte. S. G. Bullock .. | 28/11/17 .. | |
| 250532 | Pte. S. O. Byford .. | 26/3/17 .. | |
| 251034 | Pte. B. Boreham .. .. | 26/3/17 .. | |
| 251113 | Pte. E. Beere .. .. | 26/3/17 .. | |
| 250925 | Pte. W. A. Bentley .. | 2/11/17 .. | |
| 251180 | Pte. G. Baker .. .. | 2/11/17 .. | |
| 251208 | Pte. E. Brewer .. .. | 2/11/17 .. | |
| 250530 | Pte. A. W. Bell .. .. | 26/3/17 .. | |
| 251211 | Pte. W. Blanks .. .. | 19/9/18 .. | |
| 251287 | Pte. H. Bambridge .. | 26/3/17 .. | |
| 251728 | Pte. E. Bailey .. .. | 26/3/17 .. | |
| 252736 | Pte. A. E. Bint .. .. | 19/9/18 .. | |
| 250169 | L/Sergt. N. Bruce .. | 2/11/17 .. | |
| 250213 | Pte. C. Buckman.. .. | 2/1/117 .. | |
| 1947 | Pte C. Brazier .. .. | 26/11/17 .. | |
| 250317 | L/Corpl. E. Barr .. .. | 27/3/17 .. | |
| 250444 | L/Sergt. H. Byles .. | 2/11/17 .. | |
| 250913 | Pte. H. Bank .. .. | 22/11/18 .. | Died of Disease |
| 3131 | Pte. R. Buller .. .. | 26/3/17 .. | |
| 250887 | Pte. S. J. Barker.. .. | 2/11/17 .. | |
| 28748 | Pte. A. Brewer .. .. | 2/11/17 .. | |
| 43211 | Pte. F. Biggin .. .. | 19/9/18 .. | |
| 29505 | Pte. F. Brazier .. .. | 19/9/18 .. | |
| 56315 | Pte. W. G. Benoy .. | 19/9/18 .. | |
| 2495 | Pte. A. Chapman.. .. | 22/8/15 .. | |
| 2928 | Pte. C. Canham .. .. | 14/8/15 .. | |
| 1291 | Pte. F. R. Clarke.. .. | 14/8/15 .. | |
| 1453 | Pte. W. Clarke .. .. | 14/8/15 .. | |
| 3126 | Pte. C. Collar .. .. | 6/10/15 .. | Died of Enteric |
| 250238 | Pte. F. Cutter .. .. | 19/9/18 .. | |
| 250500 | Pte. E. Cook .. .. | 26/3/17 .. | |
| 250754 | Pte. E. H. Clarke.. .. | 26/3/17 .. | |
| 251390 | Pte. A. W. Chivers .. | 2/11/17 .. | |
| 251348 | Pte. G. Clarke .. .. | 28/11/17 .. | |
| 251791 | Pte. F. M. Cutter.. .. | 26/3/17 .. | |
| 250330 | Pte. A. E. Carter.. .. | 26/3/17 .. | |
| 252681 | Pte. F. Cutmore .. .. | 26/3/17 .. | |
| 250691 | Pte. H. Cornell .. .. | 2/11/17 .. | |
| 251072 | L/Corpl. A. Clarke .. | 19/6/17 .. | |
| 251036 | Pte. L. Clapton .. .. | 2/11/17 .. | |
| 251276 | Pte. W. Coles .. .. | 26/3/17 .. | |
| 251051 | Pte. E. Crye .. .. | 26/3/17 .. | |
| 250509 | Pte. J. Clayton .. .. | 18/12/17 .. | Died as Prisoner |
| 252744 | Pte. C. Chamberlain .. | 2/11/17 .. | |

| | | Date. | Remarks. |
|---|---|---|---|
| 250078 | Pte. A. Cross .. .. | 26/3/17 .. | |
| 250106 | Sergt. W. Cooper, D.C.M. | 2/11/17 .. | |
| 250135 | L/Sergt. A. Coates .. | 21/5/18 .. | |
| 250138 | Sergt. W. Chapman .. | 21/6/17 .. | |
| 1772 | Pte. E. Carr .. .. | 26/3/17 .. | |
| 250585 | L/Corpl. B. J. Clarke .. | 2/11/17 .. | |
| 36657 | Pte. H. Cross .. .. | 2/11/17 .. | |
| 36691 | Pte. Clelland .. .. | 30/8/17 .. | |
| 36776 | Pte. A. Carr .. .. | 2/11/17 .. | |
| 36777 | Pte. C. Castles .. .. | 2/11/17 .. | |
| 1984 | Pte. J. Day .. .. | 3/10/15 .. | |
| 1575 | Pte. F. Drury .. .. | 1/10/15 .. | |
| 251378 | Pte. T. Davidson.. .. | 26/3/17 .. | |
| 251368 | Pte. T. Deards .. .. | 26/3/17 .. | |
| 250590 | Pte. H. Dawson .. .. | 26/3/17 .. | |
| 251277 | Pte. W. Dunn .. .. | 26/3/17 .. | |
| 250057 | Pte. J. Devenish .. .. | 26/3/17 .. | |
| 250714 | Pte. A. Death .. .. | 26/3/17 .. | |
| 251064 | Pte. H. Darby .. .. | 26/3/17 .. | |
| 250306 | Pte. W. Ewart .. .. | 29/3/17 .. | |
| 250073 | Pte. S. W. Ellis .. .. | 2/11/17 .. | |
| 250774 | Pte. A. J. Eves .. .. | 2/11/17 .. | |
| 251040 | Pte. W. Eve .. .. | 26/3/17 .. | |
| 250503 | Pte. E. Emery .. .. | 26/3/17 .. | |
| 251084 | Pte. A. Enefer .. .. | 3/11/17 .. | |
| 251183 | Pte. H. Earey .. .. | 26/3/17 .. | Died as Prisoner |
| 251184 | Pte. F. Enefer .. .. | 26/3/17 .. | |
| 250196 | Pte. E. Everett .. .. | 26/3/17 .. | |
| 250290 | Pte. F. Eve .. .. | 26/3/17 .. | |
| 250126 | Pte. S. Everard .. .. | 26/3/17 .. | |
| 37316 | Pte. C. R. Earle .. .. | 2/11/17 .. | |
| 250876 | Pte. W. J. Fell .. .. | 27/3/17 .. | |
| 251054 | Pte. G. W. Finch.. .. | 2/11/17 .. | |
| 250481 | L/Corpl. S. J. Fryatt .. | 5/10/17 .. | |
| 251162 | Pte. E. J. Fitch .. .. | 2/11/17 .. | |
| 36694 | Pte. W. D. French .. | 2/11/17 .. | |
| 1835 | L/Corpl. W. M. Gardiner.. | 12/11/15 .. | Died of Disease |
| 250526 | Pte. A. Game .. .. | 26/3/17 .. | |
| 3892 | Pte. W. C. Gray .. .. | 26/3/17 .. | |
| 251353 | Pte. H. S. Green .. .. | 2/11/17 .. | |
| 251250 | Pte. G. Green .. .. | 29/8/17 .. | |
| 252755 | Pte. A. W. Gosling .. | 2/11/17 .. | |
| 253147 | Pte. A. Griffiths .. .. | 14/11/18 .. | Died of Disease |
| 2112 | Pte. H. Grove .. .. | 26/3/17 .. | |
| 250969 | Pte. B. Grimwade .. | 2/11/17 .. | |
| 36622 | Pte. J. Gray .. .. | 4/12/17 .. | |
| 37292 | Pte. S. H. Gibbins .. | 29/8/17 .. | |
| 1551 | Pte. W. Hedges .. .. | 27/8/15 .. | |

| | | Date. | | Remarks. |
|---|---|---|---|---|
| 2354 | Pte. A. Hynds .. .. | 26/3/17 | .. | |
| 250980 | Pte. J. C. Harding .. | 2/11/17 | .. | |
| 251035 | Pte. A. G. Harris.. .. | 28/11/17 | .. | |
| 250178 | Pte. A. L. Harris.. .. | 26/3/17 | .. | |
| 250303 | Pte. E. H. Harvey .. | 2/11/17 | .. | |
| 250364 | Pte. E. Horrex .. .. | 2/11/17 | .. | |
| 250485 | Pte. A. Hales .. .. | 2/11/17 | .. | |
| 3497 | Pte. H. G. Humphreys .. | 27/4/17 | .. | |
| 251194 | Pte. H. Hoslett .. .. | 26/3/17 | .. | |
| 251256 | Pte. H. Hart .. .. | 2/11/17 | .. | |
| 250649 | Pte. C. Hubbard .. .. | 26/3/17 | .. | |
| 250005 | Sergt. H. Halls .. .. | 26/3/17 | .. | |
| 251735 | Pte. G. Hibbert .. .. | 12/4/17 | .. | Died as Prisoner |
| 11165 | Pte. E. Humphreys .. | 2/11/17 | .. | |
| 250105 | Pte. L. J. Hasler.. .. | 3/12/17 | .. | |
| 1816 | Pte. J. W. Hamblion .. | 7/9/15 | .. | |
| 2288 | Corpl. P. R. Humphreys | 26/3/17 | .. | |
| 3210 | Pte. W. Howard .. .. | 26/3/17 | .. | |
| 250223 | Corpl. F. Hart .. .. | 26/3/17 | .. | |
| 37317 | Pte. T. Heath .. .. | 2/11/17 | .. | |
| 37318 | Pte. H. Hunnisett .. | 3/11/17 | .. | |
| 56308 | L/Corpl. R. Harrison .. | 19/9/18 | .. | |
| 1829 | Pte. H. J. Johnson .. | 17/8/15 | .. | |
| 250263 | Pte. T. Joy .. .. | 26/3/17 | .. | |
| 251389 | Pte. H. Jennings .. .. | 26/3/17 | .. | |
| 250542 | A/Sergt. R. Jarrold .. | 19/9/18 | .. | |
| 250727 | L/Sergt. H. L. Jeayes .. | 26/3/17 | .. | |
| 251163 | Pte W. Joslin .. .. | 3/11/17 | .. | |
| 250815 | Pte. H. G. Jenkins .. | 26/3/17 | .. | |
| 250079 | Pte. A. Jarvis .. .. | 26/3/17 | .. | |
| 37302 | Pte. G. W. Johnson .. | 20/7/17 | .. | |
| 2786 | L/Corpl. C. D. Knight .. | 2/10/15 | .. | Died of Enteric |
| 250525 | Pte. C. Keymer .. | 26/3/17 | .. | |
| 250195 | Sergt. H. E. Kemble .. | 26/3/17 | .. | |
| 36755 | Pte. J. C. Kavanagh .. | 30/11/17 | .. | |
| 3213 | Pte. P. H. Lazzell .. | 15/8/15 | .. | |
| 1909 | Pte. E. G. Lock .. .. | 15/8/15 | .. | |
| 3307 | Pte. H. W. Locke .. | 2/9/15 | .. | |
| 251394 | Pte. H. E. Lebau.. .. | 2/11/17 | .. | |
| 250234 | Pte. A. Lorkin .. .. | 26/3/17 | .. | |
| 250084 | Pte. A. Langley .. .. | 26/3/17 | .. | |
| 252765 | Pte. H. Lodge .. .. | 3/11/17 | .. | |
| 3152 | Pte. A. Little .. .. | 26/3/17 | .. | |
| 250862 | Pte. F. J. Lodge .. .. | 26/3/17 | .. | |
| 250883 | Pte. H. C. Lodge.. .. | 2/11/17 | .. | |
| 250966 | Pte. G. H. Legerton .. | 2/11/17 | .. | |
| 59089 | Pte. H. G. Lock .. .. | 19/9/18 | .. | |
| 87 | A/Sergt. R. W. Miller .. | 6/9/15 | .. | |

| | | Date. | | Remarks. |
|---|---|---|---|---|
| 250454 | Pte. W. L. Miller.. .. | 26/3/17 | .. | |
| 250595 | Pte. C. Mead .. .. | 14/3/19 | .. | Died of Disease |
| 250957 | Pte. F. C. Malyon .. | 26/3/17 | .. | |
| 4265 | Corpl. J. Murray .. .. | 26/3/17 | .. | |
| 251126 | Pte. J. Markham .. .. | 27/3/17 | .. | |
| 250357 | Sergt. A. Mann .. .. | 26/3/17 | .. | |
| 250630 | Pte. W. Mead .. .. | 21/4/17 | .. | Died as Prisoner |
| 251120 | Pte. H. Munson .. .. | 2/11/17 | .. | |
| 250071 | Sergt. A. Mitson .. .. | 29/8/17 | .. | |
| 250592 | Pte. F. Munson .. .. | 2/4/17 | .. | Died as Prisoner |
| 36686 | Pte. A. R. Meeson .. | 2/11/17 | .. | |
| 36797 | Pte. T. Marwood .. .. | 20/7/17 | .. | |
| 251222 | Pte. F. Mills .. .. | 26/3/17 | .. | |
| 251188 | Pte. J. Morris .. .. | 13/11/18 | .. | Died of Disease |
| 251187 | Pte. J. Monk .. .. | 26/3/17 | .. | |
| 250600 | Pte. W. Moseley .. .. | 26/3/17 | .. | |
| 250674 | Pte. W. W. Manktelow .. | 26/3/17 | .. | |
| 250382 | Pte. H. Miller .. .. | 27/3/17 | .. | |
| 251731 | Pte. H. Montgomery .. | 27/3/17 | .. | |
| 252767 | Pte. J. Marshall .. .. | 2/11/17 | .. | |
| 253232 | Pte. W. J. B. Mortimer.. | 19/9/18 | .. | |
| 250669 | L./Corpl. B. G. Newman | 28/11/17 | .. | |
| 250678 | Pte. G. T. Nelson .. | 2/11/17 | .. | |
| 252534 | Pte. J. Neary .. .. | 26/3/17 | .. | |
| 36638 | Pte. F. Nelsey .. .. | 3/11/17 | .. | |
| 36719 | Pte. W. H. Newvell .. | 2/11/17 | .. | |
| 251089 | Pte. F. Olley .. .. | 26/3/17 | .. | |
| 251128 | Pte. S. Oxley .. .. | 7/11/17 | .. | |
| 2280 | Sergt. E. Ogg .. .. | 20/8/15 | .. | |
| 250712 | Pte. C. Plummer .. .. | 27/3/17 | .. | |
| 250744 | L./Corpl. J. Podd.. .. | 30/8/17 | .. | |
| 251373 | Pte. W. G. Prior .. .. | 26/3/17 | .. | |
| 250611 | Pte. J. Peake .. .. | 16/8/18 | .. | Died of Disease |
| 250696 | Pte. A. C. Plane .. .. | 26/3/17 | .. | |
| 250761 | Pte. F. Patient .. .. | 26/3/17 | .. | |
| 251099 | Pte. E. F. Page .. .. | 28/11/17 | .. | |
| 251224 | Pte. S. Potter .. .. | 26/3/17 | .. | |
| 251235 | Pte. A. Peacock .. .. | 26/3/17 | .. | |
| 250512 | Pte. H. Perrin .. .. | 26/3/17 | .. | |
| 250654 | Pte. C. Patridge .. .. | 26/3/17 | .. | |
| 251697 | Pte. G. W. Piper.. .. | 2/11/17 | .. | |
| 251753 | Pte. L. Perry .. .. | 2/11/17 | .. | |
| 250907 | Pte. E. A. Pavitt.. .. | 26/3/17 | .. | |
| 15885 | Pte. A. Pledger .. .. | 2/11/17 | .. | |
| 36641 | Pte. J. Pickford .. .. | 2/11/17 | .. | |
| 36723 | Pte. P. Peck .. .. | 6/11/17 | .. | |
| 251225 | L./Corpl. H. Quilter .. | 2/11/17 | .. | |
| 251338 | A./Corpl. H. F. Rainbird | 26/3/17 | .. | |

| | | Date. | | Remarks. |
|---|---|---|---|---|
| 3492 | Pte. W. Ridgeon .. .. | 4/1/17 | .. | Died of Disease |
| 250158 | Sergt. (A./Q.-M.-S.) H. Read | 18/5/18 | .. | |
| 251092 | Pte. G. Root .. .. | 27/3/17 | .. | |
| 251741 | Pte. F. Rogers .. .. | 26/3/17 | .. | |
| 250323 | L./Corpl. L. Richardson | 28/11/17 | .. | |
| 2101 | L./Corpl. F. J. Ralph .. | 26/3/17 | .. | |
| 2192 | Pte. E. J. Russell .. | 5/9/15 | .. | |
| 2241 | Sergt. J. Rice .. .. | 16/8/15 | .. | |
| 3208 | Pte. R. Rouse .. .. | 26/3/17 | .. | |
| 250294 | Pte. E. Staines .. .. | 26/3 17 | .. | |
| 250639 | Pte. E. Succamore .. | 26/3/17 | .. | |
| 250681 | L./Corpl. C. W. Smith .. | 23/12/17 | .. | Died as Prisoner |
| 250805 | Pte. W. Seaman .. .. | 26/3/17 | .. | |
| 250931 | Pte. H. C. Stone .. .. | 26/3/17 | .. | |
| 250480 | Pte. A. J. Seaborne .. | 26/3/17 | .. | |
| 251055 | Pte. W. C. Stock.. .. | 21/2/19 | .. | Died of Disease |
| 250846 | Pte. A. Smith .. .. | 4/11/17 | .. | |
| 250941 | Pte. S. P. Spurgeon .. | 26/3/17 | .. | |
| 251096 | Pte. C. Simpson .. .. | 26/3/17 | .. | |
| 251122 | Pte. A. Scotney .. .. | 26/3/17 | .. | |
| 251147 | Pte. W. L. Stebbings .. | 3/11/17 | .. | |
| 251170 | Pte. A. E. Smith.. .. | 26/3/17 | .. | |
| 251242 | Pte. T. Smith .. .. | 26/3/17 | .. | |
| 251261 | Pte. A. J. Stephens .. | 2/11/17 | .. | |
| 251326 | Pte. B. Smith .. .. | 1/6/17 | .. | Died of Disease |
| 250274 | Pte. W. J. Sadler.. .. | 26/3/17 | .. | |
| 251733 | Pte. F. H. Sealey.. .. | 2/11/17 | .. | |
| 1480 | Corpl. V. F. Scruby .. | 9/10/15 | .. | |
| 1587 | Sergt. H. Stone .. .. | 27/8/15 | .. | |
| 3145 | Pte. S. A. Sadler.. .. | 14/8/15 | .. | |
| 251676 | Corpl. H. Stock .. .. | 26/3/17 | .. | |
| 1784 | Pte. A. Sharpe .. .. | 15/8 15 | .. | |
| 2651 | Pte. C. Shelley .. .. | 14/8/15 | .. | |
| 250629 | Pte. J. Smith .. .. | 18/6/17 | .. | |
| 3507 | Pte. A. Shead .. .. | 26/3/17 | .. | |
| 250892 | Pte. W. S. Skingley .. | 4/11/17 | .. | |
| 250904 | Pte. H. J. Stephenson .. | 26/3/17 | .. | |
| 250407 | Pte. A. W. Smith .. | 26/3/17 | .. | |
| 36652 | Pte. G. H. Shakespeare .. | 1/12/17 | .. | |
| 36653 | Pte. S. C. Searles.. .. | 2/11/17 | .. | |
| 1227 | Pte. C. F. Starling .. | 27/8/15 | .. | Died of Dysentery |
| 2797 | Pte. C. Smith .. .. | 23/9/15 | .. | Do. |
| 2348 | Pte. H. Stubbings .. | 30/11/15 | .. | Died of Diphtheria |
| 250295 | Pte. C. Turner .. .. | 26/3/17 | .. | |
| 250871 | Pte. G. Theadon .. .. | 26/3/17 | .. | |
| 251397 | Pte. F. Tomlins .. .. | 26/3/17 | .. | |
| 250184 | L./Corpl. A. Tasker .. | 2/11/17 | .. | |
| 251027 | Pte. C. R. Thorpe .. | 26/3/17 | .. | |

| No. | Name | Date. | Remarks. |
|---|---|---|---|
| 251153 | Pte. A. Theobald | 26/3/17 | |
| 251198 | Pte. C. Thorogood | 4/5/17 | |
| 251227 | Pte. P. Tansley | 26/3/17 | |
| 4053 | Pte. H. Teager | 18/10/16 | Accidentally |
| 1956 | Pte. A. Tye | 26/3/17 | |
| 250794 | Pte. E. Taylor | 2/11/17 | |
| 34368 | Pte. A. Thompson | 2/11/17 | |
| 36670 | Pte. H. W. Terry | 2/11/17 | |
| 957 | Pte. A. E. Thomas | 27/9/15 | Died of Disease |
| 403 | Pte. F. Tyler | 4/10/15 | Died of Enteric |
| 250153 | Sergt. B. Upchurch | 28/11/17 | |
| 36741 | Pte. J. S. Wheeldon | 13/5 18 | |
| 35568 | Pte. H. P. White | 20/11/17 | |
| 250030 | Pte. R. Wiggins | 26/3/17 | |
| 250778 | Pte. V. Wale | 4/4/17 | |
| 250145 | Pte. W. Wade | 26/3/17 | |
| 250179 | Pte. S. Wiggins | 2/11/17 | |
| 250449 | Pte. J. Wager | 26/3/17 | |
| 250847 | Pte. F. Wright | 26/3/17 | |
| 251105 | Pte. J. Willis | 2/11/17 | |
| 251125 | Pte. S. G. Woods | 5/10/17 | |
| 251155 | Pte. G. Webb | 2/11/17 | |
| 251168 | Pte. B. F. Wilson | 26/3/17 | |
| 251230 | Pte. E. Ward | 26/3/17 | |
| 251331 | Pte. H. Willsher | 26/3/17 | |
| 251199 | Pte. E. J. Wallis | 2/11/17 | |
| 251234 | Pte. J. Wright | 26/3/17 | |
| 253228 | Pte. A. C. Welland | 19/9/18 | |
| 250104 | Pte. F. Waylett | 4/4/17 | |
| 1747 | Sergt. F. Wass | 18/8/15 | |
| 1845 | Pte. H. Wheatley | 14/8/15 | |
| 250447 | Pte. F. W. Webb | 2/11/17 | |
| 250933 | Pte. B. H. Wright | 2/11/17 | |
| 1733 | Pte. L. Warner | 16/8/15 | |
| 36654 | Pte. W. G. Wright | 2/11/17 | |

2. WOUNDED. (Total, all ranks, 551).

(*a.*) *Officers.*

| Name | Date. | Remarks. |
|---|---|---|
| Lieut. B. Archer, M.C. | 2/11/17 | |
| Captain H. T. Argent | 17/8/15 | |
| Lieut. J. Avery (M.O.) | 4/11/18 | |
| Captain F. W. Bacon | 26/3/17 | |
| Do. | 2/11/17 | See 1. (*a.*) |
| Captain H. S. Calverley, M.C. | 26/3/17 | |
| Captain E. B. Deakin, D.S.O., M.C. | 2/11/17 | |
| Captain T. G. N. Franklin | 26/3/17 | |

| | Date. | | Remarks. |
|---|---|---|---|
| Lieut.-Col. T. Gibbons, D.S.O... .. .. | 5/11/15 | .. | |
| Do. | 26/3/17 | .. | |
| Do. | 2/11/17 | .. | |
| 2/Lieut. A. E. Gilmore .. | 26/3/17 | .. | |
| Major J. Heron .. .. | 30/8/15 | .. | See 1. (*a.*) |
| Lieut. J. H. Jackson .. | 3/11/17 | .. | |
| 2/Lieut. F. Lucas.. .. | 14/5/18 | .. | |
| Captain C. Portway, M.C. | 19/9/18 | .. | |
| 2/Lieut. E. H. Ryan .. | 2/11/17 | .. | |
| Lieut. F. C. Safe .. .. | 2/11/17 | .. | |
| 2/Lieut. E. Cooper Smith | 26/3/17 | .. | |
| 2/Lieut. J. Templeton .. | 19/9/18 | .. | |
| Captain E. D. H. Willmott | 26/3/17 | .. | |
| Lieut. F. P. Windsor .. | 26/3/17 | .. | |
| Captain L. D. Womersley | 1/12/15 | .. | |
| Do. | 26/3/17 | .. | |
| 2/Lieut. E. M. G. Wray, D.S.O. .. .. | 2/11/17 | .. | |

(*b.*) *Warrant Officers, N.C.O.'s and Men.*

| | | Date. | | Remarks. |
|---|---|---|---|---|
| 250393 | Pte. E. Algar .. .. | 2/11/17 | .. | |
| 250594 | Pte. A. Acres .. .. | 26/3/17 | .. | |
| 251210 | Pte. V. Allington.. .. | 26/3/17 | .. | |
| 251307 | Pte. E. Adcock .. .. | 26/3/17 | .. | |
| Do. | Do. .. .. | 30/11/17 | .. | |
| 250693 | Pte. E. Arnold .. .. | 2/12/17 | .. | |
| 250636 | Pte. A. Ager .. .. | 2/11/17 | .. | |
| 250299 | Pte. W. Arnold .. .. | 26/3/17 | .. | See 1. (*b.*) |
| 250190 | Pte. W. Ainger .. .. | 26/3/17 | .. | |
| 252733 | Pte. B. F. Allen .. .. | 19/9/18 | .. | |
| 252734 | Pte. H. R. Arbon .. | 2/11/17 | .. | |
| 253155 | Pte. D. Adams .. .. | 19/9/18 | .. | |
| 250067 | Pte. E. Alliston .. .. | 26/3/17 | .. | |
| 1350 | Pte. W. G. Akers.. .. | 20/8/15 | .. | |
| 1472 | Sergt. P. Anderson .. | 14/8/15 | .. | |
| 1849 | Corpl. W. Arthey.. .. | 14/8/15 | .. | |
| 250735 | Pte. C. H. Anthony .. | 26/3/17 | .. | |
| 251003 | Pte. O. Aves .. .. | 2/11/17 | .. | |
| 35543 | Pte. J. Abbott .. .. | 2/11/17 | .. | |
| 1558 | Pte. S. W. Adams .. | | .. | |
| 251369 | Pte. A. E. Boreham .. | 26/3/17 | .. | |
| 251391 | Pte. H. Bottoms .. .. | 30/5/18 | .. | |
| 251387 | Pte. J. E. Brady.. .. | 2/11/17 | .. | |
| 250131 | Pte. H. Binks .. .. | 26/3/17 | .. | |
| 250533 | Pte. A. E. Barker .. | 2/11/17 | .. | |
| 250721 | Pte. J. Blunden .. .. | 26/3/17 | .. | |

| | | Date. | Remarks. |
|---|---|---|---|
| 250967 | Pte. G. Banks .. .. | 26/3/17 .. | |
| 251080 | Pte. W. J. Bartrop .. | 26/3/17 .. | |
| 251130 | Pte. J. Baldwin .. .. | 27/11/17 .. | |
| 251150 | Pte. S. C. Bird .. .. | 2/11/17 .. | |
| 250539 | Pte. F. Barker .. .. | 2/11/17 .. | |
| 250596 | Pte. F. Britton .. .. | 26/3/17 .. | |
| 250753 | Pte. W. Burr .. .. | 19/9/18 .. | |
| 250951 | Pte. C. E. Bacon.. .. | 3/11/17 .. | |
| 251158 | Pte. H. Beckwith.. .. | 4/11/17 .. | |
| 251310 | Pte. A. Bucknell .. .. | 26/3/17 .. | |
| 251243 | Pte. A. Bones .. .. | 2/11/17 .. | |
| 251260 | Pte. A. E. Bewers .. | 2/11/17 .. | |
| 250680 | Pte. J. Butcher .. .. | 2/11/17 .. | |
| 250059 | Pte. W. H. Barker .. | 26/3/17 .. | |
| 252741 | Pte. F. Bullock .. .. | 28/11/17 .. | |
| 252742 | Pte. C. A. Bunker .. | 21/5/18 .. | |
| 253154 | Pte. J. Biddle .. .. | 19/9/18 .. | |
| 250100 | Pte. S. H. Brown.. .. | 16/8/15 .. | |
| 150164 | Pte. L. Brewer .. .. | 3/11/17 .. | |
| 1682 | Corpl. A. Beardwell .. | 14/8/15 .. | |
| 250288 | Pte. J. Boreham .. .. | 26/3/17 .. | |
| 250348 | Pte. W. Barton .. .. | 2/11/17 .. | |
| 2202 | Pte. E. Bearman .. .. | 3/9/15 .. | |
| 2236 | Pte. R. S. Brown.. .. | 17/8/15 .. | |
| 2296 | Pte. W. Brignall .. .. | 23/8/15 .. | |
| 2361 | Pte. F. Bonnington .. | 13/8/15 .. | |
| 2455 | Pte. A. Bentley .. .. | 11/9/15 .. | |
| 250557 | Sergt. A. E. Beard .. | 26/3/17 .. | |
| 2843 | Pte. A. Butcher .. .. | 21/8/15 .. | |
| 250634 | Pte. E. Beckwith.. .. | 14/8/15 .. | |
| 3141 | Pte. R. Bullen .. .. | 14/8/15 .. | |
| 3135 | Pte. G. A. Bareham .. | 24/8/15 .. | |
| 3203 | Pte. W. Burr .. .. | 21/8/15 .. | |
| 253266 | Pte. F. Banks .. .. | 19/9/18 .. | |
| 3248 | Pte. G. Brown .. .. | 13/9/15 .. | |
| 3268 | Pte. C. H. Bowyer .. | 14/8/15 .. | |
| 250913 | Pte. H. Bank .. .. | 21/7/17 .. | See 1. (*b.*) |
| 250994 | Corpl. L. R. Bullen .. | 19/9/18 .. | |
| 37363 | Pte. E. Brassett .. .. | 3/11/17 .. | |
| 36679 | Pte. E. Bolton, M.M. .. | 30/6/17 .. | |
| 36685 | Pte. J. Brattin .. .. | 3/11/17 .. | |
| 36747 | Pte. W. Brewster.. .. | 2/11/17 .. | |
| 36771 | Pte. W. Bowes .. .. | 2/11/17 .. | |
| 15246 | Pte. A. Bartle .. .. | 3/11/17 .. | |
| 37265 | Pte. J. Bolton .. .. | 2/11/17 .. | |
| 37267 | Pte. J. Bennett .. .. | 27/11/17 .. | |
| Do. | Do. .. .. | 20/5/18 .. | |
| 37273 | Pte. A. J. Bacon .. .. | 19/9/18 .. | |

| | Date. | Remarks. |
|---|---|---|
| 37276 Pte. N. T. Bentley .. | 19/9/18 .. | |
| 35572 Pte. R. G. Belson .. | 2/11/17 .. | |
| 3131 Pte. R. Buller .. .. | 14/8/15 .. | |
| 1466 Pte. H. Brown .. .. | 14/8/15 .. | |
| 1535 Sergt. E. A. Brown .. | 16/8/15 .. | |
| 3273 Pte. W. B. Bristol .. | 14/8/15 .. | |
| 3268 Pte. E. Boyce .. .. | 4/9/15 .. | |
| 3302 Pte. H. E. Bareham .. | 21/8/15 .. | |
| 1571 Pte. H. Binks .. .. | 14/8/15 .. | |
| 4124 Pte. W. Blanks .. .. | 20/7/17 .. | |
| 250325 Pte. A. Carruthers .. | 26/3/17 .. | |
| 250535 Pte. J. Clarke .. .. | 26/3/17 .. | |
| Do. Do. .. .. | 20/5/18 .. | |
| 250812 Pte. F. G. Chaney .. | 26/3/17 .. | |
| 250851 Pte. A. Chapman.. .. | 2/11/17 .. | |
| 251033 Pte. H. L. Creed .. .. | 2/11/17 .. | |
| 251370 Pte. (A./L./Corpl.) A. V. Call .. .. .. | 13/5/18 .. | See 3. (*b.*) |
| 251352 Pte. E. E. Challis .. | 26/3/17 .. | |
| Do. Do. .. .. | 29/8/17 .. | |
| 251347 Pte. E. W. Chinnery .. | 19/9/18 .. | |
| 250888 Pte. J. Crowhurst.. .. | 26/3/17 .. | |
| 251081 Pte. G. Clayden .. .. | 2/11/17 .. | |
| 251115 Pte. F. G. Clarke.. .. | 2/11/17 .. | |
| 251112 Pte. E. G. Chaplin .. | 2/11/17 .. | |
| 251138 Pte. W. H. Croucher .. | 26/3/17 .. | |
| 251149 Pte. J. H. Cumbers .. | 27/3/17 .. | |
| 250548 Pte. H. Cawlin .. .. | 2/11/17 .. | |
| 250609 Pte. F. Cook .. .. | 26/3/17 .. | |
| 250683 Pte. A. Cornell .. .. | 26/3/17 .. | |
| 251093 Pte. J. Cook .. .. | 26/3/17 .. | |
| 251195 Pte. F. Clarke .. .. | 26/3/17 .. | See 3. (*b.*) |
| 251212 Pte. O. Coe .. .. | 26/3/17 .. | |
| 251213 Pte. E. Coker .. .. | 2/11/17 .. | |
| 251245 Pte. A. Crouch .. .. | 26/3/17 .. | |
| 251314 Pte. M. Crease .. .. | 2/11/17 .. | |
| 250528 Pte. E. Coppin .. .. | 26/3/17 .. | |
| 251239 Pte. F. Cresswell .. .. | 26/3/17 .. | |
| 251263 Pte. A. Cox .. .. | 26/3/17 .. | |
| 251293 Pte. W. L. Coote.. .. | 2/11/17 .. | |
| 251313 Pte. F. Clarke .. .. | 13/5/18 .. | |
| 251283 Pte. H. Coppen .. .. | 26/3/17 .. | |
| 250953 Pte. S. Coe .. .. | 26/3/17 .. | |
| 251280 Pte. W. Cawley .. .. | 26/3/17 .. | See 3. (*b.*) |
| 250509 Pte. J. Clayton .. .. | 26/3/17 .. | See 1. (*b.*) |
| 252796 Pte. S. Collard .. .. | 26/3/17 .. | |
| 252773 Pte. W. G. Carter .. | 2/11/17 .. | |
| 253208 Pte. F. Chowings.. .. | 19/9/18 .. | |

| | | Date. | Remarks. |
|---|---|---|---|
| 1351 | Pte. M. Candler | 15/8/15 | |
| 1521 | Pte. R. Coller | 8/9/15 | |
| 2055 | Pte. W. Carder | 17/8/15 | |
| 250366 | C.-S.-M. J. H. Cruse | 21/8/15 | |
| 2208 | Pte. J. Coote | 21/8/15 | |
| 250491 | Pte. W. Collins | 26/3/17 | |
| 250725 | Pte. H. Curtis | 2/11/17 | |
| 250738 | Pte. G. Collar | 3/11/17 | |
| 250763 | Pte. W. Clayton | 1/9/15 | |
| 250768 | Pte. C. Challis | 26/3/17 | |
| 251002 | Pte. S. Collins | 19/9/18 | |
| 3300 | Pte. F. Cutter | 19/8/15 | |
| 250909 | Pte. R. F. Clayden | 2/11/17 | |
| 36774 | Pte. A. Chapman | 21/5/18 | |
| 37281 | Pte. C. Clark | 3/11/17 | |
| 37282 | Pte. J. G. Clayton | 3/11/17 | |
| 37298 | Pte. T. J. Corbett | 2/11/17 | |
| 37307 | Pte. J. Cassey | 19/9/18 | |
| 56338 | Pte. R. Crabb | 19/9/18 | |
| 1516 | Pte. F. Collins | —/8/15 | |
| 250113 | Sergt. F. Collins, D.C.M. | 2/11/17 | |
| 1715 | Sergt. W. Clarke | 16/8/15 | |
| 3216 | Pte. C. Collar | 8/9/15 | |
| 2736 | L./Corpl. B. J. Clark | 24/9/15 | |
| 36691 | Pte. J. Clelland | 29/8/17 | |
| 252676 | Pte. S. J. Chadwick | 20/5/18 | |
| 250938 | Pte. C. R. Downham | 26/3/17 | |
| 251377 | A./Corpl. A. Dance | 26/4/17 | |
| 250863 | Pte. A. E. Day | 26/3/17 | See 3. (*b*.) |
| 251100 | Pte. W. Doe | 19/9/18 | |
| 251178 | Pte. T. W. Dicks | 26/3/17 | |
| 251238 | Pte. C. Denny | 26/3/17 | |
| 251160 | Pte. L. Dedman | 27/3/17 | |
| 251316 | Pte. R. Davey | 2/11/17 | |
| 251317 | Pte. E. Deal | 29/6/17 | |
| 250023 | Sergt. A. J. Diss | 3/11/17 | |
| 250080 | Pte. G. Davey | 18/4/17 | |
| 252747 | Pte. H. Dennison | 4/12/17 | |
| 250050 | C.-Q.-M.-S. C. Dixon | 26/3/17 | |
| 34274 | Pte. A. T. Dedman | 2/11/17 | |
| 36751 | Pte. W. G. Dixon | 27/11/17 | |
| 36781 | Pte. J. Dixon | 21/5/18 | |
| 36782 | Pte. J. H. Dickens | 2/11/17 | |
| 37285 | Pte. E. Daw | 3/11/17 | |
| 2536 | Pte. W. W. Daley | 14/8/15 | |
| 2114 | Pte. E. J. Diggins | 14/8/15 | |
| 2230 | Pte. J. Dennis | 23/8/15 | |
| 2362 | Pte. C. Death | —/8/15 | |

| | | Date. | Remarks. |
|---|---|---|---|
| 36753 | Pte. N. W. Ditchburn | 26/7/18 | |
| 250908 | Pte. W. C. Easter | 3/11/17 | |
| 251103 | Pte. S. Ephich | 26/3/17 | |
| 251110 | Pte. E. E. Edwards | 26/3/17 | |
| 251183 | Pte. H. Earey | 26/3/17 | See 1. (*b.*) |
| 874 | L./Corpl. A. Edwards | 17/8/15 | |
| 1365 | L./Corpl. E. Everitt | 14/8/15 | |
| 250489 | L./Corpl. W. Eve | 20/5/18 | |
| 3260 | Pte. A. J. Eves | 16/8/15 | |
| 250786 | Pte. F. Elsworthy | 16/8/15 | |
| 3294 | Pte. Elmsworth | —/8/15 | |
| 2992 | Pte. Elmer | —/8/15 | |
| 250334 | Sergt. R. French | 3/12/17 | |
| 250137 | Pte. B. Foster | 26/3/17 | |
| 250811 | Pte. W. Frost | 26/3/17 | |
| 250841 | Pte. C. J. Freeman | 23/4/17 | |
| 250957 | Pte. W. French | 26/3/17 | |
| 251359 | Pte. J. M. Fletcher | 27/3/17 | |
| 250705 | Pte. W. Fitch | 2/11/17 | |
| 251154 | Pte. A. V. Field | 26/3/17 | |
| 251216 | Pte. J. Fryatt | 26/3/17 | |
| 251296 | Pte. H. Farrow | 29/6/17 | |
| 250219 | Pte. L. S. Forman | 26/3/17 | See 3. (*b.*) |
| 250505 | A./L./Corpl. W. Francis | 29/8/17 | |
| 250021 | C.-S.-M. H. Frost | 26/3/17 | |
| 1127 | L./Corpl. W. Fairclough | 14/8/15 | |
| 1213 | Pte. E. Fairbrother | 14/8/15 | |
| 250147 | Sergt. F. Foster | 29/8/17 | |
| 250375 | Pte. T. Farren | 26/3/17 | |
| 250435 | Pte. T. H. F. Foreman | 26/3/17 | |
| 2836 | Pte. L. Fletcher | 17/8/15 | |
| 2951 | Pte. A. Fisher | 15/8/15 | |
| 250747 | L./Corpl. B. Fenner | 26/3/17 | |
| 3259 | Pte. A. Francombe | 14/8/15 | |
| 36617 | Pte. J. A. Fenton | 2/11/17 | |
| 36695 | Pte. H. Fletcher | 3/11/17 | |
| 36696 | Pte. A. Fotherby | 2/11/17 | |
| 37312 | Pte. G. S. Ferris | 2/8/17 | |
| 250602 | Pte. C. Grimsey | 3/11/17 | |
| 250917 | Pte. E. Gowers | 2/11/17 | |
| 2177 | Pte. G. F. Gowers | 14/8/15 | |
| 250363 | Do. | 26/3/17 | |
| 251141 | Pte. S. Garwood | 27/11/17 | |
| 251217 | Pte. J. Gowers | 2/11/17 | |
| 250297 | Pte. L. P. Green | 10/6/17 | |
| 250943 | Pte. G. Griggs | 2/11/17 | |
| 250060 | Pte. F. W. Goodey | 26/3/17 | |
| 250386 | Pte. A. B. Groves | 26/3/17 | |

| | | Date. | Remarks. |
|---|---|---|---|
| 205 | Sergt. H. Guymer.. .. | 17/8/15 | .. |
| 250040 | Sergt. H. Goodwin .. | 20/4/17 | .. |
| 250313 | Corpl. G. J. Goldstone .. | 2/11/17 | .. |
| 2788 | Pte. W. E. Good.. .. | —/8/15 | .. |
| 250653 | L./Sergt. W. Gafney, D.C.M. | 2/11/17 | .. |
| 250897 | Pte. A. Gepp .. .. | 26/3/17 | .. |
| 36623 | Pte. J. Goodall .. .. | 2/11/17 | .. |
| 36624 | Pte. J. Gibbs .. .. | 28/11/17 | .. |
| 3155 | Pte. H. W. Gunn .. | 14/8/15 | .. |
| 3118 | Pte. H. Gooch .. | 18/8/15 | .. |
| 2112 | Pte. H. Grove .. | 16/8/15 | .. |
| 251061 | Pte. A. Gordon .. .. | 1/8/17 | .. |
| 36622 | Pte. J. Gray .. .. | 27/11/17 | .. |
| 250628 | Corpl. C. J. Housden .. | 2/11/17 | .. |
| 251351 | Pte. W. Hilsden, D.C.M. | 2/11/17 | .. |
| 250189 | Pte. J. Hammond .. | 2/11/17 | .. |
| 250257 | Corpl. H. G. Harvey .. | 2/11/17 | .. |
| 250751 | Pte. A. Harden .. .. | 26/3/17 | .. |
| 250758 | Pte. G. Harris .. .. | 26/3/17 | .. |
| 250686 | Pte. J. Hill .. .. | 13/5/18 | .. |
| 250694 | Pte. C. Hutchins .. .. | 26/3/17 | .. |
| 251185 | Pte. G. H. Hand.. .. | 2/11/17 | .. |
| 250048 | Pte. H. Hale .. .. | 5/11/17 | .. |
| 250724 | Pte. V. Hart .. .. | 26/3/17 | .. |
| 250781 | Pte. W. Hockley .. .. | 26/3/17 | .. |
| 252797 | Corpl. S. Henfreys .. | 15/1/18 | .. |
| 250473 | Pte. A. Huckson .. .. | 29/8/17 | .. |
| 1493 | Pte. G. F. Hayward .. | —/8/15 | .. |
| Do. | L./Corpl. Do. .. | 2/11/17 | .. |
| 1748 | Pte. C. Hicks .. .. | —/9/15 | .. |
| 1884 | Pte. G. Holland .. .. | —/8/15 | .. |
| 250243 | Do. .. .. | 26/3/17 | .. |
| 1915 | L./Corpl. H. G. Harvey .. | 14/8/15 | .. |
| 2007 | Pte. B. Holgate .. .. | 14/8/15 | .. |
| 2178 | Pte. E. Horrex .. .. | 15/8/15 | .. |
| 2319 | Corpl. H. J. Hitchcock .. | 17/8/15 | .. |
| 250655 | Corpl. J. Howard .. | 2/11/17 | .. |
| 3104 | Pte. J. Hawkes .. .. | 23/9/15 | .. |
| 3110 | Pte. C. Harris .. .. | —/8/15 | .. |
| 250709 | Do. .. .. | 2/11/17 | .. |
| 3148 | Pte. R. Humphries .. | 14/8/15 | .. |
| 3225 | Pte. T. J. Hickford .. | 17/8/15 | .. |
| 3274 | Pte. H. Hume .. .. | 15/8/15 | .. |
| 250780 | Do. .. .. | 3/11/17 | .. |
| 35549 | Pte. J. Hunt .. .. | 5/11/17 | .. |
| 36706 | Pte. C. W. Hinnan .. | 2/11/17 | .. |
| 36793 | Pte. J. W. Hodgson .. | 21/5/18 | .. |
| 36796 | Pte. A. Hopkinson .. | 2/11/17 | .. |

| | | Date. | Remarks. |
|---|---|---|---|
| 37314 | Pte. J. J. Hills .. .. | 2/11/17 | .. |
| 45489 | Pte. W. Hughes .. .. | 19/9/18 | .. |
| 59064 | Pte. E. Harvey .. .. | 19/9/18 | .. |
| 1384 | Pte. F. G. Honeywood .. | 14/8/15 | .. |
| 1814 | L./Corpl. F. J. Hull .. | 14/8/15 | .. |
| 21739 | Pte. P. H. Henderson .. | 3/5/18 | .. |
| Do. | Do. .. .. | 20/9/18 | .. |
| 36791 | Pte. C. Horne .. .. | 13/5/18 | .. |
| 2000 | Corpl. W. Hawkes .. | 16/8/15 | .. |
| 389 | Corpl. P. Hance .. .. | —/8/15 | .. |
| 3281 | Pte. D. E. Hart .. .. | —/8/15 | .. |
| 2277 | Pte. W. Hopping .. | —/8/15 | .. |
| 2092 | Pte. T. Harris .. .. | —/8/15 | .. |
| 173 | Sergt. J. Hinton .. .. | 14/8/15 | .. |
| 251735 | Pte. G. Hibbert .. .. | 26/3/17 | .. See 1. (*b*.) |
| 1980 | Pte. W. J. Joyce .. | 14/8/15 | .. |
| 2010 | Pte. D. W. Jordan .. | 16/8/15 | .. |
| 2438 | Pte. F. Joslin .. .. | 15/8/15 | .. |
| 2531 | Pte. H. Johnson .. .. | 13/8/15 | .. |
| 250522 | Do. .. .. | 26/3/17 | .. |
| 1910 | Corpl. J. L. Jeffries .. | —/8/15 | .. |
| 250932 | Pte. N. Jarvis .. .. | 26/3/17 | .. |
| 250895 | Pte. D. Joyce .. .. | 26/3/17 | .. |
| 251172 | Pte. F. Jennings .. .. | 2/11/17 | .. |
| 250110 | Pte. W. Juniper .. .. | 26/3/17 | .. |
| 36666 | L./Corpl. A. S. Jeffries .. | 13/5/18 | .. |
| 2041 | L./Corpl. H. Keeble .. | —/18/15 | .. |
| 250092 | Pte. A. W. Knott .. | 26/3/17 | .. |
| 250998 | Pte. W. H. Karsten .. | 2/11/17 | .. |
| Do. | Do. .. .. | 19/5/18 | .. |
| 250305 | Pte. W. Kirby .. .. | 26/3/17 | .. |
| 251028 | Pte. G. Knudson .. .. | 26/3/17 | .. |
| 251306 | Pte. L. Kerridge .. .. | 26/3/17 | .. |
| 252762 | Pte. A. King .. .. | 30/11/17 | .. |
| 250302 | A./Corpl. H. Keeble .. | 26/3/17 | .. |
| 2826 | Pte. R. Lockwood .. | —/8/15 | .. |
| 1390 | L./Sergt. A. E. Lungley.. | 14/8/15 | .. |
| 1847 | L.Corpl. W. T. Lyes .. | 14/8/15 | .. |
| 1381 | Sergt. A. Langley.. .. | 14/8/15 | .. |
| 1814 | L./Corpl. F. G. Leatherdale | —/8/15 | .. |
| 1890 | Pte. S. J. Letch .. .. | 24/9/15 | .. |
| 250499 | Pte. H. Linnett .. .. | 2/11/17 | .. |
| 250576 | Pte. A. Laver .. .. | 26/3/17 | .. |
| 251070 | Pte. A. R. Lucas .. | 2/11/17 | .. |
| 251197 | Pte. A. Lee .. .. | 3/11/17 | .. |
| 251201 | Pte. E. Leworthy.. .. | 2/11/17 | .. |
| 250884 | Pte. E. W. Lodge .. | 3/11/17 | .. |
| 251747 | Pte. F. W. Law .. .. | 26/3/17 | .. |

| | | Date. | Remarks. |
|---|---|---|---|
| 250350 | Pte. F. Long .. .. | 2/11/17 .. | |
| 2433 | Dmr. H. Marshall .. | 14/8/15 .. | |
| 251164 | Pte. Do. .. .. | 26/3/17 .. | |
| 1908 | Pte. P. L. Moss .. .. | —/8/15 .. | |
| 251278 | Pte. H. Minney .. .. | 13/5/18 .. | |
| 2050 | Pte. W. A. Mynard .. | —/8/15 .. | |
| 250165 | Do. .. .. | 26/3/17 .. | |
| 2986 | Pte. W. W. Manktelow .. | —/8/15 .. | See 1. (*b.*) |
| 2402 | Pte. W. Moore .. .. | —/8/15 .. | |
| 250494 | Pte. R. McLean .. .. | 2/11/17 .. | |
| 250529 | Corpl. F. May .. .. | 26/3/17 .. | |
| 250595 | Pte. C. Mead .. .. | 2/11/17 .. | See 1. (*b.*) |
| 251048 | Pte. C. Manhood .. .. | 26/3/17 .. | |
| 250111 | Pte. B. E. Maskell .. | 26/3/17 .. | |
| 250630 | Pte. W. Mead .. .. | 26/3/17 .. | See 1. (*b.*) |
| 250704 | Pte. G. Mannell .. .. | 26/3/17 .. | |
| 250981 | Pte. G. T. Matthams .. | 30/11/17 .. | |
| 251139 | Pte. J. Mynard .. .. | 26/3/17 .. | |
| 250286 | Pte. J. Martin .. .. | 2/11/17 .. | |
| 250280 | Pte. H. Miller .. .. | 26/3/17 .. | |
| 251012 | Pte. A. Martin .. .. | 26/3/17 .. | |
| 251745 | Pte. H. Martin .. .. | 26/3/17 .. | |
| 252769 | Pte. J. E. Maynard .. | 27/11/17 .. | |
| 250605 | Pte. A. Moule .. .. | 26/3/17 .. | |
| 36637 | Pte. W. Mills .. .. | 19/9/18 .. | |
| 36668 | Pte. W. Marsden .. .. | 3/11/17 .. | |
| 56317 | Pte. E. J. Mutter.. .. | 19/9/18 .. | |
| 56335 | Pte. R. S. May .. .. | 19/9/18 .. | |
| 250592 | Pte. F. Munson .. .. | 26/3/17 .. | See 1. (*b.*) |
| 34275 | Pte. W. Moore .. .. | 13/5/18 .. | |
| 2094 | Pte. F. C. Newman .. | 16/8/15 .. | |
| 251076 | Pte. L. W. Newman .. | 2/11/17 .. | |
| 251223 | Pte. W. Norfolk .. .. | 26/3/17 .. | |
| 251192 | Pte. C. Newman .. .. | 26/3/17 .. | |
| 250784 | Pte. C. Newman .. .. | 2/11/17 .. | |
| 35542 | Pte. T. Nash .. .. | 2/11/17 .. | |
| 36794 | L./Corpl. A. E. Neal .. | 13/5/18 .. | |
| 2205 | Dmr. J. Oatway .. .. | 14/8/15 .. | |
| 2917 | Pte. F. W. Orris .. .. | 24/8/15 .. | |
| 251021 | Pte. J. J. O'Connor .. | 2/11/17 .. | |
| 251203 | Pte. E. Owers .. .. | 26/3/17 .. | |
| 252771 | Pte. P. S. Oliver .. .. | 2/11/17 .. | |
| 3211 | Pte. G. Partridge .. | 14/8/15 .. | |
| 2078 | L./Corpl. G W. Poole .. | 14/8/15 .. | |
| 2819 | Pte. J. Peake .. .. | 14/8/15 .. | |
| 1295 | Pte. L. Perry .. .. | 16/8/15 .. | |
| 3136 | Pte. F. Pullen .. .. | 16/8/15 .. | |
| 3205 | Pte. G. F. Pudney .. | 16/8/15 .. | |

| | | Date. | | Remarks. |
|---|---|---|---|---|
| 2708 | Pte. A. G. Pegram .. | 14/8/15 | .. | |
| 2199 | Pte. S. W. Palmer .. | 16/8/15 | .. | |
| 2508 | Pte. F. C. Palmer .. | —/8/15 | .. | |
| 252744 | Pte. E. Piggott .. .. | 2/11/17 | .. | |
| 252775 | Pte. C. Piper .. .. | 2/11/17 | .. | |
| Do. | Do. .. .. | 30/11/17 | .. | |
| 250872 | Pte. F. J. Parkins .. | 2/11/17 | .. | |
| 250064 | Sergt. C. Percival .. | 27/11/17 | .. | |
| 250241 | Sergt. A. G. Piper, M.M. | 26/3/17 | .. | |
| 250767 | Pte. E. Prentice .. .. | 26/3/17 | .. | |
| 56179 | Pte. D. Phillips .. .. | 19/9/18 | .. | |
| 250911 | Pte. E. Parish .. .. | 26/3/17 | .. | |
| 250996 | Pte. L. C. Pearse.. .. | 30/6/17 | .. | |
| 250433 | Pte. A. E. Parker .. | 26/3/17 | .. | |
| 250578 | L./Corpl. A. G. Pegram .. | 18/5/17 | .. | |
| 251108 | Pte. L. H. Pryke.. .. | 2/11/17 | .. | |
| 251134 | Pte. E. Pannell .. .. | 2/11/17 | .. | |
| 250660 | Pte. V. Parsonson .. | 26/3/17 | .. | |
| 250690 | Pte. R. Parkin .. .. | 26/3/17 | .. | |
| 250806 | Pte. G. Perrin .. .. | 2/11/17 | .. | |
| 251129 | Pte. J. Potts .. .. | 2/11/17 | .. | |
| 251193 | Pte. H. Perkins .. .. | 2/11/17 | .. | |
| 250624 | Pte. E. Pannell .. .. | 2/11/17 | .. | |
| 1621 | Sergt. H. Reed .. .. | —/8/15 | .. | |
| 3170 | Pte. L. Rawlinson .. | 14/8/15 | .. | |
| 1697 | Pte. A. V. Redpath .. | 14/8/15 | .. | |
| 3278 | Pte. G. S. Rolph .. | 14/8/15 | .. | |
| 1912 | Dmr. A. E. Ruffel .. | 17/8/15 | .. | |
| 1128 | Pte. W. Ridgeon .. .. | —/8/15 | .. | |
| 3212 | Pte. J. Raven .. .. | 9/9/15 | .. | |
| 2274 | Pte. C. S. Rawlinson .. | —/8/15 | .. | |
| 250689 | Pte. C. Reeder .. .. | 26/3/17 | .. | |
| 250116 | Pte. L. Rowland .. .. | 26/3/17 | .. | |
| 251053 | Pte. L. Rushforth .. | 21/4/17 | .. | |
| 250004 | Sergt. J. Ruffle .. .. | 2/11/17 | .. | |
| 250188 | Sergt. H. Rayner .. | 26/3/17 | .. | |
| 252649 | Pte. G. E. Robinson .. | 26/3/17 | .. | |
| 250047 | Corpl. N. Rand .. .. | 21/7/17 | .. | |
| 250398 | Pte. A. Rogers .. .. | 26/3/17 | .. | |
| 32229 | Pte. S. R. Ridgewell .. | 28/11/17 | .. | |
| 56349 | Pte. S. Rendell .. .. | 19/9/18 | .. | |
| 252780 | Pte. H. Rider .. .. | 28/7/17 | .. | |
| 36726 | Pte. C. G. Reid .. .. | 27/7/17 | .. | |
| 3007 | L./Corpl. S. Symonds .. | —/8/15 | .. | |
| 1500 | Pte. G. S. Service .. | —/8/15 | .. | |
| 1778 | Corpl. C. J. Swann .. | 14/8/15 | .. | |
| 3102 | Pte. F. G. Saich .. .. | 14/8/15 | .. | |
| 1505 | Pte. P. W. Salvage .. | 14/8/15 | .. | |

| | | Date. | Remarks. |
|---|---|---|---|
| 1813 | Pte. F. S. Sutton | 14/8/15 | |
| 3293 | Pte. H. G. Scrivener | 16/8/15 | |
| 2258 | Pte. E. Sayers | 23/8/15 | |
| 1632 | Pte. J. Suckling | 23/8/15 | |
| 1675 | Pte. L. W. Skerrit | 21/8/15 | |
| 1399 | L./Corpl. G. A. Studd | —/8/15 | |
| 400 | L./Corpl. G. Smee | —/11/15 | |
| 250343 | Sergt. F. Smith | 26/3/17 | |
| 250443 | Sergt. J. Snow | 26/3/17 | |
| 250681 | L./Corpl. C. W. Smith | 26/3/17 | See 1. (*b.*) |
| 251363 | Pte. R. W. South | 26/3/17 | |
| 251388 | Pte. J. Stewart | 26/3/17 | |
| 250240 | L./Corpl. C. Sullens | 26/3/17 | |
| 250373 | L./Corpl. A. Shelley | 2/11/17 | |
| Do. | Do. | 13/5/18 | |
| 250886 | Pte. G. W. Stone | 26/3/17 | |
| 250610 | Pte. H. Saich | 2/11/17 | |
| 250860 | Pte. F. K. Smith | 5/11/17 | |
| 251037 | Pte. G. Sampford | 26/3/17 | |
| 251062 | Pte. C. M. Stevens | 26/3/17 | |
| 251135 | Pte. W. Stock | 26/3/17 | |
| 251147 | Pte. W. L. Stebbings | 26/3/17 | See 1. (*b.*) |
| 251177 | Pte. G. H. Smith | 26/3/17 | |
| 251191 | Pte. J. Sargeant | 26/3/17 | |
| 251206 | Pte. A. Smith | 26/3/17 | |
| 251325 | Pte. W. Simkins | 26/3/17 | |
| 251241 | Pte. H. Searles | 2/11/17 | |
| 251261 | Pte. A. J. Stevens | 26/3/17 | |
| Do. | Do. | 20/7/17 | See 1. (*b.*) |
| 251291 | Pte. H. Smith | 26/3/17 | |
| 250185 | Pte. A. Salmon | 26/3/17 | See 3. (*b.*) |
| 250637 | Pte. J. Sadler | 26/3/17 | |
| 250715 | Pte. H. W. Smith | 2/11/17 | |
| 250874 | Pte. S. Smith | 26/3/17 | |
| 250160 | Pte. G. P. Sutton | 26/3/17 | |
| 253181 | L./Corpl. S. Strong | 19/9/18 | |
| 253201 | Pte. S. W. Staddon | 19/9/18 | |
| 253222 | Pte. R. Stamp | 19/9/18 | |
| 250627 | Sergt. F. Smith | 26/3/17 | |
| 250769 | Pte. A. Savill | 26/3/17 | |
| 36651 | Pte. R. Scarrart | 2/11/17 | |
| Do. | Do. | 29/7/17 | |
| 36656 | Pte. R. Swatman | 2/11/17 | |
| 36816 | Pte. R. Stewart | 2/11/17 | |
| 35546 | Pte R. E. Sanson | 2/11/17 | |
| 36606 | Pte. W. H. Selwood | 31/7/17 | |
| 34345 | Pte. C. Saffon | 30/11/17 | |
| 3193 | Pte. A. T. Tarbin | 28/8/15 | |

| | | Date. | Remarks. |
|---|---|---|---|
| 1950 | Pte. J. Thurkettle .. | 5/9/15 .. | |
| 2132 | Pte. J. Turner .. .. | 9/9/15 .. | |
| 250344 | Do. .. .. | 2/11/17 .. | |
| 172 | Pte. T. W. Thorpe .. | —/8/15 .. | |
| 250418 | Pte. W. Thompson .. | 26/3/17 .. | |
| 250993 | L./Corpl. W. H. Tatton .. | 26/3/17 .. | |
| 250652 | Pte. T. E. Tucker .. | 3/11/17 .. | |
| 251103 | Pte. T. Tyler .. .. | 26/2/17 .. | See 3. (*b*.) |
| 251104 | Pte. R. J. Townshend .. | 26/3/17 .. | |
| 251327 | Pte. T. Tucker .. .. | 27/3/17 .. | |
| Do. | Do. .. .. | 18/5/18 .. | |
| 250015 | Sergt. A. E. Thompson, M.S.M. .. .. | 3/11/17 .. | |
| 250035 | C.-S.-M. J. T. Thornhill .. | 26/3/17 .. | |
| 250136 | Pte. F. Tredgett .. .. | 26/3/17 .. | |
| 250573 | Pte. G. J. Taylor .. .. | 26/3/17 .. | See 3. (*b*.) |
| 36820 | Pte. W. Thorns .. .. | 19/9/18 .. | |
| 56173 | Pte. W. Towers .. .. | 19/9/18 .. | |
| 250039 | Corpl. S. Tatam .. .. | 13/5/18 .. | |
| 251228 | Pte. F. Voyce .. .. | 13/5/18 .. | |
| 1620 | Pte. W. Wade .. .. | 17/8/15 .. | |
| 1817 | Corpl. C. White .. .. | —/8/15 .. | |
| 2235 | Pte. A. A. Wright .. | 21/8/15 .. | |
| 3095 | Pte. W. S. Ward .. .. | —/8/15 .. | |
| 1982 | Pte. W. E. Whymark .. | 14/8/15 .. | |
| 3270 | Pte. P. Wale .. .. | 16/8/15 .. | |
| 1326 | Pte. W. Wager .. .. | 27/8/15 .. | |
| 1749 | Pte. C. A. Walker .. | 9/9/15 .. | |
| 2367 | Pte. F. W. Webb .. | —/8/15 .. | |
| 3231 | Pte. F. Waylen .. .. | —/8/15 .. | |
| 250320 | L./Corpl. H. S. Weeks .. | 26/3/17 .. | |
| 250480 | Pte. H. Wood .. .. | 26/3/17 .. | |
| 250581 | Pte. A. Weavers .. .. | 19/9/18 .. | |
| 250825 | Pte. C. Wilcher .. .. | 26/3/17 .. | |
| 251366 | Pte. F. J. Whight .. | 26/3/17 .. | |
| 36823 | Pte. R. W. Ward .. .. | 20/5/18 .. | |
| 251377 | Sergt. E. White, M.M. .. | 26/3/17 .. | |
| 251367 | Pte. P. E. Woods .. | 2/11/17 .. | |
| Do. | Do. .. .. | 20/5/18 .. | |
| 250346 | Pte. W. Ward .. .. | 26/3/17 .. | |
| 251056 | Pte. L. Wicks .. .. | 2/11/17 .. | |
| 251090 | Pte. R. W. Woodgate .. | 26/3/17 .. | See 3. (*b*.) |
| 251124 | Pte. R. Wright .. .. | 26/3/17 .. | |
| 251136 | Pte. A. Wesley .. .. | 3/11/17 .. | |
| 251146 | Pte. W. J. Woolfe .. | 2/11/17 .. | |
| 251157 | Pte. E. Woodwards .. | 26/3/17 .. | |
| 251179 | Pte. W. J. Wilsher .. | 19/9/18 .. | |
| 251209 | Pte. S. Whybrow .. .. | 26/3/17 .. | |

| | | Date. | Remarks. |
|---|---|---|---|
| 251233 | Pte. S. Wilsher .. .. | 26/3/17 .. | |
| 250991 | Corpl. A. Wallington .. | 2/11/17 .. | |
| 250521 | Pte. A. Whalley .. .. | 26/3/17 .. | |
| 250426 | L./Sergt. H. Watsham, D.C.M... .. .. | 2/11/17 .. | |
| 251156 | Pte. F. G. Wood .. .. | 2/11/17 .. | |
| 250017 | C./S./M. J. T. White .. | 26/3/17 .. | |
| 1457 | Sergt. H. J. Westrip .. | 2/11/17 .. | |
| 250150 | Pte. J. Wisbey .. .. | 26/3/17 .. | |
| 250163 | Pte. E. Wager .. .. | 2/11/17 .. | |
| 1832 | L./Sergt. H. Warner .. | 2/12/17 .. | |
| 250277 | Corpl. W. Waters.. .. | 2/11/17 .. | |
| 250463 | Pte. W. W. Wright .. | 26/3/17 .. | See 3. (b.) |
| 250465 | A./Sergt. F. R. Wilson .. | 29/8/17 .. | |
| 250799 | Corpl. A. C. Willsher .. | 2/11/17 .. | |
| 250992 | L./Corpl. E. Williamson .. | 26/3/17 .. | |
| 251019 | Pte. F. C. Wilson .. | 26/3/17 .. | |
| 36740 | Pte. A. Woodrow.. .. | 5/11/17 .. | |
| 45533 | Pte. T. Wilson .. .. | 19/9/18 .. | |
| 55130 | Pte. C. F. Westson .. | 19/9/18 .. | |
| 37257 | Pte. A. H. Wilson .. | 28/7/17 .. | |
| 36744 | Pte. A. White .. .. | 20/5/18 .. | |

3. Prisoners of War, Repatriated.

(a.) *Officers Nil.*

(b.) *N.C.O.'s and Men.*

| | | Date. | Remarks. |
|---|---|---|---|
| 251370 | A./Corpl. A. V. Call .. | 13/5/18 .. | See 2. (b.) |
| 251280 | Pte. W. Cawley .. .. | 26/3/17 .. | Do. |
| 251195 | Pte. F. Clarke .. .. | 26/3/17 .. | Do. |
| 250863 | Pte. A. E. Day .. .. | 26/3/17 .. | Do. |
| 250219 | Pte. L. S. Forman .. | 26/3/17 .. | Do. |
| 250185 | Pte. A. Salmon .. .. | 26/3/17 .. | Do. |
| 250573 | Pte. G. J. Taylor.. .. | 26/3/17 .. | Do. |
| 251103 | Pte. T. Tyler .. .. | 26/3/17 .. | Do. |
| 251090 | Pte. R. W. Woodgate .. | 26/3/17 .. | Do. |
| 250463 | Pte. W. W. Wright .. | 26/3/17 .. | Do. |

Note.—The above list is as complete as it has been possible to make it from the records kept on service, but it is probable that there are many omissions, particularly from the list of wounded.

All the casualties were incurred while actually serving with the 1/5th Essex. A large number of Officers and other ranks of the Battalion became casualties after having been transferred to other units. Records of the latter are not accessible.

# APPENDIX II.

## HONOURS AND AWARDS.

### Distinguished Service Order.

Captain (T. Major) T. Gibbons
Captain (T. Major) W. E. Wilson
Captain E. B. Deakin
2/Lieut. E. M. G. Wray
Lieut./Col. P. C. Yonge (Trench Mortars)

### Military Cross.

2/Lieut. (T. Captain) A. Colvin
Lieut. H. S. Calverley
2/Lieut. C. F. J. Keeling
Captain E. B. Deakin
Lieut. J. F. Finn
2/Lieut. E. J. Lockwood
Lieut. B. Archer
Captain C. Portway
Captain F. G. Bright (Staff)
Lieut. R. H. S. Coleman (M.G. Corps)

### Distinguished Conduct Medal.

2932 Sergt. W. J. Gafney
250106 Sergt. W. Cooper
250259 C.-Q.-M.-S. J. E. V. Coote
250146 Sergt. (A./C.-Q.-M.-S.) H. Reed
1855 Corpl. T. C. Main (R.A.M.C. attached)
250747 L./Corpl. (A./Corpl.) B. Fenner
250047 Sergt. H. N. Rand
250427 C.-S.-M. F. Wilson
251351 Pte. W. Hilsdon
250113 Corpl. F. Collins
250426 Sergt. H. Watsham
250133 Corpl. (A./Sergt.) A. Drury
250369 C.-S.-M. F. James
250255 Corpl. A. E. Ruffell

### Military Medal.

251337 Sergt. E. White
250508 Pte. E. A. G. Jordan
250241 Sergt. A. G. Piper
250101 Pte. E. W. Cook
250140 Corpl. H. J. Blundon

MILITARY MEDAL—*continued.*

250506 Pte. W. J. Mears
250425 L./Corpl. W. M. Town
251244 Pte. E. Clark
251140 Sergt. W. Simmonds
251386 Pte. J. J. Smith
251266 Pte. L. G. Harvey
250874 Pte. S. Smith
36679 Pte. E. Bolton
36818 Pte. J. Story
250358 Sergt. W. A. Osborne
251107 L./Corpl. W. Beck
250142 Corpl. (A./L./Sergt.) B. W. Dann
251269 Pte. (A./Corpl.) P. Byford
250264 Sergt. C. Green
250905 Pte. B. Hockley
250261 Pte. (A./Corpl. )W. Ransom
250273 Pte. (A./L./Corpl.) E. A. Lofts

MERITORIOUS SERVICE MEDAL.

250015 Sergt. A. E. Thompson

MENTIONED IN DESPATCHES.

Captain (T. Major) T. Gibbons, D.S.O.
Captain (T. Major) W. E. Wilson, D.S.O.
2/Lieut. A. Colvin, M.C.
2/Lieut. T. E. Fry (twice)
Captain E. B. Deakin, D.S.O., M.C.
2/Lieut. E. M. G. Wray, D.S.O.
Lieut. J. F. Finn, M.C.
Lieut. J. L. French
Lieut. R. J. S. Bateman
Captain G. E. Tompson
Lieut./Col. P. C. Yonge, D.S.O. (Trench Mortars)
Captain F. G. Bright, M.C. (Staff) (twice)
Lieut. H. Moller (Trench Mortars)
1595 Sergt. W. Chapman
251378 Pte. T. Davidson
250876 Pte. W. J. Fell
250747 Sergt. B. Fenner, D.C.M.
250355 Pte. O. Rand
250047 Sergt. H. N. Rand, D.C.M.
250146 C.-Q.-M.-S. H. Reed, D.C.M.
250255 Pte. (A./L./Corpl.) A. E. Ruffell, D.C,M.
251337 Sergt. E. White, M.M.
250167 Corpl. C. Cunningham
251385 Pte. E. Jemson
250542 Corpl. R. Jarrold

MENTIONED IN DESPATCHES—*continued*.

250350 Pte. F. Long
250549 Sergt. F. Barnes
251106 Pte. T. W. Gray
251263 Pte. A. E. Cox
253186 Pte. E. Lockwood
250040 C.-S.-M. H. Goodwin
251001 L./Corpl. A. Scott
250570 Pte. H. Smith

FOREIGN ORDERS AND DECORATIONS.

ORDER OF THE NILE.

(3rd Cl.) Major (T. Lieut./Col.) T. Gibbons, D.S.O.
(4th Cl.) Captain (A./Major) F. G. Bright, M.C. (Staff)

MEDAILLE MILITAIRE.

250147 Sergt. F. Foster

SERVIAN SILVER MEDAL.

2416 Pte. L. Shergold
1585 Pte. (A./L./Sergt.) A. Coates

# APPENDIX III.

## LIST OF OFFICERS WHO SERVED WITH THE BATTALION.

| Original Rank and Name. | From. | To. | Remarks. |
|---|---|---|---|
| Lieut./Col. J. M. Welch .. | 23/7/15 | 19/8/15 | Invalided to U.K. |
| Major T. Gibbons .. .. | 23/7/15 | 27/9/19 | Demob. |
| Major J. M. Heron .. .. | 23/7/15 | 26/3/17 | Killed in action |
| Capt. H. C. Bridges (Adjt.) .. | 23/7/15 | 10/9/15 | Invalided to U.K. |
| Capt. W. E. Wilson .. .. | 23/7/15 | —/—/19 | Demob. |
| Capt. H. T. Argent .. .. | 23/7/15 | 17/8/15 | Wounded to U.K. |
| Capt. F. W. Bacon .. | 23/7/15 | 2/11/17 | Died of Wounds in U.K |
| Capt. A. Denton .. .. | 23/7/15 | 15/8/15 | Killed in action |
| Capt. C. A. Gould .. .. | 23/7/15 | 26/3/17 | Killed in action |
| Capt. K. S. Storrs (M.O.) .. | 23/7/15 | 9/10/15 | Invalided to U.K. |
| Lieut. E. B. Deakin .. | 23/7/15 | —/—/19 | To Cairo Bde. H.Q. |
| Lieut. T. G. N. Franklin .. | 23/7/15 | —/—/19 | Army of Occupation |
| Lieut. W. H. Brooks .. .. | 23/7/15 | 22/4/16 | To Bde. M.G. Coy. |
| Lieut. G. W. F. Bellward .. | 23/7/15 | 27/9/16 | To Camel Trans. Corps |
| Lieut. E. Mackenzie Taylor .. | 23/7/15 | 14/10/16 | To M.T. A.S.C. |
| Lieut. H. L. Yonge .. .. | 23/7/15 | 28/12/16 | To M.T. A.S.C. |
| Lieut. B. Carylon Hughes .. | 23/7/15 | 7/6/19 | Demob. |
| Lieut. H. Mavor .. .. | 23/7/15 | —/—/17 | R.T.O. |
| Lieut. G. M. Nobbs .. .. | 23/7/15 | 28/8/16 | Invalided to U.K. |
| 2/Lieut. H. K. Chester .. | 23/7/15 | 26/3/17 | Died of Wounds |
| 2/Lieut. L. D. Womersley .. | 23/7/15 | 18/5/19 | Demob. |
| 2/Lieut. C. Portway .. .. | 23/7/15 | 11/6/19 | Demob. |
| 2/Lieut. J. L. French .. | 23/7/15 | 4/6/17 | To Indian Army |
| 2/Lieut. R. S. Horton .. | 23/7/15 | 1/3/19 | Demob. |
| 2/Lieut. C. O. Wilson .. | 23/7/15 | 26/3/17 | Killed in action |
| 2/Lieut. A. Colvin .. .. | 23/7/15 | 18/5/19 | Demob. |
| 2/Lieut. J. F. Finn (Adjt.) | 23/7/15 | 1/9/19 | To G.H.Q., E.E.F. |
| 2/Lieut. A. E. Sheldon .. | 23/7/15 | 22/8/15 | Died of wounds |
| 2/Lieut. R. Turner .. .. | 23/7/16 | 14/8/15 | Killed in action |
| Rev. A. J. Sacré, C.F. .. | 23/7/15 | —/9/15 | Invalided to U.K. |
| Lieut. Alford .. .. | 2/10/15 | —/—/15 | Sick |
| 2/Lieut. Perkins .. .. | 2/10/15 | —/—/15 | Sick |
| Capt. L. R. Conway .. | 7/10/15 | —/—/15 | Invalided to U.K. |
| Lieut. L. Gray .. .. | 7/10/15 | —/—/17 | Died of enteric |
| 2/Lieut. R. Compton .. | 7/10/15 | —/—/16 | Killed in France |
| Rev. B. K. Bond, C.F. .. | —/—/15 | 28/10/17 | To 10th Div. H.Q. |
| 2/Lieut. B. Archer .. .. | 7/10/15 | —/—/19 | Demob. |
| 2/Lieut. E. C. Beard .. | 7/10/15 | 26/3/17 | Killed in action |
| 2/Lieut. H. M. Browne .. | 7/10/15 | 26/3/17 | Killed in action |

| Original Rank and Name. | From. | To. | Remarks. |
|---|---|---|---|
| 2/Lieut. A. V. Coates .. | 7/10/15 | 23/5/16 | Bde. M.G. Coy. |
| 2/Lieut. H. S. Calverley .. | 7/10/15 | 15/1/18 | To 1st Essex |
| Lieut. W. E. Rubens .. | 18/10/15 | —/—/16 | To G.H.Q., E.E.F. |
| Lieut. T. H. O. Capron (Adjt.) | 18/10/15 | 26/3/17 | Killed in action |
| 2/Lieut. A. F. Tompson .. | 18/10/15 | 14/1/6 | Invalided to U.K. |
| 2/Lieut. R. J. S. Bateman .. | 18/10/15 | 18/6/19 | Demob. |
| Lieut. Humphries (M.O.) .. | —/—/15 | —/—/15 | Sick |
| 2/Lieut. R. H. S. Coleman | 9/12/15 | 22/4/16 | To Bde. M.G. Coy. |
| 2/Lieut. C. B. Godhard .. | 9/12/15 | —/—/16 | To U.K. |
| 2/Lieut. A. Scragg .. .. | 9/12/15 | 26/8/16 | To Camel Trans. Corps |
| Capt. P. C. Yonge .. .. | 10/2/16 | 26/6/16 | To Salonika |
| Capt. E. D. H. Willmott .. | —/1/16 | —/11/19 | Demob. |
| Lieut. L. U. Ransford .. | —/1/16 | 28/8/16 | Invalided to U.K. |
| Lieut. H. A. Browett .. | 10/2/16 | —/—/16 | Died in East Africa 30/10/18 |
| Lieut. L. E. Hooper .. | —/—/16 | 26/9/16 | To U.K. |
| Lieut. Proud (M.O.) .. .. | —/—/15 | —/—/16 | To R.A.M.C. |
| Capt. G. E. Tompson .. | 7/3/16 | 25/3/18 | To 54th Div. H.Q. |
| 2/Lieut. P. King .. .. | 13/3/16 | 3/10/16 | To R.F.C. |
| 2/Lieut. W. M. Robertson .. | 13/3/16 | —/—/16 | |
| 2/Lieut. F. P. Windsor .. | 13/3/16 | —/—/19 | Demob. |
| 2/Lieut. Everard .. .. | —/—/16 | 3/10/16 | To R.F.C. |
| 2/Lieut. F. C. Safe .. .. | 7/6/16 | 24/3/18 | To 1/3rd County of London Yeo. |
| 2/Lieut. A. E. Kinnersley .. | —/—/16 | 29/5/19 | Demob. |
| Capt. Coffyn (M.O.) .. | —/—/16 | 24/6/16 | To R.A.M.C. |
| Capt. Ellwood (M.O.) .. | 25/6/16 | 24/11/16 | To R.A.M.C. |
| Capt. Crawford (M.O.) .. | —/—/16 | —/—/16 | To R.A.M.C. |
| 2/Lieut. E. Cooper Smith .. | —/—/16 | —/—/19 | Army of Occupation |
| 2/Lieut. H. Moller .. .. | —/—/16 | —/—/16 | To Salonika |
| 2/Lieut. C. V. Edmunds .. | —/—/16 | 26/3/17 | Killed in action |
| 2/Lieut. F. J. Bartley .. | —/—/16 | 26/3/17 | Killed in action |
| 2/Lieut. B. L. Cooke .. | —/—/16 | 6/7/17 | To A.S.C. |
| 2/Lieut. Adams .. .. | 31/7/16 | 27/9/16 | To Camel Trans. Corps |
| 2/Lieut. E. J. Howes .. | 1/8/16 | 20/3/17 | To Camel Trans. Corps |
| 2/Lieut. A. E. Gilmore .. | —/—/16 | 26/3/17 | Wounded, to U.K. |
| Capt. C. S. Wink (M.O.) .. | 20/11/16 | 20/4/17 | To R.A.M.C. |
| Lieut. H. Miller .. .. | 7/2/17 | —/—/17 | To Bde. T.M. Batt. |
| 2/Lieut. W. H. Evans .. | 1/4/17 | 2/11/17 | Killed in action |
| 2/Lieut. E. J. C. Johnston | 1/4/17 | —/—/— | To R.F.C. |
| Capt. J. H. Owens (M.O.) .. | 20/4/17 | —/—/17 | To R.A.M.C. |
| Capt. A. D. Clarke .. .. | 23/4/17 | 7/5/17 | To 1/6th Essex |
| 2/Lieut. T. E. Fry (late R.S.M.) .. | 6/6/17 | 11/7/17 | To Duty, Sch. of Instruction |
| 2/Lieut. T. J. C. Dening .. | 6/6/17 | —/—/17 | To Devonshire Regt. |
| 2/Lieut. A. J. S. Winton .. | 6/6/17 | 9/6/17 | To 1/6th Essex |
| 2/Lieut. H. R. Lancaster .. | 29/6/17 | 2/11/17 | Killed in action |
| 2/Lieut. A. F. R. Richmond | 29/6/17 | —/—/19 | Demob. |

| Original Rank and Name. | From. | To. | Remarks. |
|---|---|---|---|
| 2/Lieut. E. J. Lockwood .. | 29/6/17 | —/—/19 | Demob. |
| 2/Lieut. E. A. P. Bowen .. | 16/7/17 | —/—/19 | Demob. |
| 2/Lieut. R. H. Walker .. | 19/7/17 | 29/9/17 | To R.F.C. |
| 2/Lieut. E. H. Ryan .. | 29/7/17 | —/—/19 | Demob. |
| Rev. J. D. W. Hayton, C.F. | 4/8/17 | —/—/17 | |
| 2/Lieut. A. W. Maxwell .. | 19/7/17 | 14/8/17 | To Divl. Details Camp |
| 2/Lieut. E. M. G. Wray .. | 19/7/17 | —/—/19 | Army of Occupation |
| Lieut. D. P. Macdonald (M.O.) | 1/9/17 | 5/9/17 | Sick |
| Capt. M. Somerville (M.O.) | —/—/17 | 2/9/17 | To U.K |
| Lieut. J. Avery (M.O.) .. | 5/9/17 | —/5/18 | To R.A.M.C. |
| 2/Lieut. J. H. Jackson .. | 24/10/17 | —/11/17 | To 1/7th Essex |
| Lieut. H. S. Rogers (Q.M.) | 24/10/17 | —/—/19 | Demob. |
| Rev. H. C. Marriott, C.F. .. | 30/10/17 | 3/8/19 | To 4th Cav. Div. |
| 2/Lieut. C. E. G. Wilton .. | 17/11/17 | 2/3/18 | To Indian Army |
| 2/Lieut. C. F. J. Keeling .. | 18/11/17 | —/—/19 | Demob. |
| 2/Lieut. W. East .. .. | 18/11/17 | 10/8/18 | To Corps Reinforcement Camp |
| 2/Lieut. G. M. Abbott .. | 14/12/17 | —/—/18 | Invalided to U.K. |
| 2/Lieut. D. Jelfs .. .. | 14/12/17 | —/—/19 | Demob. |
| 2/Lieut. J. T. Buglass .. | 14/12/17 | 9/7/19 | Demob. |
| Lieut. J R. James .. .. | 5/2/18 | —/—/18 | To Indian Army |
| 2/Lieut. H. V. Stobbs .. | 5/2/18 | 11/8/19 | To Cairo Bde. H.Q. |
| 2/Lieut. D. Coney .. .. | 10/2/18 | 30/7/19 | Demob. |
| 2/Lieut. F. Eames .. .. | 10/2/18 | 19/9/18 | Killed in action |
| 2/Lieut. F. Lucas .. .. | 10/2/18 | 30/8/19 | Leave to U.K. |
| 2/Lieut. R. Baird .. .. | 10/2/18 | 22/2/19 | Demob. |
| 2/Lieut. G. B Aitken .. | 10/2/18 | 10/5/18 | To Hospital |
| 2/Lieut. W. Watkins .. | 19/3/18 | 29/5/19 | Demob. |
| Lieut. G. N. Watts .. .. | 4/4/18 | —/—/19 | Demob. |
| 2/Lieut. A. G. Eden .. | 5/4/18 | 20/5/18 | Killed in action |
| 2/Lieut. R. J. Smith .. | 23/4/18 | 25/1/19 | Leave to U.K. |
| 2/Lieut. J. A. Russell .. | 6/5/18 | —/—/19 | Demob. |
| Capt. J. P. Bracken (M.O.) | —/—/18 | 16/5/18 | To Hospital |
| Capt. M. M. Frew (M.O.) .. | 21/5/18 | —/—/19 | |
| Lieut. M. A. Popham .. | 13/6/18 | —/—/18 | |
| 2/Lieut. A. J. Harle .. | 4/7/18 | 22/6/19 | Demob. |
| 2/Lieut. J. Templeton .. | 1/8/18 | —/—/19 | Army of Occupation |
| 2/Lieut. F. J. Foley Whaling | 2/8/18 | —/—/19 | Army of Occupation |
| 2/Lieut. S. S. Barnard .. | 17/8/18 | —/—/19 | Demob. |
| 2/Lieut. E. G. P. Fenn .. | 11/9/18 | 19/9/18 | Killed in action |
| 2/Lieut. L. Steel .. .. | 11/9/18 | —/—/19 | Army of Occupation |
| 2/Lieut. T. Haggerty .. | 11/9/18 | 22/6/19 | Demob. |
| 2/Lieut. S. E. Denny .. | 18/9/18 | —/—/18 | To 1/4th Essex |
| 2/Lieut. H. H. Hession .. | 28/9/18 | 11/6/19 | Demob. |
| Lieut. B. Ritson .. .. | 28/9/18 | 3/3/19 | Leave to U.K. |
| Lieut. R. G. Deakin .. | —/—/19 | —/—/19 | Army of Occupation |
| 2/Lieut. A. Hodgkins .. | —/—/19 | 11/6/19 | Demob. |
| 2/Lieut. G. O. Smythe .. | —/—/19 | 22/6/19 | Demob. |

| Original Rank and Name. | From. | To. | Remarks. |
|---|---|---|---|
| 2/Lieut. G. G. McCombie .. | —/—/19 | 25/7/19 | Demob. |
| Capt. F. H. Rust .. .. | —/—/19 | —/—/19 | Demob. |
| 2/Lieut. A. Cooper .. .. | —/—/19 | 22/6/19 | Demob. |
| Capt. H. E. Shonk (Q.M.) | 2/3/19 | —/—/19 | Demob. |
| 2/Lieut. T. W. Cole.. .. | —/—/19 | 30/7/19 | Demob. |
| Lieut. H. L. Goldby .. | 13/3/19 | 13/5/19 | Demob |
| Lieut. R. J. Gilmour .. | —/—/19 | —/—/19 | Army of Occupation |
| Lieut. P. W. T. Elford .. | 30/4/19 | 25/7/19 | Demob. |
| Lieut. W. C. Cooper .. | 4/6/19 | 14/8/19 | Leave to U.K. |
| Lieut. A. J. Jarvie .. .. | 25/6/19 | —/—/19 | Army of Occupation |
| Lieut. F. J. Sands .. .. | 5/7/19 | —/—/19 | Army of Occupation |
| Lieut. R. E. Welti .. .. | 7/7/19 | —/—/19 | Army of Occupation |
| Lieut. E. G. Pask .. .. | 28/7/19 | —/—/19 | Army of Occupation |
| Capt. T. Trad .. .. | 7/8/19 | —/—/19 | Army of Occupation |
| Lieut. A. R. Lee .. .. | —/—/19 | —/—/19 | Army of Occupation |

www.ingramcontent.com/pod-product-compliance
Ingram Content Group UK Ltd.
Pitfield, Milton Keynes, MK11 3LW, UK
UKHW021837270726
14058UKWH00002B/201

9 781847 349798